Becoming Christian

Becoming Christian

The Conversion of
Roman Cappadocia

Raymond Van Dam

PENN

University of Pennsylvania Press
Philadelphia

10 9 8 7 6 5 4 3 2 1

Published by
University of Pennsylvania Press
Philadelphia, Pennsylvania 19104-4011

Library of Congress Cataloging-in-Publication Data

Van Dam, Raymond.
   Becoming Christian : the conversion of Roman Cappadocia / Raymond Van
Dam.
     p. cm.
   ISBN 0-8122-3738-2 (alk. paper)
   Includes bibliographical references and index.
   1. Basil, Saint, Bishop of Caesarea, ca. 329–379. 2. Gregory, of Nyssa, Saint,
ca. 335–ca. 394. 3. Gregory, of Nazianzus, Saint. 4. Christianity and culture—
Turkey—Cappadocia—History. 5. Cappadocia (Turkey)—Church history. I. Title
BR185 .V36 2003
275.64′02—dc21   2003047320

Endpapers: Asia Minor and the Eastern Mediterranean in the fourth century.

For Jan

"Laughter fills the air; your loving grace surrounds me"
—Bruce Springsteen, Mary's Place

Contents

Acknowledgments

Gregory of Nazianzus flattered one learned correspondent as an "emperor of culture." These days a career in academic scholarship requires the encouragement of more than even a tetrarchy of such guides and teachers. The publication of the final book in a trio about Cappadocia in late antiquity allows me to pause and remember with deep gratitude some of the teachers and friends who have encouraged me along the way, long ago and now: Dick Whittaker, Geoffrey Lloyd, Peter Brown, Bob Otten, Bert Vander Lee, Bob Gregg, Paolo Squatriti, Beate Dignas, and Anne Taylor. Here at the University of Michigan it has been my good fortune that so many wonderful undergraduates and graduate students have so graciously supervised my continuing education, in particular Greg Aldrete, Amir Bagdachi, Shawn Dry, Matt Herbst, Ken Heskett, Greg Highkin, Veronica Kalas, Anthony Kaldellis, Young Kim, Dimitri Krallis, Michelle Light, Ian Mladjov, Grant Nelsestuen, Ellen Poteet, David Reynolds, Geoffrey Schmalz, Adam Schor, Dmitri Starostine, Davidde Stella, David Stone, David Van Amburg, and Rob Vander Poppen. Audiences at the Catholic University of America, Princeton University, and Calvin College provided some of the best commentary on early versions of my thoughts about ancient friendship through their own friendship. As my alma mater Calvin College was also an appropriate setting for a lecture about forgetting the past and remembering the future.

Gregory of Nyssa once compared Cappadocia to Ithaca: despite its rocky terrain and cultural boorishness, at the end of his life's restlessness it was still home. The conclusion of this research project conjures up the same sense of reluctant homecoming and deferred finality that the esteemed poet Constantine Cavafy has imagined in the mind of Odysseus. The Cappadocian Fathers gave me this marvelous intellectual expedition. Without them I would not have set out.

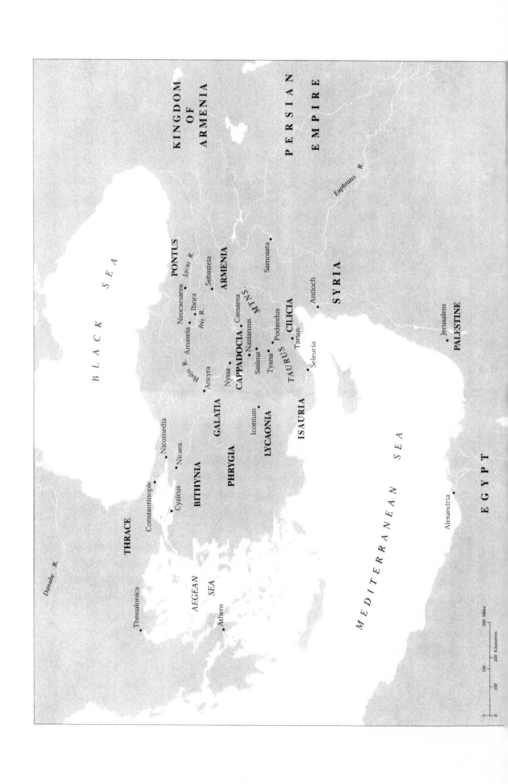

Introduction

Cappadocians were there in the crowd at the beginning of Christianity. At the first Pentecost in Jerusalem, Cappadocians were among those amazed spectators who were startled to hear the apostles preaching in their own exotic languages. Cappadocians were also present at the end of imperial hostility toward Christianity in the eastern empire. During the final great persecutions under the emperor Maximinus, some of the illustrious martyrs in Palestine were Cappadocians.[1]

But despite the participation of Cappadocians at these critical moments of early Christian history, Christianity seems to have spread into most of central and eastern Asia Minor only comparatively late. Evidence for Christian communities in Pontus, Cappadocia, and northern Galatia under the early empire is scanty and scattered. Only during the mid- and later third century did communities of Christians, of different varieties, finally become more common. Even then these communities continued to endure hostility and sometimes outright persecution, both from Roman magistrates and from local opponents. The patronage of the emperor Constantine in the early fourth century finally accelerated the process of conversion. By then Christian communities were widespread in central and eastern Asia Minor, and one ecclesiastical historian even complimented Galatia, Cappadocia, and neighboring regions for having taken the lead in the Christianization of the eastern provinces. Along with their ecclesiastical colleagues from throughout the eastern empire, bishops from Cappadocia, Pontus, and Galatia attended the famous Council of Nicaea in 325 and enjoyed Constantine's hospitality. Some thought that this council, because it had been convened under the patronage of a Christian emperor, finally marked the fulfillment of the promise of the original Pentecost. From the era of the New Testament to the origins of a Christian Roman empire, Cappadocians had contributed to the growth of Christianity.[2]

The three great Church Fathers from Cappadocia, Basil of Caesarea, his brother Gregory of Nyssa, and their friend Gregory of Nazianzus, were all born during the reign of Constantine, after the Council of Nicaea. Basil's family had been Christian at least since the later third century, and his grandparents had suffered during the persecutions under the last pagan emperors. Gregory of Nazianzus' father had converted only recently, after Constantine's demonstration of his support for Christianity, but he quickly became bishop of his hometown. Because their ancestors had become Christians by different routes, their experiences already represented in miniature two contrasting perspectives on the relationship between Christianity and Roman rule, imperial hostility or imperial patronage. The Cappadocian Fathers themselves grew up in a Christian Roman empire and in Christian families. Their distinguished careers as churchmen marked them as clear beneficiaries of the increasing significance of Christianity in Roman society.

During the later fourth century the Cappadocian Fathers were the most prominent churchmen in central and eastern Asia Minor. Basil became metropolitan bishop of Caesarea; Gregory of Nyssa served as bishop at both Nyssa and Sebasteia, and occasionally visited the new capital of Constantinople; and Gregory of Nazianzus helped his father in his episcopal duties at Nazianzus and served briefly as bishop of Constantinople. Through their writings and activities they influenced the contours of Christianity, certainly in Cappadocia but also more widely throughout the eastern provinces. Basil's treatises on ascetic spirituality shaped the organization of monasticism, Gregory of Nazianzus provided a model for the synthesis of classical rhetoric and Christianity, and Gregory of Nyssa helped to expose Christian exegesis to the influence of both Greek philosophy and mystical speculation. All three Cappadocian Fathers were instrumental in defining the doctrine of the Trinity that was accepted as orthodox at the Council of Constantinople in 381. Along with Athanasius, the famous bishop of Alexandria of a generation earlier, and John Chrysostom, the equally famous bishop of Constantinople of a generation later, Basil, Gregory of Nazianzus, and Gregory of Nyssa became the most distinguished Greek theologians of the fourth century.[3]

*   *   *

In modern scholarship their enormous reputation as theologians and ecclesiastical leaders has been both a blessing and a burden. Already in antiquity churchmen were scrutinizing the Cappadocian Fathers' doctrines in their innumerable treatises, commentaries, sermons, letters, and poems. To cope with so many texts one reader even acquired a special facility: he simply inhaled their writings like air![4] Modern specialists in patristic studies have obviously followed his inspirational example. Their meticulous research on Cappadocian theology is truly magnificent, and numerous detailed studies have culminated in the grand surveys of Karl Holl, Jean Daniélou, Thomas A. Kopecek, Hanns Christof Brennecke, R. P. C. Hanson, and Jaroslav Pelikan.

Yet the Cappadocian Fathers were always more than bishops, ascetics, and exegetes. Their extensive writings have made Cappadocia one of the best documented regions in the later Roman empire, and their lives and careers have become sterling examples of various social and cultural transformations. This volume is one in a trilogy of books about Cappadocia during late antiquity. *Families and Friends* investigates their roles as sons and brothers by analyzing their relationships with other members of their families, and it evaluates their differing ideas about friendship. *Kingdom of Snow* considers the impact of Roman rule and Greek culture in late antique Cappadocia. It discusses the roles of the Cappadocian Fathers as local brokers negotiating with emperors and imperial magistrates and as learned clerics coming to terms with the classical culture they had once studied so avidly.

This book examines the social impact of Christianity in a Roman and Greek society. If the reputation of the Cappadocian Fathers as theologians has overshadowed their other roles as familymen and local patrons, then some aspects of the modern scholarship about their theology have distorted our understanding of the religious transformation of a traditional society. In particular, a deep sense of piety and reverence still inspires many studies of Church Fathers. Somehow the study of theology and theologians, or at least of orthodox theology and orthodox theologians, frequently seems to rise above the need for historical criticism.

Studies of the making of orthodox doctrines, of the effectiveness of preaching, and of conversion to Christianity are especially susceptible to this sort of retrospective deference. Accounts of the development of orthodox theology often project a misleading sense of inevitability about the outcome of ongoing disputes that were in fact repeatedly close to veering off in different directions. Accounts of preaching likewise often ignore the precipitous obstacles to communicating with ordinary people. Educated theologians used the techniques of formal logic, the jargon of classical philosophy, and the vocabulary of an archaic, literary Greek, and still struggled to articulate their ideas. In contrast, their audiences typically included illiterate country-folk who spoke only common Greek or some local language, and whose overriding obsessions were their poverty-stricken agrarian livelihoods and their backbreaking efforts to survive from week to week. Bishops were offering the crumbs of erudition to ordinary people who were more concerned with obtaining their daily bread. Fundamental differences in language, learning, and preoccupations commonly divided preachers from their audiences. Accounts of conversion to Christianity, furthermore, often overlook the difficulties of trying to impose the new lifestyle that came along with a new religion. Older customs, older ceremonies and rituals, older myths and histories, were now all swept aside. As historians we should mourn the loss of these ancient traditions and legends, rather than tacitly conniving in a triumphalist perspective on the success of Christianity.

Only in retrospect does a single dominant vector appear in the rise of Christianity. At the time, the success of Christianity was certainly not a foregone conclusion. The single-mindedness that modern scholars often count as one of its more compellingly attractive features was in fact one of its most intrusive characteristics. Not only did Christianity eventually create an orthodox theology. It also highlighted the notion of an orthodoxy in many other aspects of society and culture. Now there was to be an orthodox speech, an orthodox lifestyle, an orthodox history. Some churchmen even started looking for an orthodox self, that one consistent trajectory of beliefs, commitments, and values that would link their past, present, and future in a single unwavering arc. The imposition of these new orthodoxies came with a price, however, that was exacted in the belittling of traditional lifestyles, the forgetting of older legends, and the condemnation of some theologians as heretics. In Roman Cappadocia the impact of Christianity was thoroughly constricting and disruptive.

* * *

Like its companion volumes, this book consists of a series of interlocking chapters with complementary interpretations. Even though its main topic is the rise of Christianity in late Roman Cappadocia, it essentially ignores doctrines, asceticism, monasticism, and spirituality. Since these were certainly important concerns for the Cappadocian Fathers, modern scholarship has already investigated them with exemplary thoroughness. Instead, this book focuses on more practical and immediate aspects of conversion to Christianity.

The first chapter discusses the social implications of the making of doctrinal orthodoxy and heresy. The Cappadocian Fathers were not the only influential theologians from Cappadocia. One of their contemporaries was Eunomius, who for much of his career was more prominent as an ecclesiastical leader and more important as a theologian. Then Basil and Gregory of

Nyssa demolished him and his doctrines through a combination of intellectual erudition and tasteless ridicule. Both were as much concerned about their personal reputations as about the search for the Christian doctrine of God. While they both went on to greater fame and glory as churchmen, Eunomius was remembered primarily to be reviled.

The next section of chapters discusses new histories. Christianity introduced new regulations about behavior and imposed a new hierarchy of clerics and bishops with lifetime tenure. To legitimate these new standards, to justify their own prominence, to ensure that the present seemed to stay in synch with the past, churchmen created new historical legends for communities and families. Gregory of Nyssa, for instance, rewrote the history of Pontus and Cappadocia to highlight the antiquity of Christianity and its regional founders. The success of these new histories then drove older histories and legends off the market. By the early fifth century the Cappadocian historian Philostorgius could barely make sense of some of these old legends about cities and their original founders.

The next section of chapters analyses preachers and their audiences. The common idiom that learned bishops shared with their audiences consisted of biblical stories and legends about local saints. This new common language was very flexible, even if sometimes difficult to use. When preaching a series of sermons about the six days of creation described in the first chapter of Genesis, Basil had to learn how to reach his audience by responding to their reactions and interests. When preaching about the cult of the Forty Martyrs both he and Gregory of Nyssa modified the incidental details in the legends about their martyrdom in order to fit with the expectations of the audiences. In the ongoing dialogue between preachers and their audiences, the listeners had essentially put the words into the speakers' mouths.

The final section of chapters looks at attempts to create legacies and afterlives. Christianity offered new ways of defining self and finding a personal identity. Philostorgius looked to the past and composed an ecclesiastical history that justified his and Eunomius' heterodox Christianity. Basil ignored the past. Once he became a cleric, he rather oddly never mentioned his earlier life. As an adult, he essentially remade himself into a foundling, a man with no family and no memories. Because he had no past to speak of, subsequent authors created various apocryphal lives to fill in the blanks. In contrast, Gregory of Nazianzus incessantly rewrote the story of his life in a series of autobiographical poems. These poems represented successive drafts of his life's story. Finding an orthodox theology had been simple compared with finding an orthodox version of his life.

In ancient society Christianity was more than beliefs, doctrines, liturgical practices, moral strictures, and ascetic lifestyles. Christianity also offered an arena within which local notables could go on competing for prestige and standing. It offered a history that communities and families could use to distinguish themselves from rivals. It offered a common language of biblical stories and legends about martyrs that allowed highly educated bishops to communicate with the ordinary believers in their congregations. And it offered autobiographies, as men made sense of the vicissitudes of their lives in terms of their enduring piety. This book focuses on the consequences of various attempts to create new orthodoxies in theology, history, language, and personal identity.

Orthodoxy and Heresy

Disputation over Christian doctrines, in all its profusion, diversity, and glorious ferocity, was a defining characteristic of the Roman empire during the fourth century. Everyone seemed to participate. Bishops and other prominent churchmen obviously took the lead in arguing these complex issues, both in their sermons and by shooting "arrows of black ink" in their treatises. Emperors and powerful imperial magistrates often imposed decisions, either cautiously through their patronage, or sometimes more implacably through edicts. Because they formed the audiences from which bishops and emperors solicited support and approval, ordinary believers were also energetic participants. In hundreds of cities people either attended or boycotted services and sermons; sometimes they took to the streets and rioted; but always, whether bustling about in the markets or relaxing at the baths, they talked and gossiped about the prominent contenders and their various doctrines. For them these disputes might as well have been the theological equivalents of sporting events that gave them another opportunity to cheer on their favorite performers. At Constantinople, Gregory of Nazianzus was dismayed to find that religious affairs had become another form of entertainment, "like horse races and the theater." It is no surprise that ecclesiastical writers filled their doctrinal and exegetical treatises with analogies to races and athletic contests. "The common life of mankind is the stadium, and for competition the stadium is available to everyone."[1]

Out of these contentious whirlpools of dissent both a sense of orthodoxy and a consensus about orthodox doctrines eventually emerged. Certification of orthodoxy appeared on several levels. Bishops and other churchmen composed lengthy tomes explaining their preferred doctrines and refuting those of their rivals. They met in councils that issued creeds of faith. The creeds of two ecumenical councils, one at Nicaea in 325 and the other at Constantinople in 381, were eventually acknowledged as indisputable definitions of orthodox doctrine. In addition, emperors issued edicts that endorsed particular formulations as orthodox, promoted the supporters of that orthodoxy, and dictated penalties for all the heretics who continued to disagree.

Yet despite this coalescence of "orthodoxy" and "heresy" within Christianity, both as conceptual constructs and as specific formulations in terms

of precise doctrines, it remains difficult to explain why some doctrinal state-
ments were accepted and so many others were rejected. The theologians of
the fourth century whose doctrines were acknowledged as orthodox knew
exactly why they had been victorious, because with the benefit of hindsight
they could detect the workings of divine will. Modern historians should
hesitate to adopt such a teleological position that removes any possibility of
interpretive contingency and that is so fundamentally ahistorical. Of the
countless theological formulations of the fourth century, few were so inherently eccentric that they were instantly discredited. All theologians were
intent upon interpreting biblical texts, and all claimed biblical authority. All
of them appealed to the precedents of past traditions and earlier interpretations by eminent theological writers. All of them were more or less familiar with the concepts and jargon of classical philosophers, often Plato or the
Neoplatonists, sometimes Aristotle or the Stoics. All of them, even those
accused of being mere logic choppers, were concerned about the relevance
of their abstract doctrines for the more practical concerns of ordinary
believers. All of them acquired supporters, sometimes many, sometimes
few. And despite the incendiary critiques of their opponents and their own
flamboyantly excessive rhetoric, all of them argued on the basis of deep
commitment and personal devotion.[2]

The oddity of doing theology has always been that the participants
themselves can sense that they are trying to explain the unknowable and
articulate the ineffable. The Cappadocian theologian Eunomius was reluctant to concede this incomprehension. "God knows no more about His
essence than we do. Whatever we know about His essence, He certainly
knows. Whatever He knows in turn, you will find without any changes in
us." Theologians of different persuasions became allies in mocking this claim
to virtual omniscience. Some scoffed that Eunomius and his supporters
must be "men who walked in heaven" to have such insights. Gregory of
Nyssa ridiculed Eunomius' claims more directly. "In human nature there is
no power for an accurate understanding of God's essence." In his estimation, small children would have more success at catching a sunbeam. The
Cappadocian Fathers instead developed a theology that highlighted the
language of negation. As a result, "it was clear that there was not, and could
not be, a perfectly adequate analogy for God."[3]

These intrinsic limitations in articulating beliefs, and the consequent
difficulties of evaluating the comparative excellence or usefulness of doctrines, should imply the necessity for modern scholars to consider the
wider social and cultural dimensions of theological debates. Some modern

interpretations in fact have been more adventuresome, in particular in their analyses of various so-called heresies during the fourth and early fifth centuries. Interpretations of the controversies over Donatism, Priscillianism, Pelagianism, and Origenism have highlighted the relationship between cities and countryside, the claustrophobic nature of life in small communities, the use of accusations of otherness and of public hearings to enforce conformity, the influence of gender roles, and the significance of networks of patronage. Whatever the specific successes of these interpretations, they have demonstrated conclusively the importance of social, cultural, and even economic factors in the shaping and reception of doctrines, and therefore in the molding of notions of orthodoxy and heresy.[4]

So far these sorts of interpretations have been limited to analyses of movements and doctrines that were eventually branded as heretical. There are no similar social and cultural interpretations of the development of orthodoxy. They also so far have not provided a comprehensive cultural analysis of the most prominent "heresy" of the fourth century, "Arianism," in all its many manifestations, however identical, similar, or dissimilar. This is a baffling oversight, for several reasons.

First, the controversies over defining the divine Trinity were the dominant theological disputes in most of the Roman empire during the fourth century, and especially in the Greek East. The issues involved filtered into all aspects of life, from imperial policies to individual prayers. Even non-Christians might be assumed to know the details of these controversies. Gregory of Nyssa once flattered Libanius, the eminent teacher at Antioch who was an incorrigible pagan, by calling him "the only-begotten erudition." In Gregory's theological vocabulary there was no higher compliment: if Jesus Christ was the only-begotten Son of God the Father, then Libanius was the only-begotten manifestation of Greek culture. People also found something to chuckle about in these controversies, since they added a humorous undertone to a riddle that presupposed familiarity with trinitarian disputes. This riddle played on the basic paradox between the one essence and the three Persons in the Trinity. What is "one from three, and three mingled in one"? Answer: a mixed drink (which was probably not the first response of early Christian theologians . . . or of modern patristics scholars).[5]

A second reason the trinitarian controversies deserve more discussion from non-theological perspectives is the possibility of engaging so many modern interpretive perspectives. Believers articulated their doctrines in many different ways. In addition to composing the predictable polemical treatises, exegetical commentaries, and moralizing sermons, theologians sometimes turned their ideas into unlikely literary genres. The infamous priest Arius, for instance, was accused of seducing the unlearned at Alexandria by composing ditties for sailors and millers, while Gregory of Nazianzus wrote sophisticated poems that followed the complex rules of classical prosody. Artists represented theological doctrines in imagery, especially in the monumental paintings and mosaics on the walls, apses, and domes inside churches. Preachers used gestures. When a deacon at Antioch smothered a bishop's mouth with his hand to prevent him from confessing an unacceptable doctrine, the bishop held up three fingers and then one to signify his notion of the Three and the One. Some churchmen found doctrinal implications in the most ordinary aspects of life. The theologian Aetius was alleged to have reduced the entire controversy to flatulent eruptions, so that three detonations of identical volume represented his rivals' claims about the Persons of the Trinity and three outbursts of dissimilar volume his own.[6]

For his theology opponents condemned Aetius as a heretic, and for his ribaldry they slandered him as "The Groaner." Aetius' fate is an indication of a further difficulty in reading and interpreting these ancient theological treatises, the inclusion of so much mean satire and ridicule and the almost complete absence of any humor or even a light touch. A few bishops did have a sense of puckishness about their theology. Eudoxius, a Cappadocian who became bishop of Constantinople, announced that "the Father is irreverent and the Son is reverent." His audience was flabbergasted, until he explained that the Father was irreverent because he revered no one, while the Son was reverent because he revered the Father; then the people burst out laughing. Sisinius, a bishop of one of the splinter sects at Constantinople, once dueled with the loquacious John Chrysostom in an exchange of quips and one-liners. "Because you are a heretic, I will end your preaching!" "And I will thank you for relieving me of such a burden!" Even Gregory of Nazianzus, who conceded that he was too kind to be witty, once tried to defuse the wrangling at a council with a mischievous announcement about the advantages of experiencing "life's many twists." "What greater pleasure is there than to have fun?"[7]

These jokes were rare, however, and in fact most bishops with a sense of humor seem to have been dismissed as unorthodox. The stern response of Gregory of Nyssa to his rival Eunomius' witticisms was more typical. In his estimation, Eunomius' clever logic may have been appropriate merriment for a tavern, but his use of humor when arguing theology clearly indicated that he needed "a teacher and a rod," a disciplinarian and a thrashing.

This seriousness, almost grimness, has unfortunately infected many modern discussions about early Christian theology too, when an acknowledgment of the comedic, a sense of playfulness, or simply a reaction of bemusement would be much more rewarding and certainly more interesting.[8]

The single chapter in this section highlights some of the social and cultural factors in the disputes among three Cappadocians over the theology of the Trinity. Both Basil and his brother Gregory of Nyssa articulated much of their theology in opposition to the doctrines of Eunomius. But doctrinal differences alone cannot explain all the animosity in their arguments. During this controversy the pursuit of local prestige and individual status was as important as any concerns about correct doctrinal formulations. Just as men selected their friends in part for utilitarian motives, hoping for assistance and support, so they chose their rivals to benefit themselves. Because Gregory of Nazianzus always loved classical culture, one of his main opponents had been a learned pagan, the emperor Julian. Because Basil and Gregory of Nyssa were concerned about doctrinal orthodoxy, one of their main opponents was a rival theologian, Eunomius. Through their disputes as well as through their friendships they hoped to enhance their own reputations.[9]

Chapter 1

"The Evil in Our Bosom":
Eunomius as a Cappadocian Father

The three Cappadocian Fathers were representatives of a long line of important churchmen from Cappadocia during the fourth century. Basil proudly claimed that the author of the creed endorsed by the Council of Nicaea had been Hermogenes, a future bishop of Caesarea. One of the early supporters of Arius, the infamously heterodox priest at Alexandria, was Asterius the Sophist, a Cappadocian theologian who seems to have spent most of his career in Syria but retained enough connections with his native region to attend a council at Antioch in 341 as the companion of bishop Dianius of Caesarea. Like the local notables who acquired offices in the imperial administration, some Cappadocians took advantage of imperial patronage or ecclesiastical connections to become bishops at cities outside central Asia Minor, including some of the great cities of the eastern Mediterranean. Euphronius, a priest at Caesarea, became bishop of Antioch with the recommendation of the emperor Constantine. Gregorius and Georgius both served as replacement bishops at Alexandria, and Eudoxius served as bishop at both Antioch and Constantinople. Perhaps the most influential of these Cappadocian churchmen was Ulfilas. His ancestors had been taken captive from their village in Cappadocia by Goths who had invaded Asia Minor during the mid-third century. Even though Ulfilas had grown up outside the Roman empire in the Danube regions, as the "bishop of the [Gothic] people" he repeatedly met with Roman emperors. He visited Constantinople during Constantine's reign, supported Constantius' doctrines, may have negotiated with Valens on behalf of one Gothic band, and argued theology with Theodosius. His most impressive achievements were his translation of the Bible into Gothic and his leadership in converting the Goths to Christianity.[1]

Some of these illustrious Cappadocian churchmen achieved their prominence outside Cappadocia, and several were considered heterodox because of their association with Arius, the doctrinal system affiliated with his theology that came to be known as Arianism, or related Arianizing doctrines. As a result, they seem to have had little direct influence on the thinking and writings of the Cappadocian Fathers. Another Cappadocian churchman, however, had a profound impact. One of their contemporaries was Eunomius, a sometime bishop, a powerful dialectician, and an outspoken theologian so highly regarded among his supporters that one described his words as comparable to pearls. Yet despite these attributes, Eunomius never became a venerated Father of the Church. Some of his opponents sneered at his prose and his rhetoric, such as one historian who rejected his theological writings as verbose, repetitious, and pointless. Others were so incensed at his theology that they responded in huge treatises, including one with twenty-five books and "forty thousand lines" that refuted him "virtually word for word." Jerome, a younger contemporary, listed more opponents for Eunomius than for any of the other authors he included in his long catalogue of Christian writers. Since Jerome often seemed to assess churchmen by the number and reputations of their rivals, he was certainly keeping an accurate scorecard on such disputes.[2]

The most prominent of Eunomius' antagonists were his fellow Cappadocians, Basil and Gregory of Nyssa. For them the doctrines of Eunomius evoked an almost visceral reaction, and their polemical responses, simultaneously learned and sarcastic, were the lengthiest and most extensive theological treatises for each. Although their hostility certainly reflected in part their profound theological disagreements, the sheer vehemence of their personal attacks suggests additional underlying motives regarding family, education, personal connections, and expectations about the success of their careers. Eunomius was the son of a working man, while Basil and Gregory were prominent notables. For such pampered scions it must have been doubly galling to have as a theological peer someone who was a native of the region in which they were making careers as churchmen but who did not share their background of wealth and privilege.

In Greek cities local notables had always measured their standing and authority by comparing themselves to their peers. Prestige and influence were comparative, not absolute. In this atmosphere of competition and constant comparison rivalries were upside-down friendships. Just as men chose their friends, they selected their rivals, the opponents with whom they would compete and whom they would try to surpass: "professional quarrels were not a luxury but a necessary medium for self-advertisement." Like a friendship, a rivalry was both instrumental, since it helped to advance careers and reputations, and emotional, since it consistently exposed hard feelings. A successful rivalry furthermore typically followed a protocol of behavior, no matter how extravagantly crude some of the comments became, and it was public, played out before an audience that was as intent on finding out about the men themselves as on learning their particular doctrines and ideas. Both friendships and rivalries were forms of self-representation, of the care for the self that had become such a marked feature of aristocratic life in the Roman empire. Friendships and rivalries were the equivalents of appearance, deportment, and gait, all the public features that people scrutinized in order to find out more about men's inner selves. Men revealed themselves both in their friendships and in their rivalries.[3]

In the case of these Cappadocian churchmen there was a close, and perhaps not wholly coincidental, correspondence between theological disagreements and contrasting biographies. These particular doctrinal disputes would focus in part on the proper language for articulating the relationship between God the Father and God the Son, with Basil and Gregory preferring the terminology of "begatting" and "birth" and Eunomius the equally biblical language of "creating" and "making." In a similar fashion Basil and Gregory always projected a sense of entitlement about the respect and honor that was theirs by birth, and they could not cope with the self-made success of an upstart like Eunomius. The formula eventually adopted as the orthodox doctrine to describe the Son could hence also serve as a reassertion of the normal source of prestige and influence in local provincial society: "begotten, not made."

The feuds between Eunomius and his rivals from his homeland, Basil and Gregory of Nyssa, were manifestations of a long-standing pattern of competition in Greek cities, but now worked out in a Christian society. In this setting these adversaries tried to acquire primacy first by arguing over theology. Then, after the theological issues had been settled, they argued over history.

Eunomius' Success

Since Basil and Eunomius were about the same age and since they both studied classical culture and biblical writings, in slightly different circumstances they might have become friends. Eunomius had acquired his education from a profoundly opposite background, however. He was not a member of a locally distinguished family. His hometown was Oltiseris, a colorless village in the far north of Cappadocia within a hundred miles northwest of

Caesarea and northeast of Nyssa. Nearby was Corniaspa, another village close to the border with Galatia that served as a way station on the east-west road between Tavium in the province of Galatia Prima and Sebasteia in the province of Armenia Prima and the north-south road between Tavium and Caesarea. Both small villages most likely resembled Sasima, yet another inconspicuous way station in Cappadocia that was "a little village with no water or vegetation, not fully civilized, thoroughly abominable and very cramped. Everywhere there is dust, the creaking of wagons, wailing and groaning, tax officials, racks and fetters. The inhabitants are strangers and vagrants." In northern Cappadocia there were no proper cities, and the entire region was filled with small settlements and imperial estates and ranches. In fact, less than fifty miles east of Oltiseris and Corniaspa was "a spa on an imperial estate" known as Basilica Therma, "Imperial Hot Springs."[4]

Eunomius' family was not quite as nondescript as his native village. His grandfather had a Romanized Latin name, and his family operated a mill and a tannery or a workshop in leather, whose laborers perhaps included slaves. The livestock in Cappadocia would have provided numerous hides, and the Roman army was a huge consumer of leather for clothing, shoes, armor, and tents. With their ready access to a main road leading toward Sebasteia and the upper Euphrates River, Eunomius' family most likely supplied grain and leather to the troops on the eastern frontier. His father furthermore owned a small farm, and during the long winter months he supplemented his livelihood by engraving letters of the alphabet for use by children. Even an opponent later conceded that he had been a "most admirable man." Eunomius' family was hence moderately successful and included farmers, craftsmen, and small entrepreneurs.[5]

Because the needs of the Roman troops had offered these men an opportunity to enhance their local standing, Eunomius would later complain that his family was concerned the attacks on him were ruining its reputation. Eunomius himself, most likely with his family's encouragement, had hoped to improve his prospects still further by taking advantage of the presence of an imperial court in the East and its demands for clerks and secretaries. He learned shorthand, perhaps with the expectation of becoming a *notarius*, a clerk in one of the many bureaus of the imperial court and provincial administration. Many young men, even sons from locally prominent families, were now learning secretarial skills. In fact, in the later fourth century some of the grandnephews of Gregory of Nazianzus would likewise learn shorthand at Tyana in Cappadocia. Some of these secretaries, because of their subsequent proximity to emperors and other

powerful administrators, even rose to higher offices and ranks in the imperial administration. One of Eunomius' exact contemporaries was Procopius,
a native of Cilicia who worked as a notary for many years before being promoted to a military command and eventually even making an attempt at
becoming emperor. Another was Sophronius, a fellow Cappadocian who
served as a notary before becoming an influential magistrate at Valens' court.
Eunomius himself initially served as a secretary for a relative and a tutor for
his children, which suggests that he had also received some formal education. He then decided to pursue an advanced education by studying rhetoric.[6]

To achieve his goal Eunomius needed more support. At Antioch a
bishop recommended him to Aetius, a cleric who already had a reputation
as a challenging theologian and a daunting logician. Born in the early fourth
century, Aetius had been raised at Antioch, where his family, like that of
Eunomius, had made a living by servicing Roman soldiers. His father too
had supplied the troops on the eastern frontier. After his father's death the
young Aetius had become a goldsmith to support himself and his impoverished mother, perhaps after first working as a tinker. After his mother's death
he began to study grammar, logic, medicine, and biblical exegesis with various teachers, among them some clerics, at Anabarzus and Tarsus in Cilicia,
Antioch, and Alexandria. When Leontius, one of his former teachers, became
bishop of Antioch, Aetius became one of his deacons, but he did not serve
long and eventually returned to Alexandria. There Eunomius finally joined
up with him; and thereafter Eunomius effectively adopted Aetius as "the
patron and the guide of his life."[7]

Aetius prided himself on his vigorous participation in intellectual debates. In disputations he had a reputation for the intimidating quickness
of his thinking: "everything seemed to be readily available at the tip of his
tongue." His own theology stressed the exact metaphysics of the relationship
between God and Son and emphasized that because God was "Ingenerate in
essence," the Son, His generate offspring, could be neither "similar in essence"
nor "identical in essence." Aetius seemed to consider theology as a form of
mathematics: "he spoke about God by using a kind of geometry and dia-
grams." His preferred technique of formulating his teachings was in a series
of terse deductive proofs, similar to syllogisms, that included "echoes of
Aristotle." It is therefore no surprise that he had earned the hostility of various bishops who did not share his theological opinions or resented his contentious demeanor, his rigid logic chopping, and his sarcastic intelligence.[8]

Two influential opponents were Basil, bishop of Ancyra, and Eustathius, bishop of Sebasteia, who promoted the doctrine that the Son was

"similar in essence" to God the Father. Rather than trying to refute Aetius' ideas directly, Basil and Eustathius plotted against their rival at the court of Gallus. In 351 the emperor Constantius had appointed his cousin Gallus as a junior emperor and sent him to Antioch. Gallus' inherent cruelty only enhanced his own insecurity about his authority, and he was quite ready to condemn men to execution or exile after hearing flimsy accusations of treason or of practicing magic. Because initially he believed the whispers of Basil and Eustathius, he ordered that both of Aetius' legs be broken. Gallus changed his mind just as quickly, however, and after bishop Leontius intervened, he accepted Aetius as his friend, appeared with him at a public spectacle, and eventually even sent him to check on his half-brother Julian, who was rumored to be drifting away from Christianity. Gallus was probably a year or two older than Eunomius, but like him, he too now accepted Aetius as his "teacher of holy doctrines."[9]

Eunomius was most likely with Aetius in Antioch, and so he too might have enjoyed special favor at the imperial court. He would also have been able to observe the end of Gallus' regime. Through reports from various imperial magistrates, Constantius had tried to keep tabs on Gallus. His cousin's behavior was disturbing enough that in 353 he sent Domitianus as the new prefect of the East with instructions to invite Gallus to visit him in Italy. Domitianus would have been an intriguing model for Eunomius, since he had started his career as a shorthand writer before acquiring senatorial rank, serving as count of the imperial revenues, and finally being appointed prefect. Eventually Domitianus confronted Gallus with a demand to leave town. Gallus' response was to encourage the soldiers to lynch the prefect and other high-ranking imperial magistrates. In 354 Constantius' envoys finally persuaded Gallus to leave Antioch, and then executed him en route to Italy.[10]

Gallus' brutish behavior had earned him a reputation for behaving like a ferocious lion that had tasted blood, and for Eunomius, a young man in his twenties, this brush with a capricious emperor could have been dangerous. Although many were soon executed or tortured for having served or been friends of Gallus, for several years it seemed that Aetius and Eunomius would suffer no penalties. Aetius tried to publicize his sophistic learning and his grievances by sending letters to the emperor Constantius, and both he and Eunomius benefited from the patronage of Cappadocians who had advanced in the ecclesiastical hierarchy. Aetius returned to Alexandria, where he served as a deacon under Georgius, a Cappadocian whom Constantius had installed as the new bishop of the city after again forcing Athanasius into exile. At Antioch, meanwhile, Eudoxius, another Cappadocian who had succeeded Leontius as bishop of the city, ordained Eunomius as a deacon. But then Basil of Ancyra and Eustathius of Sebasteia again used their earlier tactic of appealing directly to an emperor, this time to Constantius. Not only did they convince the emperor to accept their theology, but they also accused Aetius and Eudoxius of having been participants in Gallus' conspiracy. With the emperor's acquiescence, Basil's supporters seized Aetius and sent him into exile in Phrygia, and they forced Eudoxius to return to his native region. When Eunomius set out as an envoy to the emperor, he was seized on the road and exiled to Phrygia.[11]

By the autumn of 359 Constantius had returned to Constantinople to begin planning for campaigns against the Persians on the eastern frontier. His recent attempts at resolving theological disputes had become more insistent. Although he may have soon allowed the recall of the exiles, he had also sanctioned the publication of the "Dated Creed," which declared the Son to be "similar in all respects" to the Father and rejected any use of the contentious term "essence." By the end of the year he had finally compelled bishops from both East and West, after complementary councils at Seleucia in Isauria and Ariminum in Italy, to accept a creed that declared the Son to be merely "similar" to the Father. These diluted phrases were supposed to resolve as many disagreements as possible by being "a boot that fit both feet." Even though many bishops retained doubts about these reductive doctrinal formulations, they joined Constantius in agreeing that the teachings of Aetius were blasphemous. Since Aetius had recently published a short summary of his doctrines, he had made himself a convenient target. In January 360 the emperor convened yet another council, this time at Constantinople, that promulgated another creed emphasizing the "similarity" of the Father and Son, resolved a series of accusations about various bishops, and outright condemned Aetius as a heretic.[12]

The council at Constantinople also marked the emergence of some new participants in this ongoing theological debate. One was Basil of Caesarea, who attended with bishop Dianius of Caesarea. Another was Eunomius. During the previous decade Eunomius had done very well for himself. Having started out by being trained for a career as a clerk, he had since extended his education and acquired a prominent mentor in Aetius, and he had had contacts on the fringes of Gallus' court and survived the subsequent retaliatory purges. His secretarial training had not been forgotten, however, since he may have introduced some innovations in stenography that were then taught under his name. He had hobnobbed with prominent bishops like

Eudoxius of Antioch and become a deacon, and he had acquired a small reputation as a theologian himself. He would furthermore have appreciated some of the decisions of this council at Constantinople, which now deposed such bishops as Basil of Ancyra and Eustathius of Sebasteia, Aetius' old enemies who continued to prefer the doctrine that the Son was "similar in essence" to the Father.[13]

On the other hand, Aetius, and perhaps Eunomius too, also challenged the new orthodoxy, and according to the account of a later sympathizer Eunomius even assisted Aetius at this council in arguing the doctrine that the Son was "dissimilar in essence" to the Father. If Eunomius did in fact openly share Aetius' dissent, he was not penalized. Although the emperor Constantius expelled Aetius from his palace, supported his deposition from the clergy, and acquiesced in his exile first to Cilicia and then to Pisidia, Eunomius escaped sanctions. Instead, he enhanced his standing. Just as a few years earlier during the pogrom that followed the reign of Gallus, again Eudoxius came to Eunomius' rescue. At the council, Constantius had agreed that Eudoxius should be transferred from his see of Antioch to become the new bishop of Constantinople. Once he became bishop at the capital, Eudoxius obtained the emperor's approval to consecrate Eunomius as the replacement for Eleusius, the bishop of Cyzicus whom the council had deposed for his suspect behavior and unacceptable theological beliefs. In his yo-yo career Eunomius had crested again in 360.[14]

"The Clarity of His Teaching"

But in the face of stiff opposition from partisans of his predecessor he did not last long as bishop at Cyzicus. Eleusius had supported the doctrine that the Son was "similar in essence" to the Father; Eunomius now argued that the Son was "not similar in essence." Some clerics at Cyzicus then accused their new bishop of the more extreme formulation that the Son was outright "dissimilar" to the Father: "his teachings are more impious than the blasphemies of Arius." These accusations caused an uproar in Constantinople, whose bishop had supported Eunomius' consecration. Eudoxius now summoned Eunomius to the capital and gave him the opportunity to defend himself. In a series of sermons Eunomius agreed that the Son was "similar" to the Father "according to the Scriptures" although not "in essence," and he carefully did not even hint that the Son might be "dissimilar." These judicious orations were so successful that the audience praised his wisdom and piety and complimented Eudoxius for his selection of Eunomius.[15]

The reaction was different after Eudoxius invited Eunomius to preach again on the feast of Epiphany in early January 361. In this sermon Eunomius was less discreet, since he apparently argued that the Son was the slave and helper of the Father and he denied the perpetual virginity of Mary after Jesus' birth. Eudoxius nevertheless still hoped to convince Eunomius to adopt the current orthodox doctrine and even to assent to Aetius' banishment. In fact, Aetius' lingering exile became the final point of disagreement between the two. Already before accepting his consecration Eunomius had insisted upon a pledge from Eudoxius that Aetius would be released from his exile and deposition within three months. Not surprisingly, Eudoxius failed to keep this promise. Opposition to Eunomius' episcopacy at Cyzicus hence coincided with his own increasing aggressiveness in articulating his theology and his growing realization that Eudoxius was not campaigning for Aetius' recall. So Eunomius now left his episcopacy and returned to Cappadocia.[16]

Basil of Caesarea had returned to Cappadocia a year earlier after the council at Constantinople, and in the spring of 360 Constantius had traveled through the region on his way to Antioch. While resting at Caesarea the emperor had received the news about the usurpation of his cousin Julian. In 355 Constantius had sent Julian as a junior emperor to defend the Rhine frontier. Because of his military successes, Julian became so popular that his troops hailed him as a senior emperor early in 360. Constantius had nevertheless gone on to the eastern frontier and spent the winter of 360–361 in Antioch. There Acacius, bishop of Caesarea in Palestine, persuaded him to summon Eunomius for a hearing. Acacius had been one of the prominent advisers at the council at Constantinople, and he had apparently resented the episcopal consecration of Eunomius. Although Constantius ordered Eunomius, once he arrived at Antioch, to deliver an explanation of his doctrines and submit to the judgment of a council, the whole case collapsed because Acacius failed to speak up about his accusations. By then Constantius had more pressing concerns, and he eventually left Antioch and began to march west to face Julian.[17]

Constantius had been unsympathetic to Aetius and Eunomius in part because of their earlier association with Gallus. Once Julian became sole emperor after Constantius' death in November 361, however, both benefited. Julian was about the same age as Eunomius, and he too now seems to have considered Aetius as a mentor. Years earlier Aetius had called upon Julian as an emissary from Gallus; now the emperor recalled him from exile and, in memory of their "earlier intimacy," even invited him to visit. Aetius returned to Constantinople, where some of the bishops who supported his theological doctrines consecrated him as a bishop, and where Eudoxius finally began working to lift the condemnation against him. Despite Eudoxius' new energy Aetius was obviously still miffed, since among the new bishops he and his supporters consecrated was a rival bishop for Constantinople. He himself first traveled to Lydia to try to establish some of these new bishops, and then went to live on the island of Lesbos on an estate near Mitylene that was a gift from Julian. Eunomius had initially joined Aetius at Constantinople, and later went to live at Chalcedon in a villa near the coast that may also have been a gift from Julian.[18]

With Julian's support Aetius and Eunomius flourished again. Having once been threatened because of their association with Gallus and their rivals' success at securing the backing of Constantius, they had certainly remembered the importance of acquiring imperial patronage. After Julian's death in 363 they next tried to acquire the support of Jovian, the new emperor, by including two of his relatives among the new bishops they appointed for regions in Asia Minor.[19]

As one emblem of this enhancement in his prestige Eunomius published his *Apology*, a short account of his theological doctrines in which he seemed eager to defend his teachings and to establish his own reputation as a significant theologian. Under Aetius' influence Eunomius too emphasized that God was "Ingenerate" and could not share essence with a Son who was generated through God's will, and he rejected the formulation that the Son was "similar in essence." But Eunomius never mentioned Aetius in his treatise, perhaps as an attempt to disguise the background of his thinking, perhaps too because he wanted to be treated as an influential theologian in his own right. Another clear indication of his unwavering focus on theology alone was his decision not to mention any of his rivals by name. No doubt he had specific opponents in mind when he referred to "some evil men who do not hesitate to say or do anything and those inexperienced men who measure the truth by accusations of disagreements." But his treatise was remarkably moderate, especially given the sort of extravagant invective that the genre of apology seemed to encourage, surprisingly impersonal, especially given all the individual animosities that had motivated so many of the doctrinal controversies, and narrowly concentrated on theological issues and on explaining his beliefs in his own creed. At the conclusion he hinted that his rivals had distorted his case because of their wealth and influence. Even then, rather than lashing out at his opponents he only encouraged his supporters not to be misled by fallacious claims or flatteries.[20]

On its own, Eunomius' *Apology* would probably not have had much impact. Many of his ideas were by now not new. A later sympathizer in fact distinguished Eunomius from Aetius not in terms of their specific doctrines, but in terms of the ways they presented themselves. Aetius was known for "the force of his arguments and the readiness of his responses to each point," while Eunomius had a reputation "for the clarity and symmetry of his teaching and its special suitability for students." Accessibility and clarity came with a price, however, since those qualities made his doctrines inviting for refutation. Within a few years Eunomius' treatise had become notoriously celebrated because of the opposition it stirred up. The most prominent of his opponents was Basil of Caesarea.[21]

Rivalry with Basil

By the mid-360s Basil too had reached a transition point in his career. After returning to Cappadocia from his studies in Athens, he had soon decided not to assume a public career as a teacher and instead had retreated to his family's estate in Pontus to live in ascetic solitude. Eventually he had become a junior cleric at Caesarea. Then his ecclesiastical career had stalled.

Although he had accompanied bishop Dianius of Caesarea to the council at Constantinople in January 360, he had not seized the opportunity to make a reputation for himself. Participation at such public discussions had become one way for even a young cleric to distinguish himself. At the Council of Nicaea in 325, for instance, the deacon Athanasius, then in his mid-twenties, was supposed to have attracted the attention of the emperor Constantine because of his dialectical skills. At the council at Constantinople the deacon Basil was already in his early thirties, and he already had a reputation as a rhetorician. Since his skill as an orator was renowned, perhaps his reluctance to participate was due to hesitation about committing himself to specific doctrines. During this period Basil was certainly reading and thinking about these doctrinal issues of the relationship between the Father and the Son, although in a letter to a friend he admitted that he had decided not to publish his opinions. His rivals would not be so charitable, and might easily interpret his reticence as a character flaw. Years later an opponent who nevertheless admired Basil's wisdom described him at this council as someone who had "surpassed many with his power of speaking but retreated from public confrontations because of his timid resolution."[22]

In 362 Basil had not been selected to succeed Dianius as bishop of Caesarea. Even though he did become a priest, he retreated again to his life of solitude to escape his contentious relationship with Eusebius, the new bishop of Caesarea. At that point Basil's career seemed to be stymied again.

Highlighting his lack of achievement, and perhaps adding to his frustration, was Eunomius' comparative success. As a cleric at Caesarea Basil would certainly have been aware of the career of Eunomius, a native Cappadocian, and they had most likely met, perhaps for the first time, at the council at Constantinople. If Basil was feeling thwarted in advancing his ecclesiastical career, Eunomius was a rising star. He had spent time, as a guest or defendant, at various imperial courts, he had participated in the debates at the council at Constantinople, he had become a bishop at Cyzicus (even if he served only briefly) and had delivered sermons at Constantinople, and he had published a treatise outlining his own theology. Eunomius furthermore had joined Aetius in consecrating various bishops who shared their theological doctrines, among them a regional bishop for all of Galatia and Cappadocia. These new bishops considered both Aetius and Eunomius to be "common fathers and leaders" and always consulted Eunomius' opinion. In contrast, Basil had failed to become a bishop in Cappadocia and even felt himself unable to serve as a priest at Caesarea. All he had published so far was an anthology of extracts from the writings of the theologian Origen and probably some of his own writings about asceticism. By the mid-360s the most prominent and distinguished member of their generation of Cappadocian churchmen was Eunomius, not Basil.[23]

Once Eunomius published a theological treatise, however, Basil could compete with him, and try to surpass him. An argument over theology would allow him to appear high-minded, but still be confrontational. For Basil, however, confrontation was always easier than high-mindedness, and sometimes the sheer need for disputation threatened to overwhelm the actual arguments over doctrines. Theological preferences often seemed to become a matter of mere taste rather than of profound truths, "as if these were contests not over piety and faith but over a choice of colors." For Basil, the particularly galling aspect of a confrontation with Eunomius was not necessarily that his career had fallen behind, as rather that Eunomius, coming from an undistinguished family and having received his education from lesser teachers in lesser cities, was in his estimation essentially not a worthy rival. Eunomius had studied to become a mere clerk, while Basil had once had the opportunity to become an estimable rhetorician. Refuting Eunomius' theology would not be enough. If Basil wished to surpass Eunomius, he would need to protect the standing of himself and other local notables by smearing the character and the perceived arrogance of this new man from northern Cappadocia.[24]

One appropriate opportunity for such a reply was the appearance of a new imperial dynasty. In 364 Valentinian and Valens succeeded as emperors. Although Valens assumed responsibility for the eastern empire and soon traveled to the eastern frontier, support for his reign was initially uncertain. In 365 Procopius was proclaimed emperor in Constantinople. Procopius was a relative of Julian, and he now self-consciously presented himself as the true heir to the Constantinian dynasty of Julian. Among his supporters were Aetius and Eunomius, who only a few years earlier had both benefited from Julian's patronage. After Julian's death, however, both had retreated to out-of-the-way estates, and Procopius himself had been so uneasy about his standing with the new emperors that he had become a fugitive. Before he finally went to Constantinople, he had stayed for a time at Eunomius' villa outside Chalcedon. After Procopius was hailed as emperor, Eunomius visited him at his former episcopal see of Cyzicus to obtain the release of some prisoners. On Lesbos, Aetius was living with two brothers who had contacts at the court of Procopius, since their relative had become one of Procopius' most powerful advisers. This relative was able to rescue Aetius after the locals on Lesbos had slandered him as a supporter of Valens. Moving back to Constantinople was a clear indication that both Aetius and Eunomius were now openly supporting Procopius. By bolstering the new emperor's attempts to conjure up memories of Julian they were also trying again to revive their own standing and the influence of their doctrines.[25]

Valens heard the news about Procopius' usurpation while he was resting at Caesarea in Cappadocia. Since Procopius was a native of Cilicia and since some of his supporters, including Aetius and Eunomius, were from regions close to the eastern frontier, Valens responded by trying to shore up his own support among the local notables of central and eastern Asia Minor. Some of Basil's friends now acquired offices in the imperial administration. Basil himself, because he was already resentful of Eunomius' success as a churchman, may well have used this opportunity to publish a response to Eunomius' treatise and hence try to improve his own standing with the new emperor and his court.

One of Basil's theological mentors was Eustathius of Sebasteia, who had earlier tried to undermine Aetius and Eunomius by appealing to imperial courts. Basil seems now to have modified that strategy slightly by providing a theological complement to the emperor's military preparations. As Valens prepared to confront Procopius, Basil would publicly challenge the theology of Eunomius, one of Procopius' supporters. Basil was also perhaps looking to influence the theological preferences of a new emperor whose support for some specific formulation of doctrinal orthodoxy may still have seemed to be contestable. Basil's desire to compete with and defeat Eunomius and his doctrines hence conveniently coincided with the possibilities of shaping Valens' own doctrinal preferences and of acquiring gratitude from a new emperor who was actively looking to bolster his position in the eastern provinces.[26]

During his seclusion in Pontus, Basil had remained in contact with Eustathius of Sebasteia. Eustathius had occasionally visited Basil at his retreat, and in 364 in particular, during a meeting with him and other bishops who were on their way to a council, Basil had dictated some of his objections to a particular "heresy." These objections were probably some of the ideas that Basil was working on for his arguments against Eunomius' theology. In a contemporary letter he indicated that he would accept the formulation that the Son was "exactly similar according to essence" to the Father, since that phrase was equivalent to the description "identical in essence." Even though Basil himself did not attend this council, his ideas presumably had some influence, since the bishops at the council decided to endorse the doctrine that the Son was "similar in essence" to the Father. In addition, this council may have directly considered Eunomius and his activities, since one of its participants was apparently the bishop of Cyzicus who had once been deposed to make way for Eunomius.[27]

In the three books of his treatise responding to Eunomius' *Apology*, Basil articulated his own doctrines about Father, Son, and Holy Spirit at length and demonstrated his learned familiarity with both theology and philosophy. But Basil also dramatically transformed the whole tone of the debate by directly assailing Eunomius' background and character. Since he had not been involved directly in previous debates, he had most likely not been one of the unnamed opponents to whom Eunomius had alluded. Yet Basil now replied as if he had been the victim of a personal attack. His assessment of Eunomius' treatise was remarkably blunt, and from the beginning he emphasized that he would go beyond refuting his opponent's doctrines in order to expose "the falsehood, ignorance, arrogance, error, and blasphemy" in this treatise.[28]

His unveiling took various forms. He denounced Eunomius for presenting his doctrines in the guise of an apology. Since there had been no occasion during which it had been necessary for Eunomius to defend his teachings, Basil argued that he had adopted this misleading format simply to earn some sympathy from his readers. Questioning the veracity of the format then allowed him to imply that Eunomius was also untrustworthy in his theology. He criticized Eunomius for his faulty use of Aristotelian logic and his tendency to babble. He belittled Eunomius as a "Galatian." One common technique of depreciating an opponent was to feign ignorance about his background, as if it was simply too unimportant to register accurately. Since Eunomius' hometown was near the border with Galatia, it was easy enough to question his Cappadocian heritage. With this description Basil may also have been trying to protect Cappadocia, the region in which he was now serving as a cleric, from the taint of Eunomius' doctrines. Gregory of Nazianzus would likewise later be embarrassed by the career of Georgius, that "Cappadocian monster" who had been a teacher for the emperor Julian and who during his episcopacy at Alexandria had made Aetius one of his deacons. Gregory's reaction was to defame Georgius' origins and ancestry and to insist all the more firmly that Cappadocia was nevertheless "holy and known to everyone for its piety." Finally, Basil also criticized Eunomius for his open pursuit of "the love of honor." In his estimation, because Eunomius had "publicized this blasphemy with the goal of being proclaimed the leader and patron of the entire heresy," his ambition had contaminated his doctrines. "Such boasting! To think that his treatise will survive him into later times and that his memory will be preserved as immortal into the future."[29]

Rhetorically Basil's response was very effective. One later reader thought that it had reduced Eunomius to an "infant" and exposed his *Apology* as nothing more than a "lifeless joke." But Basil's complaints were also certainly disingenuous. Particularly sanctimonious was his claim that his rival was concerned primarily with the pursuit of prestige, since he was himself so intent on promoting his own reputation. Basil's castigation of Eunomius and his theology marked his own emergence to preeminence not just among members of his generation, but overall in the ecclesiastical hierarchy and in Cappadocian society. The hesitation he had shown at the council at Constantinople now gave way to an aggressive firmness.[30]

In 365 Basil returned to Caesarea to take up his duties as a priest. Then he was still so pleased with the completion of his treatise that he sent a copy to a local sophist, with the request that his correspondent decide whether it was "mere child's play" or something a bit more profound. This request was an obvious indulgence in false humility, because even though Basil asked for criticism and suggestions for improvement, he was clearly angling for compliments. In 370 he became bishop of Caesarea. This promotion as the metropolitan bishop for the province of Cappadocia would have made him the counterpart of the bishop whom Aetius and Eunomius had earlier consecrated for the region. Some of Basil's recent success was a result of his rather vicious attack on Eunomius. This denunciation was furthermore a preview of his later willingness to squash rivals (and manipulate friends) in Cappadocia to achieve his own goals. One friend who would later suffer from Basil's imperiousness was Gregory of Nazianzus, who as a result could best appreciate the impact of Basil's scorching treatise about Eunomius. In his estimation, Basil's polemical writings reminded him of "the fire that vaporized the evil lies at Sodom."[31]

Yet after boosting his career by writing this extended response to Eunomius' short treatise, in subsequent years Basil hardly acknowledged his former rival. At some time Basil talked with his brother Gregory of Nyssa about Eunomius and "compared him to the most shameless of women who transfer their own disgraces to the most chaste of women." In a memorandum to his friend Amphilochius, bishop of Iconium, he responded to various philosophical issues raised by those like Eunomius who supported the "dissimilarity" of the Son to the Father. But in all his extant letters from the period of his episcopacy he mentioned Eunomius by name only once, and then merely in passing. Having surpassed Eunomius, Basil no longer needed to consider him.[32]

Eunomius' History

In contrast, Eunomius' career spiraled downward. His mentor Aetius died soon afterward, and bishop Eudoxius of Constantinople, once his patron, had become a confidant of the emperor Valens. Eudoxius' clergy now voted to expel Eunomius from the capital. At Chalcedon people criticized Eunomius for having sheltered the usurper Procopius on his estate and even threatened to kill him. Finally the prefect sent him into exile. Although the intercession of some bishops convinced the emperor to recall Eunomius, Valens had already decided to support the doctrinal formulation that the Son was merely "similar" to the Father. Not only was Valens now not sympathetic to Eunomius or his theology, but neither was Modestus, who in 369 became the new prefect of the East. Even though he had been in Constantinople when Procopius had been proclaimed emperor, Modestus had not supported his usurpation. As prefect he was immediately hostile to Eunomius, and after condemning him for disturbing churches and cities he banished him to the island of Naxos. Demophilus, who had succeeded as bishop of Constantinople with the emperor's support, continued the insults by going to Eunomius' former see of Cyzicus to anathematize him. In their public sermons and letters ecclesiastical opponents now referred to Eunomius as "The Dissimilar." This pointed (even if somewhat misleading) reference to his theology about the Son was perhaps also meant to be a suggestive hint about Eunomius' own marginal place in the church and in society in general.[33]

During his extended banishment Eunomius presumably reflected on his career and life. Despite his current fall from grace, he remained loyal to the memory of his past mentors and supporters. Early in Valens' reign he had lost any opportunity of favorable treatment by having backed Julian's relative, the usurper Procopius. Even though this support precluded any chance at rehabilitation during Valens' reign, Eunomius seems never to have faltered in his allegiance to Julian during his exile. In fact, even a decade later, when after Valens' death he was trying to ingratiate himself with the new emperor, Theodosius, he and some of his supporters came up with the eccentric scheme of fetching Julian's body from its tomb in Cilicia, presumably to bring it for burial in Constantinople. During his exile Eunomius continued to develop his intellectual interests. In a treatise entitled "The Son" he presumably elaborated again on his trinitarian theology. He also composed a commentary on Paul's letter to the Romans, and he wrote many letters. Somewhere in his writings he even recorded some speculations about the nature of the soul.[34]

Most of all, in his exile Eunomius brooded. If Basil had shrugged off Eunomius once he became a prominent priest and then bishop at Caesarea, Eunomius certainly did not forget Basil. For over a decade he sulked over Basil's reply to his first treatise. Eventually, even though he remained true to his mentors and his theology, he did transform his approach and his outlook, in particular about Basil. In his first short *Apology* Eunomius had presented only his theology. Since Basil had replied by denouncing him personally, in his long response to Basil's reply he would now, in addition to defending his doctrines again, tell his own version of his career and attack Basil.[35]

Eunomius' *Apology for His Apology* began apparently with a long account of a dream. None of the details of this dream survives, but its inclusion was perhaps meant to conjure up a comparison with a similar experience in Aetius' career, when, after a defeat in a debate, a dream had revived his courage and convinced him of "the supremacy of his wisdom." "Thereafter it was granted to Aetius never to be bested by anyone in philosophical controversies." Leading off with this dream was a clear indication that Eunomius' initial objective was simply to convince himself, and others, that he had regained his confidence and would again be an important participant in doctrinal debates. Eunomius continued by mentioning his family, his ancestors, and their livelihoods, and he also, in order to contradict Basil's description of him as a Galatian, talked about his hometown in Cappadocia. He furthermore discussed his "labors and trials," which included his feuds with Basil of Ancyra and Eustathius of Sebasteia, his participation with Aetius at the court of Gallus, their exile to Phrygia, and his episcopacy at Cyzicus. With this narrative Eunomius was presumably trying to generate some sympathy for his tribulations, transforming his biography into an emotionally charged story of struggle against long odds (or, as a less charitable opponent would see it, into the pretentiousness of tragedy). He also apparently wanted to underline his success at acquiring imperial support, since at one point "in his treatise he boasted that he and his family were so prominent and distinguished that they were known to the emperor." Because Basil's personal attacks had turned the theological dispute into a direct feud over prestige and honor, Eunomius would now publicize his distinguished reputation too.[36]

Another of Eunomius' primary concerns in this biographical sketch was to provide his version of the circumstances surrounding the publication of his first treatise and the nature of his earlier interaction with Basil. Eunomius apparently insisted again that his original *Apology* had represented a proper defense at a "competition over doctrines." Although he did not name the place, the setting for this hearing was most likely the council at Constantinople in early 360. In Eunomius' telling, Basil had responded; but when the decision went to his opponents, Basil had fled back to "a hearth in his fatherland." Basil's alleged withdrawal then gave Eunomius the opportunity to ridicule his rival directly, not just for his cowardice at this hearing but for other flaws too. "He dared to call Basil a wicked and malicious liar, a brazen, ignorant pretender who was unfamiliar with theology." To complete his portrayal of Basil's mendacity, Eunomius tried to turn his own words against him by arguing that Basil's admission that he had received the bishopric at Cyzicus as a prize was a concession that he had actually delivered a successful apology.[37]

More than a decade of resentment boiled over in Eunomius' characterization of Basil, and the polite reticence of his first treatise now gave way to a bitter allegation about his rival's "insane madness." Already in the preface to his treatise Eunomius conceded that he was filled with an "abiding, indelible hatred," and this loathing seems to have stained his entire discussion. Once he had denounced Basil's behavior and character, Eunomius proceeded with an extended rebuttal of his opponent's theological assertions that he occasionally speckled with dismissive comments about Basil's "wavering judgment and feeble reasoning." Eunomius had now supplemented his theology with his own personal history of events.[38]

Rivalry with Gregory of Nyssa

One supporter later claimed that when Eunomius published the first book of his response to Basil's treatise, his rival was so depressed that he soon died. This claim is certainly suspect, not least because it seems to be an imitation of a story about the impact that Aetius' dialectical skills had once had on one of his opponents. In addition, because Gregory of Nyssa later had so much difficulty in obtaining a copy of Eunomius' response, it is unlikely that Basil ever read the treatise.[39]

Eunomius' reply initially consisted of two books, in which he had responded only to the first of the three books in Basil's treatise against his original *Apology*. He apparently did publish these two books at about the time of Basil's death, since Gregory conceded that death had prevented his brother from responding. In Basil's absence Gregory now claimed for himself "the inheritance of this controversy" and assumed the mantle of defending his brother's honor. His younger brother Peter strongly supported his plan to respond to Eunomius' attack. But since Gregory for years already had had to deal with, and sometimes suffer from, his older brother's imperious behavior, his readiness to take on Eunomius represented more than a defense of Basil's theology and their family's honor in Cappadocia. The relationship between Gregory and Basil had always included a combustible mixture of fraternal cooperation and fraternal rivalry. Just as Basil had once used his polemic against Eunomius to establish his preeminence in Cappadocia, so now Gregory would seize the opportunity to denounce Eunomius yet again in order to emerge from Basil's shadow and enhance his own reputation both in the region and more widely.[40]

Gregory quickly replied to Eunomius with two books of his own. He composed the first of these two books soon upon his return to Cappadocia in mid-380, after his brief interim episcopacy at Sebasteia. This first book was a refutation of Eunomius' first book. Then, after his brother Peter urged him to "stab" both of Eunomius' books with one blow, he composed a second book that responded to Eunomius' second book. According to Gregory, Eunomius had worked for "Olympiads" to compose his response to Basil's criticism: "I hear that during his long retirement Eunomius applied himself diligently for many years that exceeded those of the [Trojan] war described in the *Iliad*." In contrast, Gregory now wrote his two lengthy books, together comprising about one hundred thousand words, in less than a year.[41]

Gregory seems to have had a particular audience in mind that made him especially eager to complete his response and acquire a reputation as an important theologian. Because he had completed both books by the time of the council that opened at Constantinople in the spring of 381, he was able to present public readings to other churchmen who were in attendance, such as Gregory of Nazianzus and Jerome. Probably only churchmen who were deeply involved in the current theological disputes and thoroughly familiar with classical philosophy would have appreciated Gregory's detailed response. These two books were primarily theological treatises in which Gregory defended Basil's doctrines and developed his own. His comments droned on at inordinate length. At one point he was so upset by the "idle fussiness" of Eunomius' arguments that he complained that "the author himself would not read [his account] without falling asleep." An appraisal identical in essence is certainly also applicable to these first two books of Gregory's ponderous response.[42]

Gregory had other objectives too. One was to defend Basil's character. Eunomius had accused Basil of mendacity for calling him a Galatian. Gregory now insisted that Basil had only made an honest mistake in mentioning a nearby region rather than Cappadocia as Eunomius' homeland. Eunomius had also accused Basil of cowardice for his behavior at the council of Constantinople in 360. Gregory did not dispute that accusation directly, and in a circuitous conditional statement he essentially conceded that Basil had not "wrestled with the contenders in the competitions." Part of his response to this accusation of timidity was instead to question again the circumstances of Eunomius' own first *Apology*. The more important rebuttal of Eunomius' allegation was an extended demonstration of Basil's later courage in facing down threats from the emperor Valens, the prefect Modestus, and other court officials. By sidestepping the issue of Basil's earlier behavior Gregory had once more highlighted Eunomius' own subsequent disgrace. Basil had been courageous enough to deflect Modestus' threats of banishment and death and then to protect Cappadocia from the emperor's preference for heterodox doctrines. In contrast, Modestus had sent Eunomius into exile.[43]

Another of Gregory's objectives was to disparage Eunomius and his theology yet again. Some of his criticism was mercilessly direct. Basil had once pretended that his treatise against Eunomius might be considered "mere child's play." Gregory now, in all seriousness, called Eunomius' response a "childish treatise." Since education and familiarity with classical culture were marks of a true gentleman, by criticizing Eunomius' literary style Gregory could question his character. Gregory complained that Eunomius had borrowed much of his vocabulary from other books, resorted to too many "inevitable syllogisms and clever misrepresentations of the premises," and employed a style that was too bombastic and dense for easy comprehension. In his estimation, even a child being introduced to the study of words by a grammarian would have avoided these mistakes. With this comment Gregory was also able to slip in yet another oblique criticism both of Eunomius' education and of his teachers, including Aetius.[44]

Much of Gregory's detailed criticism of Eunomius' doctrines likewise carried subtle implications about Eunomius himself. In order to clarify the circumstances of his background, Eunomius had apparently mentioned in his second apology that his family in Cappadocia owned a mill and a workshop in leather and that as a young man he had studied to become a clerk. Gregory would now turn these true confessions against Eunomius, although indirectly, in a few artfully relevant analogies that furthermore demonstrated his own mastery of rhetorical technique. In a discussion of "energies" and their role in the making of the Son and the Holy Spirit, Gregory dismissed Eunomius' explanation as comparable to the activities of a leather worker who used a knife to cut a pattern. In a discussion of the Father as "Ingenerate" and his relationship with the Son, Gregory complained that Eunomius' argument went nowhere, "just like those [animals, or perhaps slaves] that have their eyes blindfolded and turn the millstone round and round but remain in the same place during their entire journey." In an analysis of Eunomius' comments about the relationship between the descriptions of God as "Incorruptible without beginning" and "Ingenerate without end," Gregory concluded that only those trained in shorthand could decipher this enigma.[45]

To have belittled Eunomius personally at length would not have been good sportsmanship for a notable bishop like Gregory, but his learned readers and listeners, and certainly Eunomius himself, would have understood the subversive implications of these particular analogies. Even as Gregory demonstrated through his direct arguments that Eunomius' theology was inadequate, he was also implying that his opponent was not adept at

presenting himself as a theologian. Eunomius may have prided himself on having become a famous orator, even a "second Demosthenes," but Gregory would finally conclude, with the appropriate mock sadness, that it was quite improper for him "to ridicule the ignorance of those without culture." So he had used analogies and allusions. In his estimation, for all his experience in doctrinal disputes Eunomius argued theology no better than one of the leather workers in his family's factory; he might as well have stayed home and gone on grinding grain at his family's mill; and after all his attempts at improving himself he was still qualified only to serve as a secretary and take dictation.[46]

Gregory's two books did not end Eunomius' career, however. Since Eunomius had not fared well during the reign of Valens, the emperor's death in 378 may well have been the catalyst that had finally motivated him to publish his reply to Basil's treatise. He also seems now to have emerged from his long hibernation by taking up residence again in the suburbs of Constantinople, where he held church services in private houses, attracted large audiences, and gave public readings from his writings. His activities were a counterpoint to the presence at the capital of Gregory of Nazianzus, who was leading his own services in a private house, and of Gregory of Nyssa, who would present public readings of his writings to various churchmen. Eunomius furthermore continued his refutation of Basil's treatise by composing a third book that responded to Basil's second book. After Gregory replied to that third book with a third book of his own, Eunomius composed two final books that responded to Basil's third book. For a short time he was somewhat successful in rehabilitating himself and his doctrines. Not only did some members of the imperial court seem to have supported him, but at Antioch, a city riddled with religious factions, some priests asked for communion with him and his supporters, and he consecrated a new bishop for a city in Palestine.[47]

Opposition was never far away, however, and at Antioch people ended up dismissing Eunomius and his supporters as insane "star gazers." Another obstacle for Eunomius was now Theodosius, the new emperor in the East. Initially Theodosius was willing to meet with Eunomius. But after the bishops who met at the council that the emperor had summoned to Constantinople in 381 had specifically anathematized the "heresy of the Eunomians" and promulgated the Nicene doctrine that the Son was "identical in essence" with God the Father, he issued an edict that reinforced the authority of the bishops who accepted this new orthodoxy. In 383 Theodosius gave Eunomius (and some other nonconforming bishops) one final attempt to win his

approval. Eunomius composed a short confession of his faith that he presented at the imperial palace. Theodosius rejected his confession, however,
and immediately began issuing a series of edicts that restricted the activities
of Eunomius' supporters. He furthermore expelled them from Constantinople. Imperial edicts, when enforced, were a powerful deterrent, and soon
many of Eunomius' supporters began to convert in order to join "those who
shared the beliefs of the emperors." Eventually Theodosius ordered Eunomius
himself to go into exile yet again, this time at a city near the Danube River.
The capture of this city by the Goths nullified the emperor's order; so
Eunomius was instead banished to his home region of Cappadocia, where
he was allowed to live on his own estate near Caesarea.[48]

Eunomius' career had literally come full circle, and he was back where
he had started. After having departed over thirty years earlier as a determined young man seeking to improve his prospects, he now returned as an
infamous churchman with a suspect reputation. As the glitter slowly rusted
on his once promising career, Eunomius became a broken-down reminder
of the penalties for failed ambition.

Competing Histories

Although the decisions of the council at Constantinople in 381 and the
restrictions announced in subsequent imperial constitutions effectively stifled any widespread attractiveness of Eunomius' theology, they did not silence
the arguments, and proponents of various doctrinal positions continued to
engage in theological disputes. In addition, these contestants tried to shape
the meaning of earlier events by composing and publicizing their own revisionist histories. Basil certainly had his supporters, especially in Cappadocia. Already during his tenure as a leading churchman at Constantinople,
Gregory of Nazianzus had disputed the doctrines of Eunomius and his supporters in his sermons, and he was credited with having composed two
books that refuted Eunomius directly. After he resumed residence in Cappadocia, he continued in his poems to attack some of Eunomius' teachings,
and he outright considered him as "the evil in our bosom." In the end, the
controversy had returned to its roots in Cappadocia, where Gregory lived
in retirement on his estate and Eunomius resided in exile likewise on his
estate. For all their theological disagreements, both now nursed similar resentments over their failures to find support at Constantinople.[49]

Gregory of Nyssa had already defended his brother by writing three long books that refuted Eunomius' response to Basil's treatise. Soon he added a lengthy rejoinder to Eunomius' new confession of faith. This retort snidely dismissed Eunomius' convoluted attempt to win imperial support as a superficially savory delicacy that was in fact indigestible hardtack, "bread mixed with sand." Although in his writings Gregory of Nyssa was especially concerned about theological issues, in addition, whenever he mentioned aspects of the careers of Basil and Eunomius, he underlined the clear differences between their lives. In order to highlight those contrasts he essentially had to turn their careers upside down by telling new "stories": "neither his youth nor his adulthood told the same story for each man." Gregory now defended his brother by writing both theology and history.[50]

In his retelling, although both Aetius and Eunomius had started out poor, the pursuit of wealth had soon seduced them into unscrupulous behavior. When working as a goldsmith Aetius had once stolen a bracelet, and he had pretended to be a doctor to collect payments. Eunomius likewise had transformed his patronage for a theological position into a pretext for earning fees. Even though Gregory had acquired much of his information about Eunomius and his teacher Aetius, including these rather embellished legends, secondhand from oral traditions, he nevertheless was able to invent and impose a consistent interpretive pattern. In his version of their lives their theology had been the predictable outcome of misguided ambitions to become wealthy.[51]

In contrast, Gregory never mentioned that Basil had started out with the advantages of membership in a wealthy family and an education at various university towns. He instead emphasized that by spending his ancestral possessions on the poor Basil had transformed himself into the hardscrabble scion of a distinguished family. In Gregory's view, Eunomius and Aetius had undermined their credibility by their pursuit of wealth, while Basil had improved his through his support of the poor. Even though in reality Basil had rather nonchalantly trampled on Eunomius in order to advance himself and his career, Gregory now presented his brother as the innocent victim in the controversy and Eunomius as the aggressor. In his perspective Eunomius was similar to a scoundrel who had once earned his notoriety by burning down a magnificent building in Ephesus.[52]

Eunomius was nevertheless not without his own advocates. His supporters at Constantinople continued to consult with him even after his exile, and for a while a nephew headed a congregation of "Eunomians" in the capital. In Syria one bishop was still composing refutations of Eunomius' doctrines in the mid-fifth century, and he complained about a village that was "full of Eunomians." In the early sixth century Eunomius' followers were thought to have acquired the sympathy of an emperor.[53]

Even in Cappadocia some people preferred him and his doctrines. A Cappadocian named Theophronius repeated his teachings in a treatise entitled "The Exercise of the Mind." Another supporter from Cappadocia was Philostorgius. His grandfather had been a priest in Cappadocia, and his family had converted to the doctrines of Eunomius most likely during the later 360s or the 370s, precisely the period when Basil was preeminent at Caesarea. Philostorgius himself was born a few years before Basil became bishop, and before he left the region as a young man to go to Constantinople, most likely in the later 380s, he visited Eunomius in exile at his estate. This visit was a transforming event in his life, and Philostorgius was so impressed with Eunomius' wisdom and virtue that eventually he composed an extended encomium. Decades later he decided to put his hero's life into a much larger context by writing a history of most of the fourth century that essentially justified the activities and doctrines of Aetius and Eunomius and criticized the behavior of Basil. In his estimation, by daring to attack Eunomius' writings Basil had been the presumptuous participant in these debates.[54]

Philostorgius seems to have been quite aware that by composing his narrative he was entering a long-standing polemic, since he self-consciously commemorated the completion of his history with an epigram in which he insisted that he had been "weaving together multicolored strands of the truth." In contrast, a later critic accused Philostorgius of mendacity and of having been unable to recognize and reject various "myths" in his history. In a sense both the author, with his claim on truthful memories, and the critical reader, with his dismissal of that history as myth, were correct, because Philostorgius now provided the favorable legends about his hero's life that balanced the disparaging tales of his opponents. Like Gregory of Nyssa, Philostorgius had become a storyteller. What had begun as a dispute over competing theologies had become a contest over competing histories.[55]

A generation after the composition of Philostorgius' history the exact details about Eunomius and his career had, not surprisingly, become thoroughly muddled: "some tell these stories one way, others in another way." In the end, however, the traditions and interpretations that Gregory of Nyssa and Eunomius' other opponents had reiterated monotonously were victorious. Basil had been a wealthy notable who finally earned the prominence that he and others seemed to think was entitled to him from birth, while Eunomius was in fact the unforeseen success story, the local boy from a nondescript Cappadocian family who had unexpectedly become prominent in ecclesiastical and political affairs. Upon his final return to his home region, however, he discovered that at Caesarea the inhabitants despised him for having criticized Basil. His writings were similarly reviled, and eventually imperial edicts ordered the burning of his books. As a result, Eunomius' second apology did not survive. The contents of the first three books are known almost entirely through Gregory's quotations and summaries of the passages that he intended to refute, while the contents of the last two books are completely unknown simply because Gregory never responded to them.[56]

Philostorgius' history likewise would be almost entirely lost if the eminent Photius, bishop of Constantinople during the later ninth century, had not compiled a comprehensive epitome of extensive excerpts. Photius admired Philostorgius' style and elegant vocabulary, and perhaps despite himself he may have secretly enjoyed reading a historical narrative that, as he conceded, contradicted almost all other accounts. Yet he did not appreciate Philostorgius' attempts to censure Basil's reputation, and in his collection of excerpts he occasionally scribbled his own scathing comments. Over the centuries, rhetorical abuse had changed little, and sometimes Photius' criticism of Philostorgius adopted the same technique once used against Aetius and Eunomius, malevolent puns on their names and theology. One contemporary had been annoyed that a heresiarch could have such a "false name" like Eunomius, "man of good order." As a result, Aetius had been disparaged as Atheos, "The Atheist," and Eunomius as Anomoios, "The Dissimilar." Photius now maligned Philostorgius, whose name means "fond of affection," as both Philopseudes, "fond of lies," and Kakostorgius, "evil affection." In many respects rivals often developed a dependency that was more intimate than the devotion between friends, since in their mutual loathing they pushed each other toward more extravagant and therefore more telling revelations. Preserving parts of their opponents' writings, as Gregory of Nyssa had done for Eunomius' second apology and Photius for Philostorgius' history, was an implicit concession that men needed worthy opponents to enhance their own reputations. Maligning the authors of those writings at the same time was an overt acknowledgment that they could surpass their rivals only by confronting and defeating them.[57]

Eunomius too had once admitted that disputing with distinguished opponents had enhanced his own reputation. Gregory of Nyssa predictably turned this observation into a criticism that Eunomius' underlying motive had always been only the acquisition of a reputation. Yet the same comments were appropriate for Basil's and Gregory's careers, since both were intent upon inflating their reputations. They in fact were the ones who had taken the initiative in deliberately challenging a more famous opponent. Eunomius had been more successful than Basil in the mid-360s, and more renowned than Gregory in the later 370s. As a native Cappadocian he furthermore had represented an obstacle to the enhancement of even their local reputations. For both Basil and Gregory, confronting and defeating Eunomius offered an opportunity for promotion. Gregory himself provided the best insight into the tendency of ambitious men to look for worthy opponents with an analogy to the training of athletes. As wrestlers developed and improved, they always looked to test themselves against bigger and stronger rivals. "A man who has challenged himself by such disputes to defeat his enemies creates more illustrious victories for himself, because he has wrestled with more renowned and more powerful opponents."[58]

Both Basil and Gregory furthermore thought they had been successful, as theologians and as polemicists. In their estimation, their respective treatises could serve to enhance their standing not just among other theologians, but also more widely among contemporary, even non-Christian, sophists and orators. Basil had been proud enough of his treatise to send it to a local sophist for approval, and Gregory had sent his treatise to two students of the eminent orator Libanius at Antioch and suggested that they read some of its most eloquent passages to their teacher. Neither the pursuit of honor and prestige nor the means used were new in Christian society. Men had always measured themselves against rivals, and they had all, whether orators, philosophers, athletes, local aristocrats, or now churchmen, found their identities in public competitions.[59]

Basil had once tried to free himself from this addiction. At his retreat in Pontus as he had defined the expectations of an ascetic community, he had pointedly insisted that "a Christian should not lust for the renown of men or appropriate excessive honor." But his subsequent eagerness to confront and refute Eunomius was a telling indication of the lingering seductiveness of public acclamation. The pursuit of prestige and honor, one of the long-standing characteristics that had defined the lives of Greek aristocrats for centuries, had been a decisive factor in determining the fates of Eunomius, Basil, and Gregory of Nyssa. In his theological formulations Eunomius had certainly been no less sincere and thoughtful than Basil and Gregory. But he had been much less successful in attacking them personally and refuting their own direct attacks.[60]

The careers of Eunomius and Basil are also telling indications of the consequential impact of imperial support in doctrinal disputes. While their opponents had connived against them at Constantius' court, Aetius and Eunomius had benefited from their associations with the emperors Gallus and Julian, and they had tried to acquire the patronage of the emperor Jovian and then the usurper Procopius. Eunomius' decision to support Procopius earned him the lasting opposition of the emperor Valens and his powerful prefect Modestus. Basil initially, even if in the end unsuccessfully, seems to have tried to earn Valens' approval by opposing Eunomius' teachings. With his support for the decisions of the council at Constantinople in 381, the emperor Theodosius endorsed the theology of the Cappadocian Fathers, and as a result he and his successors also strongly opposed Eunomius and his supporters. Thereafter emperors took the initiative in countering Eunomius, his theology, and his memory.

Their opposition was apparent both in Eunomius' native region of Cappadocia and at the capital. In Cappadocia the concern over Eunomius' place of exile was almost as worrisome as the disputes over his doctrines. Eutropius, the most influential adviser at the court of Theodosius' son Arcadius, was still anxious enough about the heresiarch's reputation that he instructed the prefect of the East to have Eunomius moved from his estate outside Caesarea to Tyana in southern Cappadocia. There monks would keep guard. This relocation then became an ironical manifestation of a long-standing rivalry between metropolitan capitals in Cappadocia, since Eunomius, Basil's greatest antagonist, was now moved to Tyana, Caesarea's greatest rival. Perhaps Tyana did not mind hosting Basil's adversary. After Eunomius' death Eutropius refused to allow his body to be buried in a tomb with Aetius at Constantinople. Despite numerous requests, the student would not be buried with his "teacher." Eunomius' supporters at the capital would have no shrine in honor of their founder.[61]

Instead, in order to advance his own standing, the emperor Theodosius had already denigrated Eunomius' posthumous reputation at Constantinople. Initially he resorted to a customary tactic, the publication of a series of heavy-handed edicts against heretics. Another tactic was more crudely creative. Theodosius publicized his sentiments in a much more vulgar manner by having statues of Eunomius and other notable heretics placed in one of the capital's forums and then encouraging people to spatter them with spittle, urine, and excrement. Emperors often certified their own orthodoxy by highlighting their opposition to various despicable heresies. In this decision to make Eunomius an object of public derision at Constantinople, however, Theodosius was only following the lead of Basil and Gregory of Nyssa, who had likewise enhanced their careers and their prestige by showering their rival with toxic rhetorical abuse.[62]

Fossils

During the fourth century various churchmen composed large handbooks that listed hundreds of heresies. These handbooks were the predictable, and necessary, complements to the creeds defining doctrinal orthodoxy and the canons specifying proper behavior that an endless sequence of councils kept endorsing. While the councils were delimiting orthodoxy, the handbooks were providing example after example of heresy. These handbooks should remind us also of the sheer contingency inherent in the evolution of Christian orthodoxy. Collectively they are the equivalent of the Burgess Shale, a quarry on a ridge up in the Canadian Rockies in British Columbia. This quarry has yielded a singularly wonderful collection of fossils of diminutive animals that appeared and, almost always, disappeared hundreds of millions of years ago. These miniature creatures were extraordinary for their anatomical range and taxonomic oddness. They included a comparatively large animal with eyes on stalks, a circlet mouth, and teeth lining its gullet, another animal with a frontal nozzle and five eyes, and another so uniquely weird because of its spines and tentacles that it was named *hallucigenia*. "Magnify some of them beyond the few centimeters of their actual size, and you are on the set of a science-fiction film."[63]

The largest of these handbooks appeared in the eastern empire during Basil's episcopacy. Basil had once exchanged letters with Epiphanius, a bishop on Cyprus. This was a delicate correspondence. Epiphanius already had a fearsome reputation for his rigidity about upholding orthodoxy, and he and Basil were backing different bishops at Antioch. In his letter Basil was, for one of the few times, defensive about his own theology. Even as he applauded Epiphanius' actions, he also insisted upon his own loyalty to the creed of the Council of Nicaea, although with one tiny addition. "I can add nothing to the Nicene Creed, not even the smallest change, except for the ascription of glory to the Holy Spirit. For our fathers considered this issue only partially and in haste, because the question regarding the Spirit had not yet been posed back then." In the withering gaze of a professional heresy hunter like Epiphanius, Basil was nervously trying to walk a tightrope of doctrinal correctness by professing his reluctance to "upset the simplicity of the creed," even as he admitted that he had recently published an extensive treatise about the Holy Spirit. In that treatise Basil had responded to accusations that he was an innovator by insisting that he was just a plain old-fashioned theologian. The threat of additional suspicion from a rigid conservative like Epiphanius made him uneasy again, and to ensure that he remained in Epiphanius' good graces, Basil now became an informer. Since Epiphanius had requested information about settlers in Asia Minor known as Magusaeans, who were reputed to have come from Babylon long ago, Basil cautiously supplied a few ethnographic observations about their religious practices.[64]

Other informers too must have nourished Epiphanius' vast paranoid conspiracy to find heresies everywhere by answering his questionnaires. In the later 370s he published an enormous handbook of heresies that he entitled *Panarion,* "a medicine chest for people bitten by wild animals." In this handbook he discussed eighty heresies, some of which had appeared already in Old Testament times or in the early Roman empire, while others still survived and even flourished. Sometimes he was upset by the behavior of various sects. The Daily Baptists insisted on bathing "every day in spring, autumn, winter, and summer"; in order to recreate the experiences of Adam and Eve in Paradise the Adamians met naked in a church that they thoughtfully provided with central heating; the Valesians took the biblical exhortations to chastity so seriously that they sometimes forced castration upon visitors. More often Epiphanius was offended at divergent beliefs, especially doctrines about Jesus Christ. The Ophites venerated the serpent as the source of knowledge and identified it as Christ; the Sethians claimed descent from Seth, a son of Adam, and "called him Christ and insisted he was Jesus"; the Melchizedekians honored Melchizedek, the Old Testament king and priest, by claiming he was "greater than Christ."[65]

By collecting this information Epiphanius had two objectives. One was to catalogue these heresies by constructing a proper taxonomy, just as paleontologists name and link fossils. "First there are the mothers of all heresies and their original names. The other heresies developed from these five mothers." Classification conferred power: Epiphanius' second goal was to refute these heresies, either by counterarguments or by outright mockery. With the clarity of a fanatic he hoped that all these variant forms of Christianity would become fossils. The history of the Angelics, a group that venerated angels, was his preferred fate for all these heterodox sects. "This heresy appeared suddenly in the past, but then it stopped and finally disappeared."[66]

The variety of these alternative interpretations of Christianity is still stunning. From the perspective of historical interpretation, so is the sense of loss. Like the bizarre animals in the Burgess Shale, all of these sects and doctrines had started out with a chance of surviving and developing, until unforeseen factors intruded. Neither random elimination nor inevitable success was characteristic of the search for a Christian doctrine of God during the fourth century. The disappearance of so many alternative theologies was a consequence neither of an indiscriminate culling nor of a preordained outcome. The emergence of a neo-Nicene orthodoxy that included so much of the doctrinal teachings of the three Cappadocian Fathers was certainly not a necessary result, nor even a predictable result. Other patterns of orthodoxy might have emerged, patterns that would then appear to be equally valid to us. In retrospect we modern historians would still be able to interpret these alternative pathways and make any of them seem just as sensible and unavoidable. The causes and influences behind doctrinal development, as behind natural selection, become apparent only in hindsight.[67]

Historical outcomes were contingent, and so are modern explanations. As a result, for the construction of our historical explanations it is difficult to find in these ancient theological doctrines themselves any inherent improvement or superiority in terms of intellectual excellence or practical usefulness. External social and cultural factors were more influential in determining the road actually taken. Within Cappadocia doctrinal disputes had become yet another aspect of personal rivalries over reputations and standing. Doctrines alone did not make Eunomius into a heretic. Remove the overt hostility of Basil and Gregory of Nyssa and their concern over enhancing their own prestige, and perhaps Eunomius becomes a respected Cappadocian Father.

Conversion

Explaining the eventual primacy of Christianity in the Roman world remains one of the tantalizing puzzles of ancient history. Early Christianity had started out as a splinter Jewish sect, and then slowly been transformed through interaction with Greek culture and Roman rule. As a result, it had an odd symbiotic relationship with Roman rule and Greek culture, both appreciative and distrustful. For centuries Roman emperors and magistrates had remained indifferent, or condoned local attempts at the suppression of Christians, or sometimes even initiated persecution. Early Christian thinkers had treated Greek philosophy as both a source of ideas for articulating theology and a repository of unredeemed paganism. Despite these suspicions about the influence of Greek philosophy and literature, despite a reciprocal hostility toward imperial administration, early Christianity had benefited from the extension of Roman rule and the diffusion of Greek culture, and it had gradually spread throughout and even beyond the Roman empire. In retrospect, its success might seem to have been predestined, and the patronage of the emperor Constantine merely topped off its relentless progress.

Such a triumphalist perspective thoroughly obscures the sheer contingency of the process. Just as the rise of a particular orthodoxy within Christianity would be an unpredictable outcome, so the overall ascendancy of Christianity remained doubtful even during the fourth century. Not only had Constantine's nephew, the emperor Julian, certainly not surrendered, but one of his admirers complimented him on his success in refuting Christianity. "Julian examined those books that proclaimed that man from Palestine as 'God' and 'Son of God.' Through the strength of the arguments in his long polemic he exposed these revered claims as laughable chatter."[1]

Modern studies of the rise of Christianity typically start at the beginning of the process by outlining the factors that distinguished Christianity from rival religious cults and that made Christian beliefs and behavior somehow more attractive, acceptable, and desirable. Such commonsense narratives are of course already wholly compromised. In a classic example of the uncertainty principle of historical interpretation, knowing the outcome of the process has tainted our assessment of early Christianity's potential for success. Familiarity with Christianity's eventual triumph has seemingly removed the need to question the probability of that success, as well as its attractiveness for contemporaries.

The chapters in this section focus instead on the difficulties of imposing Christian beliefs and behavior in Cappadocia. The highlands of central Asia Minor had always been resistant to the spread of Greek culture and the imposition of Roman rule. The durability of indigenous languages and local customs and the presence of so-called bandits had underscored the limitations on any cultural standardization or administrative totality. The probability of introducing religious uniformity was equally low. Despite the patronage of Christian emperors, despite their own use of Greek philosophy and literature, churchmen should likewise have anticipated the survival of pagan cults and the appearance of variant forms of Christianity. Those who were instead a bit too flush with their good fortune were simply stunned at the "numerous heresies" that continued to flourish in central Asia Minor.[2]

Nor did churchmen help themselves by trying gracefully to accommodate existing traditions. The spread of Christianity was thoroughly disruptive in local society. Churchmen introduced new regulations about behavior, in particular regarding permissible marriages and the acceptable use of violence, and they imposed a new hierarchy of clerics and bishops who all served for life. Chapter 2 investigates the implications of these new patterns both for local notables with ambitions of serving in the clergy and for ordinary Christians.

One immediate consequence was recognition of the difficulty of enforcing these new standards. Since churchmen had limited means of coercion, they instead preferred to find legitimation for this new morality and new hierarchy in the rhythms of history and the patterns of nature. Chapter 3 discusses the attempts of the Cappadocian Fathers to provide appropriate historical legends and to reinterpret the natural landscape. By insisting that Christianity had the support of both history and nature, they could claim that Christian morality and Christian hierarchy were traditional, not novel.

The intrusive impact of Christianity did not stop with introducing and then legitimating new social patterns. These new histories and new legends themselves became disruptive. Cities and families already had other legends that explained their festivals, their cults, their traditions, even their names, in terms of Roman rule and Greek culture. Chapter 4 evaluates the loss of these older legends and traditions. In many cases all that remained by the later fourth century were fragments of memories, disconnected inklings of older traditions and stories.

One of these older legends had mentioned Mosoch, the original founder of the Cappadocians. Over the centuries other local founders had displaced Mosoch, and by the later fourth century a bishop like Basil was himself being hailed as a founder. Chapter 5 discusses a final, confused attempt to make sense of the myth of Mosoch. The historian who tried to remember Mosoch was Philostorgius. Since he was a heterodox Christian who had experienced firsthand the oppressive consequences of the development of an orthodox theology, Philostorgius was perhaps more sensitive to the equally peremptory consequences of the spread of Christianity. One price to be paid for the success of Christianity was the loss of older legends and traditions.

Chapter 2
"Even Though Roman Laws Judge Differently": Christianity and Local Traditions

By the mid-370s Amphilochius, bishop of Iconium, had become Basil's closest confidant and a primary inspiration for his thinking about theological and ecclesiastical matters. Basil composed his treatise on the Holy Spirit as a response to a request for clarification from Amphilochius, and he also sent him three lengthy letters about discipline and penance. Amphilochius had asked Basil for advice on a number of issues. Although a few of his questions concerned the interpretation of particular biblical passages, most focused on the penalties for various sins and misdeeds. In the preface to his first letter Basil claimed that he was either trying to recall what he had once heard from older mentors or deducing his own conclusions based on what he had been taught; and, in fact, in many of his replies he referred to "custom" or an "old canon." His responses hence have a strongly antiquarian tinge, as if he was serving merely as a learned consultant for questions about the penalties for hypothetical sins.[1]

Yet some of the questions concerned specific cases and specific people. It is therefore possible to assume that Amphilochius, rather than merely posing imaginary situations, was raising issues of immediate concern for the pastoral duties of a bishop, that Basil accepted them as real-life contemporary problems, and that his responses were a clear indication of the impact Christianity was expected to have on traditional Cappadocian society. Amphilochius' concern over and Basil's discussion of what they both perceived to be genuine misdeeds implied the presence of such activities within or near their own communities. Three topics were especially important: the behavior of clerics, regulations about marriage, and the use of violence.[2]

Lifetime Tenure for Clerics

Basil's responses were divided into eighty-four chapters or canons, in modern editions numbered consecutively through the three letters. Several of these canons discussed penalties for clerics who had committed sins, such as sexual misbehavior. The common penalty for such wayward clerics was the loss of their offices: "the canons order a single penalty to be applied to fallen [clerics], dismissal from their office." Basil likewise suggested that clerics who took up arms against bandits should be deposed from their offices. For priests who had unwittingly become involved in an "illegal marriage," however, Basil recommended that they keep their office but be prevented from performing their liturgical duties, such as conferring the benediction or distributing the eucharistic elements. He likewise advocated that priests and deacons who had expressed merely an intention of sinning should be excluded only from the celebration of the liturgy. In two of his responses he furthermore adjudicated the cases of two priests whose ordinations and clerical service were now in question because they had once sworn misguided oaths.[3]

In his letters Basil was not only responding to various misdeeds and problems. He was also trying to cope with the more general consequences of a characteristic of the ecclesiastical hierarchy that distinguished it from other institutional hierarchies in the Roman empire. The grounds for the deposition of bishops and priests had become an important issue in part because clerics served with lifetime tenure.

Before the arrival of Roman rule, hereditary kings had ruled in Cappadocia. In addition, their relatives or other prominent local notables had served with lifetime tenure as the priests of the great temple complexes scattered through the kingdom. By encouraging the spread and importance of cities, however, Roman rule had changed these expectations about holding offices and priesthoods. Within each city local aristocrats still dominated by serving on the municipal council, holding magistracies, or holding priesthoods. Service on a council as decurions was restricted to the wealthy, was usually for life, and eventually became effectively hereditary within families. But the tenures of municipal offices and of many priesthoods were not for life. In order to encourage wide participation among its local notables, cities restricted the tenures of offices. Men held municipal magistracies usually for a year, with the possibility of repeating. Although some of the priesthoods were still hereditary and held for life and others could be conferred for life, most were held for shorter tenures. Even the priesthoods of the regional imperial cults typically rotated frequently. At Comana in Cappadocia a woman was honored for having been the "mother of five high priests." Men could also hold both municipal offices and priesthoods simultaneously, and even priesthoods in different cults. For local notables the rise of cities hence allowed the mixing of different municipal offices with service in local priesthoods. As a result, the honorific inscriptions that cities or family members set up to honor these local aristocrats often commemorated not the length of their tenures as priests or magistrates, but the number of positions they had held and the number of times they had held them. In the early second century, for instance, Sebastopolis in Pontus honored the career of a local aristocrat who, in addition to having served for life as a priest in the imperial cult, had held some municipal magistracies "many times" and had served as supervisor of the city's market "even more often."[4]

In the imperial administration a similar pattern of short tenures in office and long interruptions of retirement was common. Secretaries and lesser bureaucrats in the civil service held lifetime offices. But of the important magistrates, only emperors had lifetime tenure, and only emperors were even expected to hold their office for life. The normal pattern for imperial office-holders was occasional service in a sequence of increasingly more prestigious offices, punctuated by often lengthy periods of retirement. According to Libanius, a close observer of such trends, the tenure of these offices was so short, usually about a year, that a provincial governor would look back over his shoulder to see his successor right on his heels.[5]

The well-documented career of Symmachus, one of the most notable of the senators at Rome during the mid- and later fourth century, was typical. Symmachus held four major offices, a governorship in Italy, a governorship in Africa, the prefecture of Rome, and a consulship in 391, each for about a year and each separated by intervals of six to ten years. The three imperial magistrates from Cappadocia to whom Basil and Gregory of Nazianzus often appealed for assistance had similar staccato careers. Martinianus served as governor of Sicily, then vicar of Africa in 358, and finally prefect of Rome in 378. Aburgius was an official at court or count of the East in the early 370s before perhaps becoming a prefect in the later 370s. Sophronius started as a secretary, then served as *magister officiorum* at the court during the 370s, and finally became prefect of Constantinople in the early 380s. Even the most distinguished of aristocrats had to endure time out of office. A great aristocrat like Petronius Probus was so ambitious for office that "when not holding prefectures he withered, just like a fish removed from its water." Although Petronius Probus was powerful enough to hold an unprecedented four prefectures, one for a lengthy tenure of seven years, he too sometimes had to leave office and resume his standing as a private citizen. One of his periods of retirement lasted eight years, longer than any of his magistracies. Among pagan priests, among municipal magistrates, and even among the top magistrates in the imperial administration, rapid turnover was the normal state of affairs.[6]

In contrast, within the ecclesiastical hierarchy the normal expectation was of lifetime tenures. Once men were ordained as clerics, they served for the remainder of their lives. They could move up within the hierarchy, eventually becoming priests and perhaps even bishops, but they could not drop out to hold secular offices or to resume a life of leisured retirement and then perhaps return for another stint as a cleric. All three of the Cappadocian Fathers seem to have had difficulty adapting to this new notion of a lifetime commitment to clerical service. The first reaction of Gregory of Nazianzus to his ordination as a priest was to flee back to join Basil at his ascetic retreat in Pontus. After his consecration as bishop of Sasima he again fled to seclusion in the mountains. Eventually he became acting bishop at his hometown of Nazianzus, until he retired to a retreat at Seleucia. After a dispute with his new bishop at Caesarea, Basil simply abandoned his priesthood to spend a few more years at his retreat in Pontus, virtually in defiance of ecclesiastical expectations. As a result, Gregory's long-standing vacillation about clerical service and Basil's momentary pique at being passed over as bishop made each of their early clerical careers resemble the pattern of a secular career, moving in and out of office.

Bishops were even more restricted. Not only were they supposed to remain bishops for life, they were also expected to remain attached to their particular sees, unable to transfer to another city. Competent bishops at small sees could not move up to become bishops at larger sees. As Gregory of Nyssa described the relationship, a bishop's see was his wife, his congregation his children. Despite these regulations some bishops did nevertheless move among sees, including two of the Cappadocian Fathers. Gregory of Nazianzus challenged the expectation of permanent faithfulness by seemingly bouncing among the sees of Sasima, where he never served after his consecration, Nazianzus, where he served off and on only as acting bishop, and Constantinople, which he felt compelled to leave soon after his consecration as bishop. Gregory of Nyssa too had an odd career as a bishop. For a few years he was forced into exile from his see of Nyssa. Later, when visiting Sebasteia to help in the selection of a new bishop, he ended up being chosen himself. As he switched between episcopal service and retirement (even if forced retirement), and as he moved from one episcopal see to another, Gregory of Nyssa's career again resembled a secular career. Gregory of Nazianzus, like a successful imperial magistrate, had actually moved up in the ecclesiastical hierarchy as his episcopal sees advanced from a dusty hitching station to a venerable provincial city and then to the imperial capital. He himself was all too aware of the oddity and apparent promiscuity of his episcopal service, as he once insisted that Constantinople had been a "widow" when he had arrived and that he had never lusted after "another's wife."[7]

In its outward institutional structure the ecclesiastical hierarchy mirrored the municipal and imperial administrations. Each city had a bishop; ecclesiastical provinces generally corresponded to imperial provinces; metropolitan sees generally were the provincial capitals; bishops often met in provincial councils. But the expectations of service in the ecclesiastical hierarchy were completely different. The difficulties that might appear from this new pattern of the lifetime tenures of clerics and the lifetime attachment of bishops to their sees were readily apparent, and the careers of the Cappadocian Fathers provided many examples of these lingering ambiguities. Even as they tried to define and impose the new patterns and new attitudes of episcopal and clerical service, they were not immune from reverting to older, more traditional patterns and attitudes. Particularly troublesome were appointments and promotions.

For acquiring municipal and imperial offices probably the most important qualification was patronage, from relatives, from friends, or from connections with other magistrates and even the emperors themselves. For the selection of bishops, however, other factors were supposed to take priority. Gregory of Nyssa once advised the priests at Nicomedia about the choice of a new bishop. In his estimation, "pedigree, wealth, and worldly renown" were not necessary requirements for bishops; at best, each of these characteristics was "a shadow, following along by chance." Nor should these priests select as bishop anyone who was primarily interested in "friends and lists of honors and numerous annual revenues." Gregory's advice was that they should instead find someone "who looks only to God's affairs and does not lift his eyes to any of this life's concerns." Basil likewise once insisted that as he selected new clerics, he refused "to perform favors for some men or give in to petitions or be intimidated by fear." The exemplary model for this sort of unprejudiced selection was Gregory Thaumaturgus' choice of a new bishop for Comana in Pontus in the mid-third century. As Gregory of Nyssa told the story, Gregory Thaumaturgus had belittled the attributes of pedigree, eloquence, and beauty that others thought desirable in a bishop. Instead, he had supported a raggedy charcoal burner: "he considered virtue alone to be worthy of honor."[8]

These recommendations were rarely effective. The Cappadocian Fathers themselves had to acknowledge the important role of patronage in the selection and promotion of clerics and bishops, in part because they themselves had both benefited from it and been disappointed by it. Basil's uncle may have helped him become a priest at Caesarea. One of his supporters later hinted that Basil had missed becoming bishop of Caesarea in 362 because of the influence of rival families and factions in the city. After finally becoming metropolitan bishop Basil consecrated his brother Gregory as bishop at Nyssa. At Nazianzus Gregory the Elder had ordained his son Gregory as a priest, and then convinced him to become adjunct bishop. After Gregory the Elder's death the see of Nazianzus remained vacant for almost a decade. Gregory of Nazianzus sporadically served as acting bishop, but during his absence the people and clergy at Nazianzus were apparently unwilling to select someone else, perhaps in the hope that eventually Gregory would become the permanent bishop. Despite Gregory's reluctance, the people seem to have conceded that Nazianzus had become a family see. When a new bishop was eventually selected, he was, predictably, Gregory's relative. Despite the repeated emphasis on the importance of spiritual qualities, local aristocrats, especially those with family connections, consistently had the best chance of becoming clerics and bishops. In fact, in Cappadocia during the fourth century all the known bishops with known backgrounds were wealthy enough to have otherwise become decurions, members of their municipal councils. Even the charcoal burner whom Gregory Thaumaturgus had promoted as bishop at Comana had turned out to be educated enough to deliver a sermon that was "full of intelligence." He had deliberately accepted poverty only in order to follow a life of ascetic denial and philosophical reflection.[9]

The process for selecting new bishops was hence susceptible to the same pressures that determined the selection of office holders in cities and in the imperial administration. Local aristocrats were used to rotating offices, however, and despite their competition over prestige they maintained a more or less harmonious equilibrium by sharing civic offices and honors. Lifetime tenure interrupted that rotation. Many local notables, even those who had become clerics, never had the opportunity to become bishops. Sees became available only upon the deaths of the incumbent bishops. Gregory of Nazianzus once argued that the selection of a new bishop for Nazianzus during his lifetime was in fact not "contrary to canons." Because he had long ago been consecrated as bishop for Sasima, he had only been acting as bishop at Nazianzus. No one could complain that a new bishop would be consecrated "while the bishop was still alive," because he had never become the city's true bishop. Nazianzus "does not belong to me, and has not been assigned to me." Gregory's protest about canonical proprieties was a clear indication that the opportunities for upward advancement in the ecclesiastical hierarchy were otherwise limited. Lifetime tenure and nonstop clerical service imposed restrictions on the ambitions of local notables.[10]

The Law of Spiritual Promotion

Clerics and non-clerics, ecclesiastical insiders and outsiders, reacted to these restrictions in different ways. One reaction was the extension of higher titles and ranks to lower clerics. Basil started his episcopal career at Caesarea as the metropolitan for the province of Cappadocia. At the time this province included about ten cities, each with its own bishop. After the division of the province in 372, Basil was still the metropolitan bishop in the new province of Cappadocia Prima. But since all the other cities were now in the other new province of Cappadocia Secunda, he was the only bishop left in his own province who governed a city. Yet Basil still presided over suffragan bishops, no fewer than fifty "rural bishops." These rural bishops assisted in the administration of his ecclesiastical province, apparently by being stationed at the many villages and settlements in the countryside and on the imperial estates. In the neighboring region of Lycaonia, for instance, there were several "small communities and small villages that have possesed episcopal thrones since ancient times." These rural bishops also seem to have had some autonomy, since occasionally Basil tried to enforce his control by insisting that they not take money from newly ordained clerics and that they consult with him on possible recruits to the clergy. Even though their authority and responsibilities were unclear, and even though they did not preside in cities, these rural churchmen were certainly more than priests, since they had the rank of "bishop."[11]

Another reaction to the structural rigidities of the clerical hierarchy was the creation of alternative ecclesiastical hierarchies. The upper levels of the imperial administration accommodated many men through short tenures and rapid turnover. At Rome, for instance, there were over one hundred known prefects of the city during the fourth century, some of whom held the office for only a few months. In 351 alone five men held the office. In contrast, lifetime tenure made the upper levels of the ecclesiastical hierarchy much less accommodating, since fewer men became bishops at the big cities. During the entire fourth century there were only twelve bishops of

Rome, and there would probably have been fewer if hostile emperors had not driven some of them to early martyrdom or exile. At other cities too few men became bishops. In Cappadocia Gregory the Elder was bishop of Nazianzus for forty-five years. After a vacancy of almost a decade a relative became bishop in 383. Nazianzus hence had only two official bishops during over sixty years. During the period from about the death of the emperor Constantine in 337 to about the accession of Theodosius in 379 only three or four men served as bishop at Caesarea. Only more opportunities could compensate for such slow turnover among bishops.

One consequence of the doctrinal controversies of the fourth century was the appearance of competing Christian sects. Each had its own organization and leadership, and some became prominent enough to appoint bishops and clerics in various cities. At Constantinople and Antioch there were usually two or three rival bishops, each representing different doctrines. In Asia Minor the supporters of Aetius and Eunomius appointed bishops to represent their doctrines, including a regional bishop for Galatia and Cappadocia. These rival hierarchies increased the opportunities for becoming a bishop. One result of doctrinal controversies, perhaps even an unstated motivation for such feuding, was an increase in the number of bishops.

Local grievances and local frustration over the restrictions on upward advancement might also lead to the appearance of alternative or shadow clerics. Young clerics in particular could see the strictures on upward mobility. In Cappadocia Basil and Gregory of Nazianzus once had to cope with a junior cleric who challenged their authority. Gregory had ordained Glycerius as a deacon to help a priest in a small village, even though he knew that the young man was pompous and surly. Glycerius was clearly not content with his new office, and he soon began to challenge his mentors. He scoffed at his priest, his rural bishop, and Gregory himself. He began to recruit followers, both young men and young women, and he assumed both the title and the robes of a patriarch. He and his supporters then interrupted the celebration of a festival with lascivious dancing. Some revelers laughed, but the parents of the young women wept. Gregory responded by writing directly to Glycerius and threatened him with the loss of his rank as deacon. He also wrote to Basil and suggested he investigate. If Glycerius were to return with a letter from Basil, then he would receive indulgence and could remain a deacon. Basil was apparently a bit tardy in disciplining Glycerius, since Gregory later chided him for his negligence. Perhaps Basil had had the good grace to remember that he too had once been a new priest who had given his bishop the cold shoulder. While Gregory clearly interpreted this young man's sedition as a problem of discipline and disrespect, Glycerius was perhaps suddenly realizing the rigidities of the ecclesiastical hierarchy he had just entered. The only way he could accelerate his progress past the older clerics was by essentially founding his own sect. With his own congregation of young people he could now present himself as a "patriarch."[12]

The extension of prestigious titles and ranks to lesser clerics was one possible reaction to the constraints introduced by the restrictions of lifetime tenure; another was the appearance of alternative ecclesiastical hierarchies, either as a consequence of doctrinal controversies or as a result of local ambitions. Yet another reaction was, very simply, whining and grumbling. Gregory of Nyssa once complained at length about Helladius, who had succeeded Basil as bishop of Caesarea. Gregory had already heard the rumors that Helladius was angry at him and considered him to be "the source of his greatest misfortunes." As he was returning from a festival at Sebasteia, Gregory learned that Helladius was commemorating some martyrs at a little village in the mountains. At first Gregory continued on, thinking it more appropriate to meet at Caesarea. Then he heard Helladius was ill and decided to turn aside. After riding and walking through the night in order to arrive at this village at dawn, Gregory was miffed at his tepid reception. Although Helladius went inside to rest until midday, Gregory and his companions were left to doze outside in the oppressive heat, while the people in the village stared and pointed at him. When Gregory was finally allowed in, Helladius neither returned his greeting nor invited him to sit down: "I thought the silence was a representation of life in a tomb." During their conversation Gregory was first solicitous about Helladius' health, then unapologetic about his own actions. Helladius did not invite Gregory to share his meal, and instead sent him off that same day. As a final indignity, on the trip to rejoin his traveling companions Gregory was drenched in a violent thunderstorm.[13]

This meeting infuriated Gregory. After a tiring journey on a hot day the lack of hospitality had been an annoyance. More significantly, Gregory was enraged by Helladius' apparent lack of respect. In comparison, Jesus had received even the traitor Judas with a kiss, and He had complained when a host with leprosy had not greeted him with a kiss. Now, as Gregory snidely noted, "I was not considered the equivalent of [even] a leper." Gregory thought himself slighted because, in his estimation, he and Helladius had "equal rank." Gregory listed the similarities with regard to their families, their education, their access to influential patrons, and their knowledge of theology. The council at Constantinople in 381 had furthermore recently charged both of them with "correcting the common affairs," and the emperor Theodosius had confirmed this mandate in an edict that named them both as arbiters of orthodoxy: "we both had equality in this." If that were not enough to establish their equality, Gregory noted that they were both sinners who needed redemption! After cataloguing these comparisons Gregory could explain Helladius' presumptuous behavior only in terms of "the sickness of vanity."[14]

Helladius was in fact a thin-skinned bishop. Gregory of Nazianzus once tried to get him to change a decision that many thought slanderous: "set aside your anger and distress." Even after Helladius agreed with some of this advice, Gregory still found part of his reply "painful." Yet in this confrontation with Gregory of Nyssa, Helladius was not solely to blame. Gregory's vanity was equally prickly. Although Gregory noted in passing that Helladius was a metropolitan bishop, because of the division of Cappadocia into two provinces Helladius was in fact not Gregory's own metropolitan. The key was the see of Caesarea. The true irritation for Gregory was seeing someone else as bishop of what had been his brother's see. Gregory had inherited many of Basil's theological projects and some of his reputation, but he had been unable to assume his older brother's see. Because Gregory had already become bishop at Nyssa, he had not been eligible to succeed his brother as bishop of Caesarea. Once again, in Gregory's perspective, the selection of clerics and bishops had not followed a predictable pattern of steady and meritorious promotions. As a priest Basil had once been annoyed to find himself the subordinate of Eusebius, the new bishop of Caesarea who had never before held clerical office. A few years later his uncle Gregory had been miffed at becoming a suffragan bishop to his nephew, the new metropolitan bishop at Caesarea. Now Gregory of Nyssa could not bring himself to accept an unexceptional bishop as Basil's successor.[15]

Perhaps adding to Gregory's dismay was a realization of Helladius' success at finding an episcopal see for a supporter. Gerontius was skilled in medicine and rhetoric, and he had once been a deacon at Milan. After Gerontius used his connections at Constantinople to obtain a position at the court for Helladius' son, Helladius joined in consecrating him as bishop at Nicomedia. When Gregory advised the priests at Nicomedia to disregard secular reputation and influence in their selection of a new bishop, he may well have been belittling both Gerontius and his patron Helladius.[16]

In his letter to Nicomedia Gregory stressed the spiritual and moral qualities that bishops should display. Because bishops were propaedeutic models for other people, they had to be entirely irreproachable: "a teacher forms a student into what he is himself." In order to learn about humility, moderation, and virtue, people had to see these qualities in a teacher. This emphasis on the moral qualities of bishops, and of clerics in general, was an attempt to create an ethos to match the new realities of the ecclesiastical hierarchy, both in terms of promotion and dismissal. Lifetime tenure for all clerics and the permanent attachment of bishops to their sees hampered the potential for upward advancement. It hence became all the more important both for the men who became bishops and for those who remained lesser clerics to agree that moral and spiritual qualities alone had been the differentiating factors. The only standard was to be a "law of spiritual promotion."[17]

Lifetime tenure stifled upward mobility; it also made it difficult to remove wayward clerics. Municipal magistrates and most pagan priests typically rotated their offices annually, high-level imperial magistrates served at the pleasure of emperors, and even emperors themselves could be replaced through usurpations. In contrast, if clerics misbehaved, it was not possible to wait for the end of their tenures and then replace them. The only way to censure or remove clerics was through penalties for moral offenses. By clearly connecting clerical service with a proper lifestyle, bishops had the authority to remove or penalize clerics for moral lapses. The canons that Basil defined for Amphilochius about penalties for clerics who had sinned were another aspect of these attempts to come to terms with some of the implications of lifetime tenure for bishops and clerics.

Sex

As metropolitan bishops both Basil and Amphilochius were concerned about discipline among the clerics and their own roles in imposing and enforcing penalties. They were also concerned about the behavior of the members of their congregations. Many of the issues that Amphilochius raised for Basil's consideration involved the morality of the Christians in their communities. In particular, Basil's replies discussed what he and Amphilochius perceived to be sexual misbehavior and the improper use of force. Since both bishops seem to have been a bit uneasy about their episcopal authority, Basil because of confrontations with the emperor, imperial magistrates, and other local bishops during the early years of his episcopacy, Amphilochius because he had only recently become bishop of Iconium, it is perhaps not surprising that both were so conservative and even fierce in their outlooks. They were especially severe about the two issues that over the centuries seem consistently to have been perceived as the greatest challenges to entrenched paternalistic authority, sex and violence.

Several of Basil's canons discussed permissible marriages. Basil was particularly intent upon insisting that a man or a woman could not marry the sister or brother, respectively, of a first spouse, or that a man could not marry his brother's wife (that is, the same prohibited marriage from the opposite perspective). Such marriages were presumably among those that he classified as "a union of forbidden kin," and that were subject to the same penalty as adultery.[18]

For elaboration Basil referred Amphilochius to another letter in which he had discussed such second marriages. In that letter Basil had countered the possibility of marriage between in-laws with several different arguments. He directed one argument against the apparent endorsement of another cleric. The recipient of Basil's letter was Diodorus, and Basil was motivated to write after a man had shown him a treatise with Diodorus' signature that sanctioned the possibility of marriage between in-laws. This man then claimed that he had "written permission" to marry the sister of his deceased wife. Since Basil disagreed, he suggested that someone had impersonated Diodorus and he asked for his colleague's assistance in attacking both "that counterfeit document" and the practice itself. A second argument was necessary to contradict the implication of a verse from Leviticus that seemed to allow a man to marry his wife's sister after his wife's death. Basil countered by claiming that this legislation applied only to "those in the Law," that is, to Jews. Yet another argument highlighted definitions of kinship. Basil argued that because marriage made husband and wife into "one flesh," as the gospel of Matthew had described the union, the wife's sister acquired kinship with the husband. Hence the husband could no more have a relationship with her than with his own sister. And since "the regulations about kinship were applicable to both men and women," a woman could likewise not have a relationship with her new "brother," her husband's brother. Basil furthermore argued that a marriage between a man and his wife's sister would cause too much turmoil for the man's children. The children from his first marriage would be uncertain about his new wife, since they would not know whether she would behave with the hostility of a stepmother or the affection of an aunt, and the children from his second marriage would be uncertain whether they were the siblings or the cousins of the children from his first marriage.[19]

These were disingenuous arguments. Even though, by suggesting the possibility of impersonation, Basil was trying to give Diodorus a graceful way out, it is likely that there was no consensus among bishops and clerics about the practice. Diodorus had probably in fact signed off on the possibility of marriage between in-laws. The biblical passages about the practice were ambiguous, and Basil had to stretch his exegesis to claim that ties by marriage were equivalent to ties by blood. He furthermore had to resort to conventional stereotypes about the hostility of stepmothers to claim that they would be unkind to their new stepchildren. Pretense, forced exegesis, and stereotypes were not convincing.

The primary weakness of Basil's arguments, however, was that they seemed to take so little account of actual practices. Within the senatorial aristocracy of Rome during the late Republic, for instance, the demands of shifting political alliances had made divorce and remarriage very common and created blended families that often included a stepparent and half-siblings. Among Roman senators of the fourth century, marriage between kin was still a common strategy. The premature deaths that resulted from high mortality rates would likewise have left surviving spouses who were still young enough to contemplate remarriage. Even though Basil's general reaction was to impose sanctions on widows and widowers who remarried, he might still have had to make exceptions. Gregory of Nazianzus' mother may well have been his father's second wife. Since older men often remarried with women of a younger generation, it would have been common for a young stepmother to be close to the age of her adult stepchildren, a likelihood that Basil seemed to acknowledge by classifying the infatuation between men and their stepmothers as the equivalent of incest. Remarriages were hence common, and so was uncertainty over permissible relationships among stepsiblings, half-siblings, and relatives by a former marriage.[20]

Basil tried to clarify these relationships by imposing penalties. Yet by concentrating so exclusively on patterns of kinship he had again ignored other important, perhaps overriding concerns. Strategies of marriage involved more than simple definitions of permissible relationships, since apprehensions about fiscal arrangements, dynastic succession, and perpetuation of the family name also entered the calculus. "Marriage strategies as such must . . . not be seen in the abstract, unrelated to inheritance strategies, fertility strategies, and even pedagogical strategies."[21]

One concern involved dowries and any other transfers of property between families. Marriage of a deceased wife's sister would presumably imply that a husband could continue using his first wife's dowry, and that the father of his second wife could keep any gifts he had earlier received from the husband when he had courted his first wife. Another concern involved the family legacy. Marriage of a deceased husband's brother would preclude a man's children from being absorbed into another family if a woman remarried, and would prevent a woman from being forced into a disadvantageous marriage that might produce a competing set of heirs, or simply from being left unmarried. Elsewhere Basil himself recognized the problem of inheritances when he acknowledged that it was an offense against nature when a father who remarried forgot the children of his first marriage. He also conceded that a widow might "live with another man and ignore her previous children." Marriages between in-laws were hence attempts to preserve already existing connections between different families, and to maintain claims to succession and inheritance.[22]

Within Roman aristocratic families such concerns about property and succession would sometimes lead to marriages between even closer kin, such as first cousins, stepsiblings, and descendants of half-siblings. In Roman law restrictions on permissible marriages had focused less on ties by blood or marriage and much more on concerns about differences in legal rank and social status. In the early sixth century, for instance, even the future emperor Justinian still needed a special imperial edict in order to contract a valid marriage with Theodora, a notorious actress and courtesan. In the end, Basil too seems to have recognized that he was facing a difficult fight in trying to restrict marriages between in-laws. At the conclusion of his letter to Diodorus he simply hoped that this "sacrilegious practice" would remain where it was now common and not contaminate his own region.[23]

Another practice to which Basil objected was the abduction of women, also known as bride theft. In one of his canons Basil insisted that a man who had abducted a woman who was already betrothed must return her to her fiancé (who could then decide whether to accept or reject her). An abductor was also to return an unengaged woman, this time to parents, brothers, or other relatives. The girl's guardians would then decide whether to return the girl to her abductor and accept the relationship as binding. An abductor who seized a married woman, however, was liable to the penalty for fornication. Other canons added some nuances to these general regulations. A man who abducted a girl before marrying her could keep her as his wife, but was liable to the penalty for abduction. An unmarried girl who willingly ran off with a man without her father's knowledge was herself liable to a penalty. A widow who pretended that she had been abducted in order to remarry was liable only to the penalty for bigamy.[24]

In part Basil may have been reacting to this violent practice because the possibility of abduction had in the past threatened his own family. His mother, when a young woman, had once worried that one of her suitors might become so passionate over her beauty as to abduct her. So she had quickly married. In another instance Basil defended an aristocratic woman from being forced against her will into an unacceptable marriage. Since the coercion came from an influential advisor at the court of the vicar of Pontica, the woman fled for asylum to a church. This woman was vulnerable to this pressure because she was a wealthy widow who had recently lost her husband; Basil's mother had been unprotected because she was by then an orphan without parents to negotiate an engagement and marriage.[25]

The more common scenario, in traditional societies in which abduction is still prevalent, is for bride theft to function as a device to sidestep a betrothal that parents or guardians have arranged for young girls. The marriage of a daughter was supposed to be a carefully choreographed transfer of a young woman from her father's family to her husband's family. In his discussion of virgins, bishop Basil of Ancyra once described the safeguards used to protect a woman's honor during this transfer. "A young woman does not step outside her father's house until she has been married to a lawful husband and has been registered to him as the master and patron of her life. Then finally she may leave her father's house in the name of the husband who has taken possession of her." Marriages were designed to protect the interests of families and their patriarchs, rather than the feelings of the bride and groom.[26]

To dodge this protocol young men and women had to be bold. A rejected suitor might resort to abduction; so might a betrothed fiancé who was impatient over a delay in the arrangements or fearful of another suitor. In order to seize the girl an abductor would typically gather supporters to help. In one of his canons Basil conceded that some people provided assistance to abductors. In another case Basil was indignant to learn that an entire village had sheltered an abductor and even fought to prevent the girl's rescue. Sometimes the girl was also a willing, or perhaps even enthusiastic, participant in her own abduction, since it gave her the opportunity effectively to choose her own husband. In that case the abduction was more of an elopement. Whether violent kidnapping or consensual elopement, the end result was the same, the upsetting of arrangements that parents, and especially fathers and male guardians, had made to benefit their families and their communities.[27]

From the perspective of patriarchal figures of authority, the feelings and intentions of the abducted women were irrelevant: "abduction was a crime against the parents, and against organized society." Bride theft was dangerous to families, since it might upset the alliances with other families that fathers or male guardians hoped to consolidate or their plans for the eventual distribution of property. Bride theft was also a challenge to the harmony of communities, because it might initiate feuds between families. In his canons Basil had therefore rejected a distinctive strategy employed by young people to impose their own preferences and instead decided in favor of the social stability inherent in arranged marriages. With these canons Basil had also explicitly supported the patriarchal authority of fathers and male guardians. In his blunt opinion, an abductor was "a snake or some other wild animal."[28]

Violence

In his canons Basil also discussed the general use of violent force, in particular by making a distinction between voluntary and involuntary homicide. The most important consideration was an evaluation of a person's intent. A man who accidentally struck and killed someone with a stone that he threw to protect himself from a wild animal, or a man who beat someone to death while merely wanting to discipline him, or a man who while defending himself killed his attacker, were all, in Basil's estimation, not guilty of voluntary homicide. In contrast, those certainly guilty of voluntary homicide included bandits, because they killed for money; soldiers, because they slaughtered their enemies during warfare; poisoners, "because of the meddling and forbidden quality of their skill"; and the women who supplied the drugs to induce abortions. Even these descriptions needed qualification, however, since Basil also argued that it was necessary to evaluate the lethalness of the weapon, the severity of the victim's injuries, and the likelihood of whether the victim could walk again with a cane.[29]

The use of violent force was widespread in Roman society. The imperial administration itself sanctioned some of it, since it tried to control so-called banditry by appointing "prefects for repressing bandits" and seconding troops to help out. Provincial governors sometimes hired bounty hunters and professional killers. Cities likewise had police forces, posses of "pursuers" led by men with the ominous titles of "watcher" or "peacemaker." The exasperation in imperial edicts about the unceasing futility of trying to repress these bandits was itself an indication of the difficulty of transforming a traditional lifestyle that had always included thievery, rustling, and strong-arm extortion. Emperors and their magistrates increasingly reacted to misdeeds and crimes by resorting to torture, mutilation, and execution. In their struggles against pagans and heretics, Christians too sometimes used violence, as gangs of monks razed pagan temples, communities rioted, or rival groups of Christians pelted each other with stones. Individuals and families resorted to violence, often in the form of feuds and vendettas. In Pontus two brothers almost came to blows in a dispute over control of a marshy lake. In one of his sermons Basil provided an illustration of true loyalty by casually mentioning "a recent misfortune" in which devoted dogs had flushed out some murderers.[30]

In a society that so emphasized the importance of honor and prestige the use of violence was commonplace. As a supplement to stray textual references, the most explicit indications of the atmosphere of violence were the imprecations on tombstones in Pontus. Men took their resentments and their macho prickliness to their graves. People considered a tomb to be a "home" that they tried to protect after death with curses and imprecations. On one tombstone a man warned others not to open the tomb or bury someone else there. On another tombstone the penalty for "breaking something or knocking off a piece of marble or erasing one of the inscriptions" was a much more elaborately harsh curse on the malefactor: "May this wretched man perish wretchedly, entirely and utterly, [and likewise] the children of his children and his family and his reputation and the hearth of his house and the graves of his ancestors." In order to preserve the integrity of his ecclesiastical community Basil too sometimes had to resort to similar threats of social exclusion. One man was accused, examined before witnesses, and then examined again at the church. When he still refused to accept this judgment, Basil proposed excommunication: "let it be announced to the entire village that this man is forbidden from all the intimate interaction of life." In life men resorted to threats or the use of violence; after death they relied on curses to protect themselves and their families in their tombs.[31]

By concentrating so single-mindedly on the intent behind homicide and violence, Basil had again ignored the larger context. Rather than being aimless or random, the deliberate employment of violent force was often an attempt to manage difficult situations. In particular, violence was a response to situations involving power and prestige. Its use defined and publicized mastery and submission in personal relationships, and it preserved the honor of families and communities. "The use of violence and intimidation was part of the regional culture; the capacity to coerce with physical violence was valued in itself." Basil may have been trying to recast notions of the proper use of violence and aggression by introducing a distinction between voluntary and involuntary homicide, deliberate violence and accidental violence. But even he, in one of his canons, had had to concede the difficulty of determining a person's intent, and he hence recommended that Amphilochius had the authority to modify the penalties for involuntary homicides. Without the suggestion of an alternative, a peaceful way of responding to perceived slights and outrages, this distinction between deliberate and accidental violence, even with its attached penalties, would have little effect.[32]

"Our Laws Are Useful and Generous"

The rise of Christianity had a powerfully disruptive impact on Cappadocian society. It transformed cities, not just in the sense that bishops now took over functions once performed by municipal councilors and magistrates, but more profoundly in the sense that it created a caste of clerics, religious specialists who did not participate in municipal political life and who served for life. More widely, regulations like those proposed by Basil now tried to modify common marriage patterns and the customary use of violence by insisting upon conformity to particular interpretations of biblical injunctions.

Basil and other bishops were aware that the imposition of this ecclesiastical hierarchy challenged the usual expectations of municipal service among local notables, and that the enforcement of these canonical regulations about Christian morality would be disruptive in traditional society. In fact, sometimes they conceded that their new Christian morality even conflicted with Roman law. Gregory of Nazianzus once offered advice to a father who was pushing his daughter to divorce. He noticed that while the girl's words agreed with her parents, her tears indicated she still loved her husband. Gregory hence supported the girl's lingering feelings for her husband against her father's narrow-minded duress. He then reinforced that suggestion by noting that ecclesiastical canons did not sanction divorce: "even though Roman laws judge differently, divorce is completely disagreeable to our laws." Gregory was clearly hoping to preserve this marriage. When he wrote directly to the girl's father, he included an explicit comparison to public magistrates: "public executioners are servants of the laws, but there is nevertheless no admiration for an executioner." With this comparison Gregory had implied that if this father insisted upon his rights under Roman law to terminate this marriage, he would receive the same reproach. Rather than merely hiding behind rigid obeisance to ancient laws or continuing to follow older traditions, in a Christian society people should commit themselves to new patterns of behavior and new values.[33]

Throughout the empire Roman law and imperial edicts were difficult to impose. In support of their own pronouncements emperors often resorted to threats of grievous penalties and punishments. When Diocletian and his fellow emperors had issued an edict against the practice of close-kin marriage, including marriage between in-laws, they had threatened whippings "of appropriate severity." When Constantine had issued an edict that condemned bride theft and marriage by abduction, he imposed tortures and penalties on the nurse for not being watchful enough, on the abductor and his partners, on the girl for not staying indoors, and even on the parents if they decided to accept the marriage.[34]

These outlandish threats were a sure sign of frustration at imperial impotence. Even if these edicts were promulgated at all in outlying regions like Cappadocia and Pontus, their impact was most likely minimal. One handicap was language. Latin was still the language of power, and Greeks found Latin difficult or rude. Although one young man from Pontus with ambitions of becoming an advocate had considered Roman law to be "very Greek" because of its wisdom and precision, he had nevertheless faltered at the thought of learning "the language of the Romans": "it seemed vulgar to me." A second handicap was the low probability of enforcement. Not only could provincial administrators, municipal magistrates, and communities easily ignore these edicts, they also seemed too harsh to be effective. As Gregory of Nazianzus noted, "Roman laws are excessive, harsh, and susceptible to blood penalties, while our laws are useful and generous, and they do not permit any use of anger against wrongdoers."[35]

Basil composed his canons in Greek, of course, and he tried to enlist the support of other bishops like Amphilochius by providing the appropriate biblical justifications. In addition, the sanctions that he proposed, such as penance, exclusion from prayers, or excommunication, were presumably meant to reflect the new clemency and generosity associated with Christianity. Yet even with this claim about the leniency of the penalties, the newness or oddness of these preferences that Basil wanted to introduce about clerical service, permissible marriages, and the use of violence makes it difficult to understand how they might acquire wider normative authority. Their acceptance and enforcement would be problematic.

Chapter 3

Remembering the Future: Christian Narratives of Conversion

From our vantage point it is all too easy to applaud some of the changes that Christianity introduced. The academics among us fully appreciate the benefits of lifetime tenure; and regulations about permissible degrees of marriage, condemnation of the use of violence in abducting women, and restrictions on the use of lethal violence seem to be markers of the progress of civilization. A progressive theory of social development would then assume that people in the Roman provinces would naturally have embraced these new restrictions too.

In fact, systems of morality are themselves social constructs, arbitrary configurations of acceptable and unacceptable behavior that acquire, and indeed require, sanction and approval from public law and popular opinion. As Basil defined the penalties for fornication, adultery, and the use of improper violence, he was also trying to impose a new configuration of moral and immoral behavior. He needed more than threats and discipline, however. Basil and other bishops had to have history on their side. To reinforce their new ideas and their own prestige, churchmen required new legends and new myths. By publicizing new histories for cities and regions they could suggest that Christian patterns of behavior had long been characteristic of their communities, and by advertising new histories for families they could justify the prominence and lifetime tenures of bishops and clerics like themselves. In addition to rewriting history, the Cappadocian Fathers reinterpreted the natural landscape to suggest that Christian morality was inherent even in the behavior of animals. The new patterns of Christian behavior that they promoted would then appear instead to be as permanent as the landscape and as timeless as history.

Regional Histories

The Cappadocian Fathers rewrote the histories of their regions in different ways. One was by stressing the roles of prominent individuals as founders in both Pontus and Cappadocia. For Pontus, Gregory of Nyssa highlighted the career of Gregory Thaumaturgus and his importance for spreading Christianity. In his account Gregory Thaumaturgus had been a native of Pontus who studied overseas before returning to his homeland in the mid-third century. There, a local bishop recruited him into the clergy. Upon becoming bishop of Neocaesarea Gregory Thaumaturgus was remarkably successful in expanding Christianity. Gregory of Nyssa explained his success in various ways. Gregory Thaumaturgus delivered public sermons, and he introduced a new ceremonial rhythm for the city that highlighted the festivals of martyrs. In addition, Gregory "the Wonderworker" performed amazing wonders. He dried up a lake that was the cause of a feud between brothers, he stopped a raging river from flooding, he exorcised a demon from a young man, he had a vision of a future martyrdom, and he foresaw the coming of a plague. Gregory of Nyssa applauded his success with a graceful, but highly implausible, compliment: when Gregory Thaumaturgus had arrived in Neocaesarea there were only seventeen Christians, but upon his death only seventeen pagans were left.[1]

The career of Gregory Thaumaturgus provided a history, a myth that located the spread of Christianity in Pontus within an era long before emperors had converted and begun to patronize Christians. Various cities could claim a connection to Gregory Thaumaturgus, including Amaseia, whose bishop had originally consecrated him, and Comana, for which Gregory Thaumaturgus selected a bishop. The people of Neocaesarea had certainly tied its reputation to the activities and teachings of their famous bishop. Locals had hoarded his "sayings" and passed them on to their children, "preserved in the sequence of memory." The congregation continued to celebrate the liturgy exactly as in the "time of Gregory the Great." In fact, this congregation was so devoted to these ancient practices that Basil would criticize its rigidity. The clerics and congregation at Neocaesarea simply ignored this sniping, and the cult of Gregory Thaumaturgus continued to grow. Even though there was apparently no tomb known for Gregory Thaumaturgus when Gregory of Nyssa composed his biography, eventually the church acquired a proper tomb. This church that Gregory Thaumaturgus himself had constructed was now the rock-solid warranty for these legends. Not only was it still standing over a century later, but engraved on its walls was the text of a creed that was attributed to the saint. Gregory of Nyssa insisted that this was in fact an autograph copy that preserved "the characters of his blessed hand." Both the church building and the copy of the creed were historical texts that would verify this narrative for a skeptic: "let him listen to the church."[2]

The church was one solid guarantee; another was the land itself. Gregory of Nyssa found additional reinforcement for this new history in the natural landscape of Pontus. Memories of Gregory Thaumaturgus now dominated the region around Neocaesarea. In fact, in one story Gregory of Nyssa claimed that Gregory Thaumaturgus had once literally become a part of the countryside. During a persecution, he and a companion had escaped detection when their pursuers saw only "two trees standing a short distance from each other." Gregory Thaumaturgus had blended into the landscape.[3]

In his own day Gregory of Nyssa still saw traces of the saint everywhere in the countryside. When he looked at a pasture, he remembered a miracle performed by Gregory Thaumaturgus. Once two brothers had almost come to blows over a small lake, until Gregory Thaumaturgus had resolved their feud by turning the marsh into a dry field. The evidence to prove the miracle was still there: "at the edge of the former marsh a few traces of the bubbling water are preserved even today." When Gregory of Nyssa looked at a tree near the Lycus River, he remembered another miracle. Once, when the river was overflowing its bed, Gregory Thaumaturgus had stopped the flooding by stabbing his staff into one bank. The staff then took root and grew into a tree. "Still today the tree is a sign and a memorial for the inhabitants. . . . Still today the tree is called 'the staff,' a lasting reminder for all time of Gregory's grace and power." The life of Gregory Thaumaturgus was now deeply grounded. It had taken root. The landscape too was a text, and trees and fields were the equivalents of the "sayings" that conjured up stories about Gregory Thaumaturgus' miraculous powers.[4]

For Cappadocia, Gregory of Nyssa hinted at a legend about another founder. Early traditions had already claimed that Jesus' apostles had scattered as missionaries to various regions and cities. Gregory himself noted that Thomas had gone to Mesopotamia, Titus to Crete, and James to Jerusalem. Although an earlier Christian historian had suggested that the apostle Peter had preached in Pontus, Cappadocia, and central Asia Minor before proceeding to the West, Gregory associated him only with Rome. Instead, according to Gregory, "we Cappadocians received the centurion who acknowledged the divinity of the Lord at his crucifixion." Although the gospel accounts had mentioned a centurion who had glorified Jesus at the foot of the cross, Gregory's comment was apparently the first reference to his leading role in the Christianization of Cappadocia. Later traditions would of course expand on this legend by naming the centurion as Longinus, identifying him as a native of Cappadocia, and describing his martyrdom and subsequent cult at Caesarea. Eventually a shrine to this centurion was established in Cappadocia.[5]

This legend about the centurion implied that Christianity in Cappadocia had an ancestry that went all the way back to the moment of Jesus' death. As a result, Gregory of Nyssa could think that Cappadocia was as much of a holy land as Palestine itself. In one of his letters Gregory argued against the need to visit Palestine and "see the places in Jerusalem where the souvenirs of the Lord's sojourn in the flesh are visible." This viewpoint was less an argument about the futility of pilgrimage and more a comment on the importance of Cappadocia in the Christian world. Gregory naturally worried about the temptations pilgrims might encounter on the road and the difficulties for women, in particular of maintaining their modesty. His most surprising argument, however, was the suggestion that Palestine could no longer claim to be a special holy region because of the exclusive presence there of the Lord or the Holy Spirit. "If it is possible to infer the presence of God from visible signs, then someone might think that God was living in the region of the Cappadocians rather than in remote places." Even though Gregory had traveled to Jerusalem on official ecclesiastical business in order to mediate a dispute, he insisted that this trip had not been necessary in order to confirm his beliefs. "I confessed the incarnation through the virgin before I witnessed Bethlehem, and I confessed the resurrection from the dead before I confirmed the shrine." Cappadocia was itself an ancient holy land, and rather than leaving, people only needed "to travel from their bodies to the Lord." "Believers here become participants in the grace [of the Holy Spirit] in proportion to their faith and not because of a journey to Jerusalem." Even the centurion had felt no need to stay in Jerusalem after the crucifixion. He had instead gone to Cappadocia.[6]

Gregory of Nyssa was obviously not above indulging in some regional pride when he talked about the origins of Christianity. In the process he had linked early Christianity in Cappadocia with the life of Jesus Christ himself. His historical arguments were compelling precisely because of their circularity. Just as faith now was a proof of God's presence then, so Cappadocia's reputation as a long-standing holy land was an incentive to accept Christianity and its new demands about a proper lifestyle.

Gregory's brother Basil provided additional confirmation by arguing that Christian morality and theology were inherent in the natural landscape of Cappadocia. In a series of sermons about the six days of creation Basil highlighted the moral implications of the flora and fauna. Birds in particular provided examples of proper and improper behavior. The cranes that kept watch at night, the storks that cared for their elderly, and the crows that guarded the storks were all appropriate examples of vigilance, affection, and hospitality. Basil also used the example of the turtledove that remained alone after losing its mate as an argument that women should prefer the nobility of widowhood to a second marriage. In contrast, the behavior of eagles that abandoned one of their nestlings was not worthy of imitation, since it was reminiscent of "parents who under the pretext of poverty exposed their children or who were unfair to their children in the division of the inheritance." Basil also made some theological deductions from the behavior of birds and insects. One was about the possibility of a virgin birth. Because a vulture could lay an egg without coupling, "the history of birds" has indicated that it was "not impossible or contrary to nature for a virgin to give birth while preserving her virginity immaculate." Another theological implication concerned the transformation of the human body at the moment of resurrection. As an appropriate analogy Basil mentioned the metamorphosis of the Indian silkworm from a caterpillar into a flying insect. In the minutest customs of birds and insects in Cappadocia, Basil was now able to find examples of proper morality and orthodox theology. This exegesis implied that the Christian lifestyle he was promoting was not new, since it had been inherent in nature from the very moment of creation.[7]

Basil and Gregory of Nyssa were the recorders, and not necessarily the inventors, of these legends and traditions. Like the stories they had heard from their ancestors about Gregory Thaumaturgus, these legends had no doubt been circulating already in oral traditions, and perhaps even in other written accounts. But, as bishops, they could now link them with their own notions of Christian morality. The legends about founders like Gregory Thaumaturgus and the centurion Longinus made Christian behavior seem quite traditional, and its connections with the natural landscape and the behavior of animals made it seem perfectly natural. History linked Christian morality with the life of Jesus Christ, and scriptural exegesis with the moment of creation.

Family Histories

These legends about the heroic founders of Christianity in Pontus and Cappadocia blended into a second type of legendary history that focused on the significance of particular families. Gregory of Nyssa in fact had made an explicit segue from Jesus' life at Jerusalem to his own family back in Asia

Minor. He reminded a friend that they had once met at Antioch because he was on his way to Jerusalem in order "to see in those places the traces of the Lord's sojourn in the flesh." Once they had started talking, however, Gregory had preferred to tell him about "the memory of a distinguished life," the life of his sister Macrina. Already during his trip to the Holy Land Gregory had been more interested in talking about his own family than about the life of Jesus.[8]

Local legends in his home region were just as attractive, and attachment to the legacy of Gregory Thaumaturgus directly benefited at least two prominent families in Pontus. The first person at Neocaesarea to offer lodging to Gregory Thaumaturgus was reputed to have been a local notable named Musonius. At the beginning of Basil's episcopacy a century later the bishop of Neocaesarea was likewise named Musonius, and it is likely that he was a descendant of this earlier Musonius. His ancestor's generosity seems to have boosted the standing of his family by associating its prominence with the introduction of Christianity under Gregory Thaumaturgus: "the passage of time has transmitted to his descendants the memory of such a distinction."[9]

The other family in Pontus that attached itself to the legacy of Gregory Thaumaturgus was the family of Basil the Elder, father of Basil and Gregory of Nyssa. Basil the Elder had become a local teacher at Neocaesarea, and his family owned many estates in the region. This family had hence become wealthy under Roman rule and had flourished because of Basil the Elder's familiarity with Greek culture.

Yet Basil and Gregory of Nyssa preferred to tell a different history of their family. In their version the defining event had been the suffering of their ancestors during the persecutions of Christians at the beginning of the fourth century. Their maternal grandfather had been executed, and their paternal grandparents had spent seven years hiding in the mountains of Pontus to escape the persecutions of the emperors Diocletian, Galerius, and, in particular, Maximinus. Two generations later Basil and his siblings were able to find a sense of pride in the horrors their grandparents had experienced. The mementos of those final persecutions were always with them. In Cappadocia, rather than discarding the public portraits of Maximinus, people had kept them on display, apparently as reminders both of the heroic behavior of martyrs and of divine vengeance upon a persecutor. "His icons bear the marks of a stroke at that time. They are still on display in public places, and they publicize the mutilation of his body." Basil and some of his siblings eventually adopted an ascetic life, and he and some of his brothers became priests and then bishops. In order to emphasize the continuity of their lives and careers they preferred to situate the history of their family in a longer tradition of martyrdom and hostility to Roman rule, of withdrawal and uneasiness about classical culture, and of clerical service. For this sort of family history neither Roman rule nor Greek culture was necessary. Their prominence was a consequence of the suffering of their ancestors in the name of Christianity.[10]

Basil and Gregory of Nyssa also stressed the family's link to various saints' cults. One was the cult of the Forty Martyrs of Sebasteia, forty soldiers who had preferred to die on a frozen lake rather than offer sacrifice to pagan deities during the persecutions of the early fourth century. As a young boy Gregory had attended the saints' festival, and later in life he confessed that he still had a relic of the saints. His parents had been buried in a shrine dedicated with relics of the Forty Martyrs.[11]

Another saint to whom his family was attached was Gregory Thaumaturgus. This attachment went back almost firsthand to the saint's life, since their paternal grandmother had memorized some of the sayings of Gregory Thaumaturgus and passed them on to her grandchildren. Basil mentioned some of the episodes from the saint's life in his letters, and he had read a treatise attributed to the saint's authorship. Gregory of Nyssa finally collected many legends and sayings and composed a long *Life* of Gregory Thaumaturgus. In this biography Gregory of Nyssa offered a distinctively self-serving interpretation. Most notably, he conveniently overlooked an alternative viewpoint about the saint's early life. In his own recollection of his early education, Gregory Thaumaturgus had mentioned that he had once tried to learn Latin in order to study Roman law at Beirut. After abandoning that ambition he had ended up studying at Caesarea in Palestine with Origen, a Christian theologian who was deeply influenced by Greek philosophy. Gregory of Nyssa mentioned none of this early education in Roman law and Greek culture. Instead, he included a legend that sent the young Gregory Thaumaturgus to Alexandria, where he was a "student of the Gospel." To supplement this viewpoint Gregory of Nyssa also included episodes in which Gregory Thaumaturgus had himself downplayed the importance of familiarity with classical culture, and in which he had had to flee during a persecution initiated by an emperor.[12]

In the construction of this *Life* Gregory of Nyssa had decided to include legends that distanced Gregory Thaumaturgus from the benefits of Roman rule and the attractions of Greek culture in order to associate him from his youth with biblical studies. In their own lives he and Basil had also made decisions about their careers. As he set out to shape these legends about the patron saint of the region, Gregory could make choices about this *Life* that corresponded to the similar choices he and his brother had made about their lives. Gregory Thaumaturgus did not become a Roman lawyer or a Greek sophist. Instead, with "the power of prophecy," a local bishop could see that Gregory Thaumaturgus was destined to become a bishop himself. The history of the saint hence conveniently reinforced the revised history of Basil's and Gregory's father's family, and thereby helped to promote the local standing of family members as clerics and bishops. Basil and Gregory became bishops in Cappadocia and their brother Peter at Sebasteia, while the successor to Musonius as bishop of Neocaesarea was one of their relatives. Several members of this family had benefited from its devotion to the memory of Gregory Thaumaturgus.[13]

In Cappadocia the family of Gregory of Nazianzus favored a different sort of history. Gregory of Nazianzus could not outright belittle the benefits of Roman rule, since his brother would eventually serve in the imperial administration as a treasury official. Since he had himself studied at Athens and had even wanted to stay, he was also quite reluctant to abandon the pleasures of familiarity with classical culture. His family's history hence focused on his father's conversion to Christianity.

Gregory the Elder had not suffered during the persecutions. Instead, he had quickly realized the implications of Constantine's patronage for bishops. Within a few years he had become bishop of Nazianzus, his hometown. In Gregory's estimation, because his father had inherited a church that was in ruins, he was now responsible for the expansion of the Christian community there. For forty-five years Gregory the Elder dominated his community as bishop, "the father and teacher of orthodoxy." At Nazianzus, Gregory the Elder had effectively become the founder of Christianity, and the success of his long career seemed to be a guarantee of the continued success of the Christian community there. By reviving the Christian community Gregory the Elder had also revitalized the city. "I am an ancient city afflicted by demons. Through Gregory's efforts I have been energized again." The history of the city had merged with the history of this family.[14]

The memorial that explicitly linked city and family was the new church that Gregory the Elder had begun and his son Gregory had completed. After Gregory the Elder's death the people of Nazianzus seem to have preferred continuity. Gregory the Elder had groomed his son to become his successor. Over the years, as Gregory vacillated in his thinking about service at Nazianzus, the Christian community never selected a new bishop. The hope that Gregory the Elder's son might become bishop was apparently more attractive than finding a proper fulltime bishop. When the city finally did acquire a new bishop, it is not surprising that he was Gregory of Nazianzus' relative.

An Old Destiny

The Cappadocian Fathers were all, whether deliberately or in passing, re-writing history. They were certainly not alone in doing so. Other Christian communities were also inventing or refurbishing charter myths. In order to promote a community of heterodox Montanist Christians at Ancyra one supporter commemorated some Montanist martyrs from the early fourth century. He wrote his account most likely during the reign of the pagan emperor Julian. Novatians were rigorist Christians whose communities were common in northwestern and central Asia Minor. In the early sixth century they composed a *Life* of St. Autonomus, a local martyr, that neatly accounted for the geographical spread of their version of Christianity. In these revisionist historical narratives Christian authors were of necessity deliberately trying to overturn earlier Greek and Roman histories. Their primary concern was to locate the narratives of their regions, their communities, and their families in the longer traditions of biblical and ecclesiastical history.[15]

In his *Life* of Gregory Thaumaturgus, Gregory of Nyssa compared his hero with illustrious heroes of the Old Testament like Abraham, Joseph, and Moses. Gregory of Nyssa also composed an encomium of Basil in which he compared his brother with Moses, Elijah, John the Baptist, and the apostle Paul. Gregory of Nazianzus compared his father and mother to Abraham and Sarah and himself to Samuel. These comparisons with biblical figures provided some chronological depth. They implied that the rise of Christianity in Pontus and Cappadocia was not a novel and unexpected phenomenon, and that neither was the prominence of certain families. The emphasis in Basil's family on martyrdom linked it with ecclesiastical history going back to the origins of Christianity, and the comparisons with biblical figures linked his family and Gregory of Nazianzus' family with a misty past that was older than Roman history and rivaled Greek mythology. Since the history of his family had coalesced with the history of the community, Gregory of Nazianzus was also prepared to refer to his small hometown of Nazianzus as Bethlehem. And in a panegyric he referred to Basil as the metropolitan bishop not just of Caesarea, but of "the Jerusalem above." In these new traditions even the cities in Cappadocia had been inserted into biblical history. Cappadocia was not just a region in the Roman empire or a part of the Greek cultural world. It was a holy land, an ancient domain in a Christian realm.[16]

The ecclesiastical hierarchy had created a new institutional structure and new expectations about service. Yet despite its claims about open recruitment and the importance of spiritual values for advancement, it had not freed itself from the traditional pressures of patronage and the conventional importance of wealth and ancestry. Most of the men who became bishops would otherwise have dominated their communities as municipal councilors, magistrates, or priests, or they would have gone on to hold offices in the imperial administration. But to explain their continuing prominence as bishops, to justify their lifetime tenures, churchmen provided a rationale that associated these men and their families with earlier legendary heroes of the spread of Christianity. With such heroic pedigrees no one could complain that these men might serve as bishops or clerics for life.

Churchmen likewise justified the values of the new Christian lifestyle they promoted in the weight of history and in a correspondence with nature. In their estimation, ancient history and the natural landscape had converged with the expectations of a new Christian society. With these sorts of warranties they could not be accused of having merely invented new legends and new interpretations. Once the natural environment was interpreted properly, once the past was understood correctly, the future would become apparent. Theirs was an old destiny. All they had done was remember the future.

Chapter 4

"Everything in Ruins":
Ancient Legends and Foundation Myths

The most conspicuous change in the local landscape came with the construction of new shrines and churches. In the past, local aristocrats had used their wealth to finance the construction of municipal buildings, such as porticoes, baths, theaters, stadiums, walls, and temples, on which they would of course inscribe their names. By the later Roman empire, many cities no longer had the resources to maintain these buildings and monuments. Even at Caesarea, the largest city in Cappadocia, some older buildings were in disrepair, "broken down by time, their remains jutting up throughout the city like rocks." Many local notables were by now becoming clerics and bishops, and they instead preferred to fund the construction of churches and Christian shrines. The most conspicuous relic of the memory of Gregory Thaumaturgus was the church he had built at Neocaesarea. Gregory of Nyssa was especially impressed that, more than a century after its construction, this church had survived a recent earthquake. "When almost everything else was completely demolished, municipal buildings and private homes, everything in ruins, that church alone was unshaken, without any cracks." Gregory Thaumaturgus had constructed this church "as if a foundation and a footing for his own priesthood," and its survival implied that the legends about him would be just as durable and his significance in the history of Pontus just as prominent.[1]

In contrast, other buildings and the memories they represented were not as sturdy. Gregory of Nyssa once commiserated with the people of Nicomedia on the decline of their city. In the recent past Nicomedia had still been a prominent provincial capital, even a residence for the emperor Diocletian: "you know your legends better than anyone, and how the court long ago resided in your city." Diocletian had initiated so many construction projects, including meeting halls, a hippodrome, a mint, and other factories, that he seemed to want to make Nicomedia the equal of Rome. Then Nicomedia had lost its prominence. One reason was of course "the expansion of your neighboring city." Once the emperor Constantine had transformed the nearby town of Byzantium into the new capital of Constantinople, it drew resources away from other cities. Another reason for the decline of Nicomedia was the devastation resulting from an earthquake in 358. This earthquake had completely demolished the city and its suburbs, and a subsequent fire had destroyed any remaining temples and houses. In Gregory's estimation, the one benefit of this devastation was that it had in addition erased the earlier history of Nicomedia. The city's earlier legends were as much rubble as its buildings. In the Christian society that had emerged from Constantine's reign, Nicomedia could now start over, and it would no longer have to be embarrassed by its association with Diocletian, one of the last emperors to have persecuted Christianity. As it started rebuilding, it could start rewriting its history. "Even if the splendor of your buildings has vanished, the city and its people equal its ancient beauty through the number and the reputation of its inhabitants." All the citizens of Nicomedia needed was a new bishop who could guide them in the disclosure of these new legends.[2]

Gregory's rather unruffled reaction indicates that rivalries with other cities and seismic disasters were not necessarily the most powerful catalysts toward the loss of older legends and histories. To justify the disruption arising from the imposition of an ecclesiastical hierarchy and new regulations about proper behavior, churchmen had publicized new legends about the rise of Christianity. But at the same time that these new legends explained and justified the new hierarchy and the new lifestyle, they were themselves disruptive. Once established, those new legends eclipsed older histories. The fourth century was not only a marvelously fertile period for the creation of new histories. It also marked the end of an earlier era when cities and families throughout the Greek world had carefully associated themselves with older legends about Greek myths and Roman history.

Greek and Roman Legends

Roman emperors and magistrates had generously encouraged the revival of interest in the Greek past. Even though cities in Pontus and Cappadocia were on the fringes of this Greek world, they too promoted traditions and rituals that linked themselves with Greek culture and Roman history. Strabo was a learned Greek from Pontus who had been a contemporary of the first emperor, Augustus. The rise of Roman rule had allowed him to expand his intellectual horizons. He had been educated in the old cultural centers of western Asia Minor, had hobnobbed with Roman aristocrats, and had traveled to Italy and Egypt. His writings included the *Geography*, an extensive survey of regions, cities, and temples in the Mediterranean world and Near East. As a native of Amaseia in Pontus he was especially familiar with central and eastern Asia Minor. He had furthermore certainly visited the region of Cappadocia. In fact, since the region of Pontus was for a long time included in the large Roman province of Cappadocia, later authors who used Strabo's writings even identified him as a "Cappadocian."[3]

In his geographical survey Strabo included more than mere references to topographical features, because he also liked to mention local stories and local myths. Everywhere he looked, Strabo saw history and legends in the landscape and the monuments. Although he himself may not have been fully aware of the chronological details, the legends he recounted stretched back endlessly. For him, the starting point was the epic poems of Homer, and he often provided exegesis on verses from these sacred books. At one point Strabo launched into a lengthy argument about whether Homer had mentioned some peoples from Pontus in the list of the allies of Troy, since their inclusion would indicate that the poet had certainly visited the coast of the Black Sea.[4]

Strabo had to concede that Homer had in fact not mentioned Cappadocia by name in his poems. He was nevertheless pleased to note that in his day the inhabitants of Pontus and Cappadocia still publicized legends that located their cities and shrines squarely in Greek mythology. Legends about Orestes were especially popular. Orestes was the son of the great king Agamemnon, the commander of the Greek forces during the Trojan War. Because Orestes eventually joined his sisters to avenge their father's murder by killing their own mother, classical Greek tragedians in particular had been entranced by the creative possibilities of the tensions within his dysfunctional family. According to legends current in Pontus and Cappadocia, Orestes had eventually traveled to central Asia Minor. At Comana Strabo discovered that people had already identified an indigenous deity named Ma with Enyo, a Greek goddess of war. They also claimed that Orestes and one of his sisters had introduced the cult in honor of this goddess, and that they had deposited at its shrine the "hair of sorrow" from which the city had derived its name. As Strabo commented of the people at another temple, "they find an etymology for the name by presenting a myth." Near Tyana was another shrine whose foundation locals also associated with a visit from Orestes. When Strabo visited, "some people there kept repeating the same history about Orestes."[5]

In Pontus, local legends highlighted the importance of Jason or one of his fellow Argonauts, including Hercules, who had once sailed in the Black Sea. The legend associating Heraclea Pontica with Hercules in fact became an example of the kind of foundation myth that orators might use to praise the origins of a city. "Cryptic myths" about Jason were confirmation of the region's prominence "in the past," and memorials in honor of Jason dotted the countryside. At Sinope there was a statue of Autolycus, one of Jason's companions, "whom the people there called their founder and honored as a god." The Heniochians, "chariot drivers," a people who lived at the east end of the Black Sea, claimed to be descendants of some of the charioteers who had accompanied the Argonauts. "They apparently arrived with Jason's expedition. The myth states that they were left behind and settled in these regions." Various cities also claimed the Amazons as their founders.[6]

During his journeys Strabo sometimes questioned these stories. In his account of the Amazons he tried to distinguish between "myths," which were "ancient and false and filled with marvels," and "history," which "searches for the truth, whether in the past or in modern times, and includes no marvels." Since Strabo then immediately conceded that this distinction did not apply to the Amazons, "about whom the same stories are told, both now and long ago," he was not simply trying to define a more sophisticated view of historical writing. Strabo was already sensing the clash between older legends and newer stories. The rise of regional kingdoms had generated rival histories, the expansion of Rome rule had accelerated the process, and as a result some older traditions seemed irrelevant to the current circumstances. They were now myths, too marvelous to be classified as history any longer.[7]

Even as local traditions began to highlight the role of genuine historical figures, they were nevertheless not reluctant to embellish the achievements of their new heroes. Legends about Alexander the Great were particularly widespread. During his march through Asia Minor Alexander had skirted along the western and southern coasts, until making a quick trip to Gordium and Ancyra in the interior. He had then marched through Cappadocia to return to Cilicia on the south coast. In outlying regions Alexander's failure to visit was not a handicap, but rather an opportunity to provide suggestive links with other legends. Some people claimed that Alexander had mated with the queen of the Amazons, others that a mountain range in northern Armenia was in fact in India. In Pontus and Cappadocia stories about the regional kings who followed Alexander's conquests were also common. The most dominant were the Mithridatic kings in Pontus, and especially king Mithridates Eupator, who expanded his rule over much of eastern and central Asia Minor in the first half of the first century B.C. Mithridates transformed both cities and the rural landscape through his construction projects. At Amaseia there were palaces, monuments, and royal tombs. At Cabeira he built a palace and a water mill. To demonstrate his mastery over wild beasts, and by implication over his subjects, Mithridates built a zoo to keep the animals alive for display and game parks for hunting them. Throughout the countryside he built numerous garrisons.[8]

Memories of king Mithridates and his dynasty survived for centuries. Three hundred years later Strabo's hometown of Amaseia still minted a coin that depicted the tomb of one of Mithridates' ancestors. But the coming of Roman rule to central and eastern Asia Minor devastated the countryside, left cities impoverished and ruined, and undermined local ancestral traditions. During his campaigns against Mithridates the Roman general Lucullus had at the same time been collecting souvenirs, paintings and statues that eventually ended up on the grounds of his magnificent villa in Rome. After capturing Sinope he made off with the statue of Autolycus. The Roman general Pompey continued this destructive meddling, but on a much grander scale. He pompously renamed many cities. Eupatoria, which king Mithridates Eupator had named after himself, now became Magnopolis, named after Pompey Magnus, Pompey "the Great," and Cabeira, one of Mithridates' royal residences, now received the Greek name of Diospolis, "City of Zeus." Pompey also confiscated Mithridates' most precious treasures and deposited them on the Capitoline Hill in Rome. The imposition of a formal imperial administration did not end this destruction of local customs and traditions. Pompey had reassigned regions from Mithridates' former kingdom in order to augment an existing province and to reward loyal partisans. Subsequent Roman administrators occasionally modified these territorial assignments and the standing of cities: "Roman magistrates imposed one division after another." The city of Amaseia had once been a "gift for kings"; "now it is [part of] a province." The result for Pontus and Cappadocia would have been the same as the consequences for the region around Troy: "because a different division of the region has been imposed under Roman rule, many people have already lost their languages and their names."[9]

The renaming of cities, the realignment of regions, and the theft of statues and monuments would have destroyed whatever etymological myths these cities and regions had previously developed about their names, titles, and cults. Already when Strabo surveyed cities in Asia Minor he was sadly resigned to the great loss of past traditions. One city on the coast of the

Black Sea conjured up no legends at all: "Tieium is a small town that has nothing worthy of memory."[10]

Cities instead tried to accommodate the realities of Roman rule. In Cappadocia, Caesarea assumed an imperial name already during the reign of Augustus. Soon after the region was annexed as an imperial province, the city acquired a temple in honor of the imperial cult. It also over the decades initiated a series of "Roman" festivals, one to honor the emperor Commodus, another to honor the two sons of the emperor Septimius Severus, another to honor the emperor Gordianus III. In Pontus, the royal city of Cabeira had already received the Greek name of Diospolis from the Roman general Pompey. In the early first century A.D. the widow of the last Cappadocian king changed the city's name to Sebaste, the "August City," a Greek equivalent to honor the emperor Augustus' name. By the end of the first century the name of the city had been changed once more, this time to Neocaesarea, the "new foundation of Caesar." The city's chief municipal cult kept pace with this process of cultural and political assimilation. First its local deity was identified with Zeus, the ruler of the Greek gods, and the city hosted a regional festival in honor of Zeus. Then statues of emperors were added to the sanctuary in order to link it with the imperial cult, and the city initiated games to honor the emperors. Its legends also kept pace. Even into the later fourth century Gregory of Nyssa still remembered some hints, but no details, of a myth about the imperial etymology of "Neocaesarea." "A distinguished emperor, one of the rulers of the Roman empire, was captivated by his love and affection for the region. Since he was named Caesar, he decided that this city was worthy of being called by his own name." Both Caesarea and Neocaesarea now redefined themselves in terms of Greek culture and Roman rule.[11]

In Greece and the western regions of Asia Minor, the area around the Aegean Sea that had always been the heartland of the old Greek cultural world, Greek culture flourished under Roman rule. Both rulers and subjects could see the advantage of linking the new realities of imperial administration with the traditional structures and ancestral legends of Greek cities. In outlying regions like Pontus and Cappadocia, however, the imposition of Roman rule offered an opportunity not to revive Greek culture, but simply to acquire it at last. These regions had always been under-Hellenized, ridiculed and satirized for their general boorishness. "It is easier to find white crows and flying turtles," one highbrow epigram claimed, "than a distinguished orator from Cappadocia." Pausanias, a native of Caesarea who went to study at Athens in the mid-second century, was praised for his skill at improvised oratory, but mocked for mangling his pronunciation because of his "thick accent, as is customary among Cappadocians." Once Roman rule linked Cappadocia and Pontus with the Mediterranean world, however, these regions could finally embrace Greek culture fully. Pausanias ended up teaching at both Athens and Rome. Another man, who may also have studied at Athens at about the same time, returned to his hometown of Neocaesarea in Pontus. There he composed a funerary imprecation that revealed his interest in archaism and that protected his family's tomb by appealing to various traditional Greek deities.[12]

Under Roman rule cities in Pontus and Cappadocia acquired new names, new cults, and new legends. Individuals likewise acquired a new culture, and they too assumed new names. Indigenous Cappadocian personal names and eastern "oriental" names gradually disappeared. Families now preferred Greek personal names, or names that conjured up aspects of Roman rule. They were now Greeks and Romans.[13]

The Challenge of Christianity

Roman rule had encouraged the formation of new local customs and legends that replaced older traditions and that linked regions, cities, and families with aspects of Greekness and Romanness. The rise of a Christian society during the fourth century in turn posed a similar challenge to these Greek and Roman legends. Personal names with Christian connotations became increasingly common. In Cappadocia a son might be named Longinus, presumably in honor of the centurion who had introduced Christianity to the region. In the region around Euchaita in Pontus men were named Theodorus and women Theodora, in honor of the local martyr St. Theodorus. If the families of Basil and Gregory of Nazianzus were representative, in both Pontus and Cappadocia "Gregorius" became a popular name, most likely because of the reputation of Gregory Thaumaturgus. In Basil's family men named Gregory included his brother and an uncle, in Gregory of Nazianzus' family his father, himself of course, a grandnephew, and a former slave designated as his heir. Gregory of Nazianzus once commented to Gregory of Nyssa on the honor of the name they shared. "If a man is worthy of being named after one of those [heroes] whom Scripture honors as men of God, this is already a gift of God."[14]

Basil's name also became popular. In one revealing example, a young man named Diogenes, "offspring of Zeus," changed his name to Basileios, perhaps after baptism or after becoming a monk. Basil's name was itself a palimpsest of all these historical transformations. "Basileios" was a "grand name," according to Gregory of Nazianzus. Within Basil's family it was apparently an ancestral name, one that he had inherited from his father. More broadly, from its association with the Greek words *basileus* and *basileia*, "king" and "kingdom," "Basileios" conjured up the royalty that had long ago ruled in Pontus and Cappadocia. Once *basileus* became the standard title for a Roman emperor in the Greek world, Basil's name was also a reminder of imperial rule. Yet even though Basil's name recalled family associations, Greek monarchs, and Roman emperors, Basil and his friends would have interpreted it differently. They were interested not so much in his name's association with the past, even with his family's memories, as in its capacity for invoking a Christian future. The realm they looked forward to was God's kingdom in heaven.[15]

From the reign of Constantine, Christian names, traditions, and myths became increasingly dominant in the Roman empire. By the later fourth century gangs of monks and fanatical clerics were marauding about, smashing pagan temples and shrines. No longer was it necessary to wait for earthquakes or the gradual deterioration of age, since these hooligans were themselves equated with natural disasters, "rivers flooded by rain." In their frenzy they also destroyed the traditions and myths that had defined cities and communities. "Shrines are the opening hymns of a foundation, passed down through many generations to the people of today." The legends disappeared with the shrines and temples. Without the cues provided by these memorials, memories were no longer remembered.[16]

Although overshadowed and frequently demolished, fragments of memories of older traditions nevertheless lingered in this Christian society. People and cities had many different reactions to these ancient legends. One reaction was to insist that these legends were still meaningful and relevant, and that they could still define the identity of a city or a family. Non-Christians argued, predictably, for the revival of the ancestral pagan cults and rituals. Even Christians were sometimes reluctant to abandon these old traditions and myths. Pagan temples might become churches. At Comana, for instance, Christians transformed the shrines that the Greek hero Orestes was thought to have founded directly into churches, "without making any changes at all in the structure." Pagan heroes seem likewise to have become Christian saints. In the same way that some local deities had once been

identified with gods in the Greek or Roman pantheon, mythological founders and heroes were assimilated into a Christian civic liturgy. At Caesarea
bishop Basil celebrated the festivals of two rather obscure local saints, the
centurion Gordius and the shepherd Mamas. In his commemorative panegyrics he hardly knew what to say about them. Since their names were
apparently traditional indigenous names, perhaps he was simply trying to
embellish some local traditions into full Christian cults. Basil and the metropolitan bishop of Tyana once feuded over the revenues from a shrine dedicated to "the holy Orestes," located in the Taurus Mountains in southern
Cappadocia. This St. Orestes and his shrine are otherwise completely unknown. Perhaps it is not too fanciful to imagine that this saint's cult retained
a memory of an earlier cult at Tyana that the locals claimed had once been
founded by the Greek hero Orestes.[17]

Another reaction was to drain all the meaning out of these old legends, and then disregard them or smile at them as irrelevant folklore. Some
people turned these old legends into academic curiosities, and then either
studied them as intellectual relics or ignored them as dangerous influences.
Once Greek cities had represented themselves in performances of tragedy
that correlated mythology and society. Newly Hellenized cities in Cappadocia had appropriated the same mythology and claimed as their founders
mythological heroes like Orestes. In the Christian families of the fourth
century, however, such mythology was not proper reading. Macrina, Basil's
older sister, was not allowed to read classical tragedies or comedies: "the
misfortunes of tragedy were inappropriate, and comedy was indecent."[18]

Other people transformed these ancient legends into public entertainment. Gregory of Nyssa once described how actors earned their title as
"wonderworkers" during their performances in the theaters. "As the subject
for their wonderworking they choose a myth from history or a subject from
the old legends, and they narrate this history to the spectators. This is how
they narrate the sequence of events. They don costumes and masks. They
depict the city with an approximate similarity on curtains [hung] over the
stage. They adapt this place that until now has been empty into a glittering
representation of events. The actors, the imitators of these historical events,
become an object of wonder for the spectators. So do [the scenes on] the
curtains, [as if] truly the city." In these theatrical presentations old legends
had become amusements, stripped of contemporary meaning and significance. In their imaginary city on stage actors still played out the old myths.
In a Christian city of the fourth century, however, these legends were now
just entertaining stories, and no longer momentous foundation myths or

an integral part of a city's collective self-representation. Now the audience laughed at these ancient marvels, and could not remember how or why they had ever been meaningful.[19]

One other reaction was to replace these old legends with direct equivalents. This reaction acknowledged the lingering social authority of these legends, but then tried to trump them. In Pontus many cities had progressed through a series of incarnations, each represented by a new name. The city that became Neocaesarea had once been Cabeira, a royal residence that king Mithridates had turned into a theme park to his own glory. In the later Roman empire the imposing ruins of the great construction projects of the Mithridatic kings were still scattered around Pontus. Despite these reminders, Gregory of Nyssa never mentioned any of this royal heritage for the city. In his estimation Gregory Thaumaturgus had effectively surpassed the impact of these earlier kings. Controlling and using rivers was one obvious test of power. Mithridates had constructed a water mill at Cabeira. In Cappadocia king Ariarathes had blocked a river in order to flood a plain and create a lake for his childish games. In contrast, Gregory Thaumaturgus had once dried up a marshy lake that was the cause of a feud between brothers, and he had prevented a river from overflowing its banks. The miracles of Gregory Thaumaturgus had both reversed and replaced the marvels of these earlier kings. Audiences thought actors were working wonders by recreating on stage these stories about an ancient king. In fact, Gregory "Thaumaturgus" was the true "Wonderworker," and legends about him were now the charter myths of Neocaesarea. As Gregory of Nyssa phrased it, Gregory Thaumaturgus had become the founder and lawgiver for the city, although in a Christian context he had acquired these titles to signify that he was the "founder of virtue" and the "lawgiver of life."[20]

At Caesarea legends about Basil would likewise replace earlier myths. Caesarea too had gone through a series of different names. Once it had been called Eusebeia, "Piety." Perhaps a dim memory of that earlier name motivated Gregory of Nazianzus to highlight his friend's piety in a commemorative oration. Basil's consecration as bishop of Caesarea provided Gregory with another opportunity to play with this allusion. Basil's predecessor had been Eusebius, "who bore the name of piety." One of the bishops who consecrated Basil was Eusebius of Samosata, "known for his piety." All these allusions reinforced the perception that Basil's episcopacy was itself the embodiment of piety, although now, of course, Christian piety. Another dim memory may have influenced another of Gregory's comparisons. When he described his friendship with Basil, he claimed that together they had exceeded Orestes and Pylades. These two mythological heroes had been cousins, comrades-in-arms, and paradigmatic examples of a close friendship. Orestes had also once been appropriated as a founder for cities and shrines in Cappadocia. According to Gregory, Basil had surpassed Orestes in his friendship; by implication, perhaps he had also replaced him as a founder at Caesarea.[21]

Although in Gregory's oration these comments about piety and Orestes were puns and metaphors, they were also fragments of older memories. Myths about Basil had not just succeeded earlier myths; they had also updated and replaced them. Mythology conferred authority and respect. The bishop, and not the city, was now the personification of piety, and Basil had replaced Orestes as a local founder. As a result, he now had the moral authority to introduce new laws and regulations. However new and disruptive were the disciplinary canons that Basil now proposed, people would respect them if at the same time they hailed him, like Gregory Thaumaturgus, as a lawgiver and founder.

Chapter 5
The Founder of the Cappadocians

In the early fifth century a Cappadocian scholar wrote an extensive ecclesiastical history that surveyed the developments of the previous century. In his homeland Philostorgius had grown up in the shadows of the great Cappadocian Fathers. Despite their prominence, Philostorgius did not embrace their version of orthodox theology. Instead, he and his family accepted the doctrines of Eunomius, another Cappadocian theologian whom Basil and Gregory of Nyssa would personally discredit and vilify. Nor did Philostorgius remain in Cappadocia, since eventually he moved to Constantinople.

In his ecclesiastical history Philostorgius was hence both ecumenical and local. He included many tidbits of odd information about biblical events and the Roman empire, and he was interested in legends about Cappadocia. When he mentioned Mazaca, the original name for the city that eventually became Caesarea, he noted that this name was derived from "Mosoch, the founder of the Cappadocians." Mosoch's name suggests some sort of Semitic derivation, and his reputation as the founder of the Cappadocians seems to hint at a foundation legend for the region that was older than the adoption of Greek myths. In the early Roman empire people outside Cappadocia had heard of Mosoch too. The Jewish historian Josephus even tried to fit him into biblical genealogies by equating him with Meshech, one of the grandsons of Noah.[1]

Although Mosoch is an intriguing primal ancestor, he unfortunately remains completely obscure. Philostorgius in fact knew so little about the legend that he could not match up the consonants and vowels in order to make sense of the postulated link between the city's name of Mazaca and Mosoch's name. So he shrugged and invented a makeshift phonetic transfer: "after the passage of time [the city] was called Mazaca through a 'swerving.'" In the later Roman empire all that survived of whatever legends there may have been about Mosoch were his name, his reputation, and his enigmatic connection with the name of a city. The myth of Mosoch the Founder was a lost memory, a fragment of an abandoned past, a casualty of the adoption of Greek mythology, the imposition of Roman rule, or the expansion of Christianity. In a society that defined itself in terms of Greekness, Romanness, or Christianity, Mosoch the Founder had become meaningless.[2]

The renaissance of Greek culture in the early Roman empire had included several aspects. One was an emphasis on the Greek past, especially its classical era. In particular, cities linked their foundation legends, civic myths, municipal and religious festivals, political institutions, and names and titles to Greek mythology and ancient history. Another component of this revival of Greek culture was an emphasis on linguistic and stylistic purism. Imitation of the style, vocabulary, and grammar of classical Athenian authors was to be the new standard of excellence. This period of the so-called Second Sophistic in the early Roman empire was supposed to be a self-conscious revival of the First Sophistic when literature had flourished at Athens during the fifth and fourth centuries B.C. The Second Sophistic hence combined a distinctively pure language with an interest in Greek history and mythology to differentiate the learned elite from everyone else, and to promote the standing of cities and regions. "Language purism . . . played a key role in establishing a coherent and recognizable identity for the Greek elite at this time. Complementary to it was the general role of the Greek past as a source of authority and commentary in the present."[3]

Educated Greek authors of the fourth century likewise prided themselves on their ability to maintain language standards and imitate Attic Greek, and their revival of classical standards defined what might be called a Third Sophistic during late antiquity. Christian authors like the Cappadocian Fathers also used this purist Greek, and they criticized their rivals for their linguistic failures. Gregory of Nazianzus kept with him a volume of the speeches of the great Athenian orator Demosthenes, and a bishop of Amaseia studied one of Demosthenes' speeches for hours on end. The theologian Eunomius likewise presented himself as an imitator of Demosthenes. Gregory of Nyssa thought otherwise, and before he refuted Eunomius' doctrines, he indulged in some literary criticism. His comments about Eunomius' prose were merciless: "who would not properly burst out laughing upon seeing the tastelessness in his selection of words and figures of speech, and the aimless effort without any proper model?" Yet although this Third Sophistic included expectations about language standards, among Christian authors it did not encourage another revival of allusions to Greek myths and Greek history. Christian authors preferred to use purist classical Greek to discuss instead their own myths and their own history.[4]

Christian bishops like Basil had introduced new patterns of hierarchy and new expectations of behavior for local communities. Because those new patterns conflicted with established behavior and traditional expectations, churchmen reinterpreted both the natural landscape and history itself in order to link this new morality with much longer traditions. Even through they wrote in classicizing, Atticizing Greek, they did not locate their new worldview in Greek myths and Roman history. Instead, they focused on biblical and Christian history. Their interpretations linked their communities with ecclesiastical history back to Jesus, with biblical history back into the Old Testament, and even with the original moment of creation. Local legends that had situated communities in Greek and Roman history were hence lost. At best they remained curiosities, occasionally collected by ethnographers or historians.

A miniature version of this entire process was the change in names of Caesarea, Basil's episcopal see. The original name of the city had been Mazaca, somehow derived from the name of Mosoch the Founder. During the Hellenistic period the kings of Cappadocia had renamed the city with a respectable Greek name, Eusebeia, "Piety." This renaming presumably reflected their goal of introducing Greek culture and the amenities of a proper Greek city. At the end of the first century B.C., Archelaus, the last of the Cappadocian kings, had renamed the city again as Caesarea in order to honor the emperor Caesar Augustus. Archelaus himself was hailed as a "founder," and Caesarea became a proper city in the Roman empire. In the fourth century bishop Basil founded a "new city" in the suburbs of Caesarea that included a church, a clerical residence, a poorhouse, and a hospital. Rather than simply renaming Caesarea, Basil had founded a replacement settlement, a vatican outside the city's walls. The name for this new foundation was, not so surprisingly, "Basilias," Basil's place. Mazaca, Eusebeia, Caesarea, Basilias: each new name was an entire history in one word, and as a community changed its name and cults, it changed its local history and legends. With each new name the city had also had to acknowledge a new founder or eponymous hero. Mosoch, a Hellenistic king, a Roman emperor: the next member of this series was a Christian bishop. By the later fourth century Basil was hailed as the "second founder and protector" and the "guardian and patron of the community." Legends about him now defined his community.[5]

Heterodox History

How quickly they forgot. At Caesarea memories of Basil were beginning to erode perhaps already soon after his death. Two processes contributed to this forgetting, one that looked to the future, the other that looked to the past.

One process was a continuation of the tendency of Basil, Gregory of Nyssa, and other churchmen to construct new histories that were more relevant to contemporary circumstances. Basil's immediate successor as bishop of Caesarea was Helladius. Since Basil seems not to have mentioned him in his extant correspondence, he may well not have been a special favorite. Helladius would furthermore have disputes with Gregory of Nyssa and Gregory of Nazianzus, who in their commemorative panegyrics had both helped burnish the myth of Basil at Caesarea. Helladius hence had no particular reason to promote Basil's memory.[6]

Another successor as bishop of Caesarea in the early fifth century was Firmus. Basil's foundation for the poor was still in operation, and Firmus was involved in its administration. But when he mentioned the Basilias by name, he did not take the opportunity to mention Basil. Firmus was instead all too ready to find a new founder for Caesarea. He once offered an imperial magistrate the opportunity to earn some honors from the city. Firmus suggested that this magistrate should restore some buildings, or that he might increase the number of cities that would be subordinate to Caesarea and hence to its metropolitan bishop, himself. These concerns were of course similar to Basil's earlier concerns about the city's standing, and they nicely indicated how cities and their bishops continued to struggle to maintain their local prestige. In this case Firmus was nevertheless prepared to discard earlier reputations to help his own cause. If this magistrate were to show his generosity, Firmus noted that in return the people of Caesarea would hail him as "benefactor and second founder." The earlier founders whom this magistrate would surpass and replace would have included Basil. But by now Firmus politely downplayed their contributions. "Those [founders] brought the city into existence, but you will help it become more glorious." When this later bishop of Caesarea needed support, he was certainly ready to push aside the legends of Basil and rewrite the city's history to accommodate a more recent founder.[7]

The other process that undermined Basil's reputation was antiquarianism. Philostorgius deserves credit for breaking away from this powerful mythology about the significance of Basil. His curiosity was a valued attribute, especially for a historian, since it made him critical as well as inquisitive. Reinforcing this inherent skepticism was a sense of grievance about the treatment of Eunomius. Basil and Gregory of Nyssa had reviled Eunomius and his theological doctrines; in contrast, Philostorgius made a pilgrimage to visit his hero in his retirement on a Cappadocian estate. Philostorgius then wrote his ecclesiastical history in part to defend Eunomius' reputation and to criticize Basil's behavior. "His historical account contradicts almost all other ecclesiastical historians." As one later Byzantine reader noted with both horror and fascination, his history was "an indictment of the orthodox" and a "eulogy of heretics."[8]

Philostorgius was hence a heterodox Christian who wrote a heterodox history. He had clearly not followed the new orthodoxy either about theology or about history. Even when writing about his own homeland of Cappadocia and adjacent regions, he broke ranks. Gregory of Nyssa had rewritten the history of Pontus in order to highlight the significance of Gregory Thaumaturgus; Philostorgius seems not to have mentioned either Gregory Thaumaturgus or Gregory of Nyssa. Basil's supporters had not been reluctant to rearrange the past to correspond to their vision of a better future, and they had emphasized the significance of the Basilias for Caesarea and Basil's own reputation in Cappadocia. Philostorgius was simply a better historian than that. Realizing that the entire past was relevant for interpreting the present, he preferred to mention Mosoch the Founder and Mazaca, the region's original founder and the city's original name, even if the shards of their memories left him puzzled about the connections. Rather than wanting to forget old legends about Cappadocia, Philostorgius struggled to recollect and record them. He was still trying to remember the past.

Preachers and Audiences

People had always watched and listened to the Cappadocian Fathers. Always they had lived in public and performed in public, as students praised by their teachers, as patrons interceding on behalf of friends and cities, as clerics ministering to congregations, even as ascetics who publicized their ideas about the benefits of seclusion. As bishops one of their primary responsibilities was to preach. In their sermons they articulated their own theology, criticized rival doctrines, offered hortatory advice about proper morality, commemorated new buildings, honored saints and their cults, and consoled people over their misfortunes. Sometimes they commented on current events, a devastating drought, the fire that almost destroyed a church "yesterday," the heavy drinking that filled long winter nights. Their sermons were hence not simply theological treatises, moral homilies, or laudatory panegyrics. In the small towns of eastern Asia Minor they were the equivalents of today's newscasts and editorials.[1]

Modern historians have carefully sifted sermons as historical sources for biographical details, political events, and many aspects of everyday life. But for all their success at extracting these golden nuggets of information, modern studies have often overlooked the most obvious question about these sermons. Did ancient audiences actually understand them? Both the theology and the language posed formidable obstacles. The Cappadocian Fathers were highly educated orators who articulated complex theology by means of intricate philosophical ideas and the techniques of formal rhetoric. The overwhelming output of modern exegesis on patristic writings is a more than adequate indication of our own difficulty in interpreting the theology, and it should raise hesitations about the ability of ancient audiences to comprehend these doctrines.

In addition, in many cases the grammar and vocabulary of the language were as sophisticated and complex as the theology. The Cappadocian Fathers and other bishops were participants in the movement to revive the Attic Greek that had been used centuries earlier during the classical period. In their writings, and frequently also when delivering sermons, they used a rather archaic literary Greek that was quite different from the common spoken Greek. Because much of the New Testament had been written in this vulgar Greek, some of these learned bishops and clerics were embarrassed by their own biblical texts. Whenever they cited passages from the Septuagint, the Greek translation of the Old Testament, or from the New Testament, they seemed to incorporate "words and expressions from these texts in their own archaizing language like technical terms or quotations from a foreign language." Sometimes citation became translation. When one bishop in Cyprus quoted a saying of Jesus in his sermon, he carefully substituted a classical word for the common Greek word. Basil once turned this distinction on its head to distinguish himself from his baroque critics by associating his own archaizing language with traditional homespun values. "The language of the country folk is still now old-fashioned, while the words of these artists are branded with the new sophistry." In this case Basil's portrait of himself was thoroughly disingenuous, since he too was a new-fangled sophist.[2]

Nor was diglossy, the distinction between purist literary Greek and common spoken Greek, the only language problem the Cappadocian Fathers faced in their preaching. Despite centuries of exposure to Greek culture, in the highlands of Asia Minor Greek was not the only spoken language. Long ago one regional king in eastern Asia Minor had finally consolidated his authority only by learning dozens of local dialects. Basil once noted that "we Cappadocians," like people in Mesopotamia, had "a regional language." Gregory of Nyssa conceded that Cappadocians had their own word for "heaven." In Cappadocia people used purist Greek, common Greek, Cappadocian, and no doubt other languages too. As a result, many preachers were all too aware that both subject matter and language might make their sermons difficult to understand. Pedantic theology and highbrow Greek were genuine impediments to effective communication with their audiences, and as they thought about one obstacle, they could not help but also reflect on the other. When Gregory of Nazianzus once commented on the chaos of doctrinal controversies, he immediately thought of the Tower of Babel, "which completely confused languages." In his own sermons Gregory struggled to talk "like a fisherman," one of Jesus' apostles, rather than "like Aristotle."[3]

Despite these difficulties, sermons were popular public events. In a typical traditional society in which "the little town tended to be deadly dull," at the very least a sermon might be good entertainment and offer an opportunity for a social occasion. A crowd once gathered at a shrine in Cappadocia at midnight in anticipation of a sermon that would not begin until noon. Even if people did not understand all the theology or the language, as Christians they shared an acquaintance with the Bible. Just as a mastery of classical literature was a means for connecting educated elites horizontally across the empire, so familiarity with biblical stories provided a common idiom between clerics and the ordinary people in their congregations. People paid careful attention to these sermons, and afterward talked about them. Everyone was a critic. At a dinner party a monk challenged Gregory of Nazianzus. This monk had once heard Gregory preach on the Holy Spirit, he had recently heard Basil preach on the same topic, and now he wondered why they had used different terminology. Gregory was affronted enough to ask this man for his own credentials as an "expert on dogma."[4]

Most people's familiarity with theology came from listening to sermons. At Sebasteia some people questioned the orthodoxy of Gregory of Nyssa's theology. Gregory sent them a formal treatise; they then asked for an oral confession. Their preference for a personal appearance is a pointed reminder of an often forgotten characteristic of sermons. Preaching was not like lecturing, with a speaker droning on before a quiet audience. Instead, preaching was a theatrical performance. Like orators, preachers knew they were entertainers. The famous sophist Libanius once admitted with pride that he had been accused of being more an actor than an orator. Like old-time revivalists, preachers strutted, ranted, pointed, and cajoled. Their audiences shouted back their questions, their agreement, their taunts. Every sermon was a dialogue, an animated conversation between preachers and audiences. The people at Sebasteia wanted Gregory to come and perform.[5]

The two chapters in this section are attempts to imagine the vividness and immediacy of these public dialogues. Each recreation is possible only because of unique circumstances. Even when information is available about dates, locations, and contexts, most of the extant sermons of the Cappadocian Fathers were disconnected, one-time events. But a few sermons, because they were interconnected, encourage inventive speculation about the interactions between preachers and audiences.[6]

Basil once delivered a series of nine sermons about the account of creation in the first chapter of Genesis. In this case he was preaching before essentially the same audience, in the same place, on five consecutive days. In order to sustain his listeners' interest, he had to respond to their reactions and needs. After his first sermon he clearly began to extemporize. Basil and Gregory of Nyssa also delivered some sermons about the cult of the Forty Martyrs. In this case they were preaching on the same topic, but at different times, in different places, and before different audiences. Even as they repeated the same basic narrative about these martyrs, they modified the precise details to fit the different situations.

All of these sermons were hence readings, as Basil reacted to the responses to his earlier sermons, and as he and Gregory manipulated the details to present their own ideas and interpretations. As the audiences listened to their sermons, preachers watched and listened to their audiences. While talking about creation Basil began to ad-lib on his prepared script. While talking about the Forty Martyrs he and his brother were improvising on the traditional score. The audiences had essentially put the words into the speakers' mouths.

Chapter 6
Listening to the Audience:
The Six Days of Creation

Among Basil's many extant orations is a series of nine sermons on the Hexaemeron, the "six days" described in the first chapter of Genesis during which God created the heaven and the earth. For Jewish intellectuals and then for Christian theologians, the first chapter of Genesis had long posed as many problems of interpretation as opportunities for exegesis and speculation. Basil was of course familiar enough with classical philosophy and current Christian theology to have written commentaries on books of the Bible. But he apparently decided to display his biblical exegesis instead in treatises on particular subjects, in polemical works that refuted others' ideas, in epistolary responses to others' questions, and in his sermons.

Once published, however, later readers considered this series of sermons about the first chapter of Genesis to be a nearly definitive commentary. Even though Peter of Sebasteia, one of Basil's younger brothers, raised questions about some interpretations, and even though Gregory of Nyssa, another brother, responded to those questions with supplemental comments, both admired "the sublime voice of the teacher." Modern scholars have tended to follow the brothers' lead and have likewise evaluated these sermons of Basil as a work of systematic exegesis or "scientific popularization" for a Christian audience, a commentary in disguise about the first chapter of Genesis and the theological meanings of creation. As such, these sermons have been assumed to be "the clearest expression of his mature thought," an attempt "to present a complete cosmology," and the natural culmination of his convictions about "the interplay between individual and community." One result of these assumptions is to turn Basil's sermons on the Hexaemeron into a lasting monument to his erudition and intellectual insight. Another, more problematic consequence is to diminish their immediate significance and meaning for both the preacher and his audience.[1]

The deepest difficulty with these assumptions is in fact the presence of a large audience of ordinary people, among them municipal notables, manual laborers, and rural peasants, who would not have been very familiar either with the philosophical and theological traditions that Basil drew upon or with Basil's own earlier inner musings about individual ideals and a disciplined community, and perhaps did not care that much about these ideas either. With its emphasis on a careful explication of the theological themes or philosophical echoes modern scholarship has often distorted the immediate impact and significance of ancient sermons. This misrepresentation reflects a failure to acknowledge the differences between the textual context so beloved of modern historians and patristics scholars and the oral context characteristic of ancient sermons. Modern audiences for these sermons consist of readers, but ancient audiences were primarily listeners. Because they did not have the luxury of comparisons with other treatises or even of rereading a sermon, their immediate reactions were focused on their local and current concerns.

Dialogues

The need for effective and meaningful communication with audiences of varying backgrounds and interests compelled ancient preachers to use all their rhetorical skills and persuasive eloquence. When Gregory of Nazianzus once imagined himself preaching before his congregation at Constantinople, he clearly outlined his difficulties in accommodating a diverse audience that included both clerics and young virgins, as well as noble matrons in the upper galleries. Some in attendance wanted a sermon that was "low to the ground and free flowing, because they did not wish to look up," while others wanted a sermon that was "high flown and nimble, because they wanted to investigate the foundations of both types of wisdom, both external [philosophical] wisdom and our [biblical] wisdom." And to make quite clear their contrasting preferences for easy platitudes or sophistical punditry, people were outright shouting at Gregory: "my sermon was hampered by contending desires."[2]

Gregory's solution was simply to preach his doctrine of the Trinity and rely upon the seductiveness of his rhetorical skills: "my eloquence enchanted everyone." He certainly knew how to play to his audience, as he once explained to an enthusiastic admirer. "When all the people are applauding me in a church, you will be forced against your will to agree with what you do not know. If you remain silent, everyone will dismiss you as stupid." For all his confidence, Gregory's recollection of his experiences nevertheless acknowledged that the interaction between preacher and audience involved competing preferences and needs, and that to be successful he had to generate instant satisfaction and comprehension. In Gregory's case, people were so intrigued by his sermons that they pressed up to the chancel screen, murmuring "like bees."[3]

The sermons that Gregory eventually delivered included, of course, the magnificent theological orations that seem far too intellectually high-powered for most in his audiences (and for many modern readers too). Later Byzantine commentators were in fact so impressed that they mined these sermons for examples of the most erudite techniques of formal logic; the noted polymath Michael Psellus thought that only Gregory could compare to the old classical orators. Audiences at Constantinople were nevertheless surely curious about theological controversies. Since so many bishops and churchmen came to the capital to attend councils and jockey for standing at the imperial court, the people there probably had more opportunities to hear about many doctrines, and they were perhaps more familiar with rhetorical techniques. They were certainly knowledgeable enough to recognize a clumsy speaker immediately. One such inept preacher was Demophilus, Gregory's predecessor as bishop of Constantinople, who presented his thoughts in a "disorganized heap" and included too much "rubbish," too many digressions, in his sermons. They also had enough of a passing familiarity with theological doctrines, or at least with the simplistic maxims that became shorthand for various doctrinal stances, that reciting these slogans provided an instant means of identifying theological loyalties. According to Gregory of Nyssa, the hubbub in the alleys and markets of the capital echoed with these abbreviated chants. "If you ask about coins, a vendor discourses to you about 'Generate' and 'Ingenerate.' If you inquire about the price of bread, he replies that 'the Father is greater and the Son is subordinate.' If you ask whether the bath is ready, he offers the definition that 'the Son is from the nonexistent.'"[4]

Yet this obsession with theological arguments does not necessarily imply that audiences at Constantinople were more sophisticated and learned than elsewhere. Gregory of Nyssa in fact included this description of people's fascination with doctrinal slogans in a critique of their ignorance about biblical narratives. The famous rhetorician Libanius had been much more unforgiving when he had complained that at Constantinople the majority of his audience was unable to comprehend his public orations and could instead merely watch his gestures. His assessment suggests that many in an audience were in fact only watchers, and that for most people the most memorable aspects of a public oration or sermon were the theatricality of the speaker and his dramatic presentation, rather than the precise content or specific ideas. Both prominent orators and effective preachers never forgot that in addition to expounding a topic they were addressing an audience. In one of his orations Gregory of Nazianzus candidly conceded the vital role of the audience as arbiter: "like a knowledgeable judge, the listener stands between my oration and the truth." Since an audience often based its assessment of the value of an orator's ideas on his competence as a speaker, in a successful public oration or sermon the presentation was more important than the content. An ancient audience was listening to the rhetoric, and not just the content.[5]

Basil may not have been an especially fluent or dynamic speaker. Gregory of Nazianzus once described his friend's oratory as "methodical, usually thoughtful, and internally compact." Out in Cappadocia Basil hence compounded a speaker's usual concerns about the audience's comprehension with his own spare and proper rhetorical style. According to Gregory of Nyssa, Basil delivered his sermons about God's creation "to a large crowd in a packed church." "Among his listeners there were many who had heard of the more complicated ideas. But for the most part the listeners did not understand a subtle examination of these ideas. They were uneducated men, laborers engaged in ordinary occupations. The group of women was unfamiliar with this knowledge; there was a cluster of children as well as some people who were older in years. All of these people were expecting the sort of sermons that, after some comprehensible persuasion about the visible and beautiful aspects of creation, would lead them by the hand to an understanding of the Creator of everything."[6]

These sermons were hence part of an ongoing dialogue with the members of his ecclesiastical community, and although the gave-and-take of that dialogue was only occasionally made explicit, the sermons were expected to be understandable and meaningful to the listeners. In return, as Basil spoke, he could watch the eyes and faces of the people in the crowd, and to be successful he had to respond to their reactions. Whatever significance the sermons had for Basil as a means of demonstrating his familiarity with previous exegetical traditions, and whatever importance they acquired for later readers as a learned commentary on the biblical account of creation, at the time they were indicative of his attempts simply to communicate with his audience.

Basil delivered these nine sermons almost certainly sometime during his episcopacy, perhaps during the later years. He presented the first four sermons as two paired sets, morning and evening, on two consecutive days, the fifth by itself on the next day, and the final four again in paired sets, morning and evening, on the next two days. The five days on which he delivered these sermons were apparently part of a week of fasting, which may have been a week during Lent.[7]

Even though the exact circumstances and date of the sermons remain uncertain, their delivery on consecutive days in rapid succession offers a unique opportunity to examine aspects of the dialogue between a preacher and his audience. Evaluations that highlight the philosophical and literary sources or the overall moral thrust tend to conflate the nine sermons into an undifferentiated whole. In fact, to understand the impact of these sermons on the audience it is necessary to consider them one by one in sequence and to assume that day by day, even from the morning to the evening, Basil learned from and reacted to the responses of his listeners. Each sermon after the first one represented a reading, an interpretation, of the previous sermon, as Basil listened to his audience. Not only could his listeners not anticipate his specific interpretations, but their reactions clearly influenced his remarks and in some cases diverted him from his prepared comments and motivated him to improvise. In these sermons Basil was both overtly responding to his listeners' reactions and implicitly commenting on his own earlier sermons. Even as he listened to the audience, he was listening to himself.[8]

Philosophical Erudition: First and Second Sermons

Each sermon was a virtuoso display of learning. Even though in most cases Basil was probably drawing upon manuals of excerpts from philosophical and scientific treatises, his own notes, or his memories of his earlier reading rather than actual copies of the complete treatises by other theologians or philosophers, his discussions were still overwhelming erudite. They were also most likely quite baffling to many of the people in his audience. The first sermon in particular, with its discussion of the creation of heaven and earth, was intellectually the most challenging, and the inclusion in its opening remarks of a verbal pun, an ambiguous allusion, and an implied identification immediately set the intellectualist tone.[9]

The initial text for explication was, of course, the first verse of Genesis that mentioned God's creation of heaven and earth "in the beginning." Basil started out by noting that an appropriate "beginning" or "origin" for his

sermon was an analysis of the "origin" of visible things. This rather arch
pun created a context of highbrow expectations that he could then use to
highlight his own intellectual qualifications while implicitly questioning
those of his audience. His next suggestion, that his listeners were perhaps
not yet worthy of hearing "the greatness of these words," also set the scene
to his advantage, since it was not clear whether "these words" were the biblical texts or Basil's own comments. Basil then provided a brief history of
Moses, who, he claimed, had composed Genesis by reporting what he had
heard directly from God himself. Although this short biography was intended
to establish the credibility of the author, by implication it also established
the credentials of the preacher. Basil seems to have been implying that, like
Moses, he too was articulating "the teachings of the Spirit," and that he
shared with Moses the same concern, "not for the approbation of those
listening but for the salvation of those instructed." With these initial comments he had situated his sermon within a long-standing debate among
intellectuals, acknowledged that his audience might not understand everything, and implied that his listeners should simply take his interpretations
on faith. Basil had long had a reputation for intellectual (and personal)
arrogance, and the opening remarks of his first sermon seemed to imply
that he was preparing to do his audience a favor by allowing them to listen
in on his ideas.[10]

Although ostensibly an exegesis of the first verse of the first chapter of
Genesis, this first sermon quickly became a commentary on others' commentaries, loaded with allusions to various "wise men of the Greeks" and
their writings about the nature of things. Having posed the rhetorical question of how he should initiate his discussion, Basil decided to begin with
"the follies of outsiders," that is, with the doctrines of pagan philosophers.
Even though his subsequent presentation was entirely unsystematic and a
bit haphazard, he consistently highlighted philosophical tenets. Some philosophers argued that the primary components of the world were various
material substances or atoms that had coalesced by chance; Basil insisted
that God had provided the initiative and the direction. Some philosophers
argued that heaven and earth were eternal with God or even that heaven was
God; Basil insisted that God had created everything within time and that
it would all be ended within time. An emphasis on the origin of things
implied different notions of time; Basil nevertheless insisted that the world
had come into existence through the will of God that operated outside
time.[11]

Since in this first sermon Basil did not cite or allude to many other biblical passages, much of the agenda came from his engagement with earlier philosophers. The most important of these Greek cosmographers was Aristotle, whose various treatises had certainly influenced many subsequent discussions of nature and cosmogony. In this sermon, however, even though he demonstrated his familiarity with some of the writings of Aristotle, Basil never mentioned him by name and instead confronted him and other earlier thinkers anonymously. One advantage of anonymous criticism was an implicit denigration of the ideas in these treatises, as if they were so embarrassing that their authors did not deserve mention by name. Another was to disguise his own reliance upon and sometimes acceptance of those ideas, as in his discussion of the various significations of the Greek word for "beginning" that in fact used Aristotle's definitions.[12]

Yet another advantage was to conceal the difficulty Basil was having in trying to dispute these ideas. Some of the teachings of Basil, and of many Christian theologians in general, clearly were baffling in the context of mainstream Greek philosophy. At Athens, over three centuries earlier, Greek philosophers had burst out laughing upon hearing the apostle Paul's claims about Jesus' incarnation and resurrection. Basil conceded that still now some "let loose a loud guffaw" upon hearing about the end of the world and the regeneration of life through God's judgment. When he was unable (or unwilling) to offer a convincing refutation, he had to resort to other strategies. One was to claim that the issue was unimportant, not worthy of "a long and irrelevant digression." Another was to insist that people should simply "set limits on the investigation," lest their curiosity lead them astray. Yet another was to assert that "the simplicity of faith was stronger than logical deductions." This last option in particular was the equivalent of an intellectual shrug, an unspoken acknowledgment that the speaker did not in fact have all the answers. All these options, however, nicely indicated the difficulties Basil faced in presenting himself as the Christian equivalent of a philosopher as he analyzed the creation of the world, ready to refute classical cosmogony even as he offered his own interpretations. At the end of the sermon he characterized any further discussions of cosmogony as merely more of "the same frivolity." Instead, his audience should simply trust Moses. By implication, they should also trust Basil.[13]

Given his initial readiness to analyze the treatises of Greek philosophers about nature, Basil's conclusion may have surprised even himself. It may also have influenced his discussion in his second sermon that evening. At the beginning of this sermon he conceded that "this morning while spending some time on a few words [of Genesis] we found such hidden depth of meaning as to despair completely of what follows." Rhetoricians had often employed such deprecating concessions as a means of highlighting their own skills and insights, since they could then go on to demonstrate that they were in fact capable of providing the appropriate interpretations. But given Basil's warning at the end of his sermon that morning about indulging in "frivolous bantering," perhaps he had by now realized that confronting earlier philosophical treatises was not a very productive technique for interpreting the story of creation in Genesis. Perhaps, too, during the midday interlude between the sermons some of his audience had suggested a preference for a different approach that was less intellectualist and more accessible. Whatever the reasons, in this second sermon he was less intent on criticizing, even anonymously, the ideas of earlier philosophers and more intent on simply preaching about the biblical texts.[14]

Basil also wanted to speed up his discussion a bit, because while in his first sermon he had focused on only the first verse, in this second sermon he analyzed the next five verses that filled out the account of the first day of creation. His primary objective was to determine "the purpose of Scripture." To do so he still sometimes refuted or simply denied others' interpretations, although now he was more interested in rival religious interpretations rather than strictly philosophical positions. Some he criticized again anonymously. In his arguments against the suggestion that matter once had been invisible or even uncreated he rejected "the falsifiers of the truth," who may well have been Gnostics. Others he criticized by name. In his rejection of the notions that the darkness covering the abyss was an evil power or that it was evil itself, self-begotten and opposed to the goodness of God, he explicitly mentioned two Gnostic sects and "the disgusting heresy of the Manichees." Although these references to Gnostics and Manichees were largely generic, without much detail or any specific citations, it is significant that Basil was now mentioning some opponents by name. The ideas themselves were still perhaps not any more simple or even understandable, but a reference to specific opponents had the effect of making their claims more immediate and his own disagreements more timely. He also explicitly referred to a commentator with whom he agreed. In a discussion about the assertion in Genesis that the Spirit of God was carried above the water, he admitted that "a Syrian" had provided an explanation that properly understood the sense of the Hebrew text.[15]

In this evening sermon Basil had hence changed his tactics, and he now seemed to be more interested in citing a biblical verse to initiate his discussion rather than in proceeding directly to his summations and refutations of various philosophical positions. In order to enhance his points he also began to rely more upon two techniques that he had hardly employed in his morning sermon.

One was the use of practical illustrations from everyday life. In his criticism of the "falsifiers of the truth" who suggested that matter was uncreated and that God had therefore only shaped and formed it, Basil could easily have drifted into a discussion of philosophical ideas. Instead, he decided to refute this notion by introducing some examples from daily life. Craftsmen did in fact follow this pattern of using materials from elsewhere, since wool was supplied to weavers and wood to carpenters who then transformed it into spears for soldiers. These particular examples carried a special resonance in Cappadocia, where many worked in the imperial factories that produced clothing and armor. But Basil now insisted that these examples were not comparable to the handiwork of God, who had simultaneously conceived the form of the cosmos and created the appropriate matter. Later in his sermon he used an example that perhaps reminded his listeners of how some of them had spent the interlude between sermons, since in his discussion of the causes of darkness he suggested that his listeners imagine a man who entered a dark tent in the middle of the day. The use of such allusions to aspects of everyday life suggests that he had decided after his first sermon that he needed to use examples that would have more significance for his audience: "understand my explanation from this clear example."[16]

Another technique that Basil now began to employ was to emphasize the specific moral obligations for his listeners. In his morning sermon the implications of God's involvement in cosmogony had been largely abstract and remote from human affairs. In this evening sermon, in contrast, he made a pointed application to people's lives. In his argument that evil did not have its origin from God, he suggested that it was instead "a condition in the soul that was opposed to virtue and that appeared in sluggish people because they abandoned the good." Evil was not something that came upon people from without, it was not something that just happened naturally, like old age or illnesses, and it was not something that happened by chance, like finding a treasure while digging a well or confronting a rabid dog while walking to the market. Instead, Basil was very explicit that people were to accept responsibility for their own evilness: "each person is to recognize himself as the author of the evil in himself."[17]

By working more directly off the biblical verses and by using more practical examples this second sermon was hence more relevant and friendly. By insisting upon moral responsibility it was also more challenging to its audience, although that challenge was itself another way of making the sermon more meaningful. At the end of the sermon Basil discussed the differences between day and night. This discussion provided a convenient segue to conclude his sermon, since the coming of nightfall had overtaken his comments on the night.[18]

Questions and Complaints: Third and Fourth Sermons

On the next day Basil delivered two more sermons. In the introduction to the first of these sermons he evaluated his two sermons of the previous day by suggesting that the one in the morning had provided nourishment for people's souls and the one in the evening joy for their souls. This distinction seems to suggest that he himself now conceded that his first sermon had been intellectually much more high-powered than its sequel. It also hinted that he might be intending to follow the same pattern with the two sermons for this day.

Yet Basil's next remarks stressed that in fact he was not planning to deliver another presumptuously overwhelming sermon. He first admitted that in his upcoming discussion of the marvelous works of the second day of creation he planned "to promote not the power of the exegete but rather the charm of the written words." On the previous day he had started by implicitly identifying his exegetical skills with the credentials of the author, Moses himself; now he was giving more credit to the biblical texts. In addition, he included a specific reference to "the many workers in manual crafts" who were in his audience and whose presence compelled him to be brief in his comments, so that they could return to their occupations. On the previous day Basil had begun by pointing out the difficulties many would have in understanding his remarks. Now he was explicitly acknowledging not only the presence of ordinary workers in his audience, but also their concerns about their livelihoods. With these comments he effectively conceded that he had reoriented his outlook about the goals of his sermons. Perhaps it is appropriate to guess that some listeners had grumbled about the length of his sermons or about the obligation of listening to so many sermons on consecutive days.[19]

Basil's presentation in this sermon was also more similar to the accessible format of the previous evening's sermon than to the austere format of the previous morning's. The topic for this sermon was the creation of the firmament and the division of the waters. Basil could hence still indulge himself in citing opinions by "the wise men of the Greeks," in this case the various (anonymous) "philosophers who wrote about heaven." But in most cases he cited opinions without fully engaging them. Instead, in his analysis or refutations of these opinions he often introduced comparisons with aspects of ordinary life that would have had special relevance to those workers about whose attention he had worried at the beginning of his sermon. In his discussion of the distinction between heaven and firmament he mentioned the theory that the movement of the planets in their seven circles produced a sweet sound, and then mocked the inability of its proponents to explain why that sound was inaudible by comparing them to "workers in forges whose ears are constantly deafened." When he argued that so much water was necessary to offset the effects of fire and heat, he noted that fire was necessary for "the essential occupations of our life" such as weaving, shoemaking, house building, and farming. These comparisons would certainly have connected with farmers and the workers in the imperial weaving mills and armor factories.[20]

Other examples were also aimed specifically at particular characteristics of life in Cappadocia. In his discussion of the spherical shape of the firmament Basil used a comparison with "the stone vaults of the baths and the structures of cavelike buildings" that had semicircular vaulted ceilings inside but flat roofs outside. Public baths were common enough in Greek cities. But Caesarea was also quite uniquely distinctive, since the surrounding region was probably already honeycombed with some of the fantastic stone churches and houses carved out of the volcanic rockscape that would become so common in the later Byzantine period. Basil was now suggesting that his listeners visualize the shape of the firmament in terms of buildings with which only they as Cappadocians would be familiar. In his subsequent analysis of the nature of the firmament, in contrast, he insisted that the obvious analogies from Cappadocia were misleading. While conceding that the firmament was associated with water, he nevertheless claimed that it was not similar to ice, common enough during winter, or to the rocks thought to be formed from filtered water, such as the rock crystals and reflective marble for which the local mines and quarries were noted.[21]

In this sermon not only had Basil been quick to introduce comparisons and examples from the experiences of his audience, he also had an exegetical alternative to the ideas of classical philosophers. Interestingly enough, he now introduced this alternative by focusing on the reaction of his audience. Basil still enjoyed mentioning alternative opinions about some issue and letting them contradict each other, but he also admitted that refuting these opinions was "not appropriate for a man who knows how to manage time or who is concerned about the comprehension of his listeners." This remark seems to be an admission that an audience of farmers and manual laborers would not understand or benefit from detailed discussion of classical philosophy. Instead, by "leaving the arguments of outsiders to outsiders," he decided to highlight "the teaching of the church." In his sermon of the previous evening he had stressed some of the moral obligations of his listeners; in this sermon he began to hint at some of the basic doctrines and terminology that he had used elsewhere in his campaigns against heresies. In his discussion of God's command about the creation of the firmament he suggested that it was necessary to consider the "Person" who had received this command, that is, "the Only-Begotten" who was already present. Later he insisted that his discussion of the nature of the firmament had likewise provided "clear arguments about the Only-Begotten." This stress on the teachings of the church also apparently included recognition of earlier ecclesiastical teachings and traditions, although Basil remained predictably true to form by having to disagree with some earlier Christian writers about an allegorical interpretation of the division of the waters.[22]

In this third sermon Basil had hence continued his trend away from the strongly philosophical and rather remote emphasis of his first sermon and toward the more immediate characteristics of his second sermon. He even ended this sermon with another recognition of his listeners' concerns by suggesting that during the interval before the evening's sermon some people could review his comments, while others could work at their livelihoods. God would certainly be sympathetic, since as creator of everything he too was a "craftsman" who labored in "the huge and elaborate factory of divine workmanship."[23]

Basil must have appreciated the irony of being able to claim that none of the immense imperial enterprises that dominated Cappadocia, the weaving mills, the armor factories, even the sprawling estates and ranches, could compare to God's own workshop of the entire world. Not all of his listeners may have been so entranced by hearing the details of creation, however, because at the beginning of his fourth sermon in the evening of this second day he seems again to have had to deal with some weariness and hesitation. His response was to label as laziness people's preferences to spend their time watching jugglers, listening to music, or just daydreaming about their favorite race horses and charioteers, especially since they had the opportunity to contemplate instead "the arrangement of everything."[24]

The sermon this evening was a discussion of the gathering of the waters at the beginning of the third day of creation. Two characteristics of this sermon were especially significant. One was again Basil's preference to work more directly with the biblical texts. He in fact initiated his exegesis with the comment that his listeners would understand the nature and arrangement of water "from what has just been read to us." This comment was an explicit acknowledgment that a reading from the Bible had preceded this sermon (and most likely the others too), and that it was the basis of his subsequent remarks. In fact, in this sermon Basil was so intent on explicating the actual text that he included a discussion about the correctness of a particular sentence in the Greek translation of a verse.[25]

A second notable characteristic was the comparative chattiness and informality of this sermon. Basil complained, mock-seriously, that some people had raised questions about his previous sermons. In particular, someone had "demanded an explanation for the invisibility of the earth." Basil had first discussed this issue in his sermon of the previous evening, and he now admitted that "perhaps my comments do not seem to be adequate to you." His reaction was to use the biblical text currently under discussion to illuminate the earlier text that described the earth as unseen: "listen now to Scripture as it reveals itself." Basil has here responded to a question from a listener not by citing more philosophical doctrines but by discussing another biblical verse. A bit later he reacted to a complaint that "my account of the creation of the world is contrary to experience." Since this objection concerned his discussion in this sermon about the gathering of the waters, it was presumably not a question that had been raised earlier about an issue in a previous sermon but perhaps a reaction shouted out while he was preaching now. His response was a classic example of how to belittle a heckler with a polite but still overwhelming display of erudition, which in this case was a long list of lakes and seas. Basil also posed other issues by presenting them as rhetorical questions that other members of the audience might raise: "the thought might come to you as you stood beside a spring that was pouring out abundant water."[26]

By responding to actual questions and by attributing rhetorical questions to his listeners Basil had become much more adept at engaging his audience. As yet another indication that he was being more responsive, perhaps in particular to people's grumbling about the use of their time, he made this a short sermon, only about two-thirds the length of each of his previous three sermons. The end of this sermon turned into an ode on the usefulness of water for people's livelihoods. Equally praiseworthy, according

to Basil, was the "congregation of this church" that was not troubled by
heretical teachings. This compliment was an encouragement for people to
gather again the next day. It was also an open acknowledgment that he had
now placed the emphasis on his audience, their concerns, and their needs.[27]

The Morality of Agrarian Life: Fifth Sermon

On the next day Basil delivered his fifth sermon. Two characteristics immediately distinguished this sermon from its predecessors. First, its discussion
about the creation of plants and trees was a continuation of the discussion
in the sermon of the previous evening about the activities of the third day
of creation. Basil had split his exegesis of the activities of the first day of creation between morning and evening sermons, and he would do the same for
his discussion of the activities of the first half of the sixth day of creation in
his final pair of sermons, but this sermon marked the only time that he
started again on the next day with the activities of the day of creation he had
been discussing during the previous evening. One possible explanation is
that Basil simply decided to separate the two major acts of creation on the
third day, the gathering of the waters and the creation of flora, as topics too
disparate to be discussed together. Another possibility, however, is that he
had originally intended to discuss the entire third day of creation in his sermon of the previous evening, until he decided instead to cut that sermon
short, perhaps after hearing some complaints about the excessive time people had to devote to these sermons.

A second characteristic of this sermon might support this suggestion
that Basil had modified his original intentions. Unlike his previous sermons,
this one had no preamble in which he introduced his topic or bantered with
his audience. Instead, he simply launched directly into a discussion of a verse
from Genesis about the sprouting of vegetation. As it stands, this introduction is somewhat abrupt and disconcerting; but presumably if he had included all the activities of the third day of creation into one sermon, the
appearance of dry land after the gathering of the waters would have served
as the logical bridge to the appearance of plants. In fact, in this sermon
about plants Basil nevertheless retained a connection with his discussion
of the previous evening about seas and other bodies of water, since in his
discussion of grain he noted that originally, before there ever was inclement
weather or crop failure, "the fertility of the fields that rippled with crops
offered the image of a sea surging with the waving of the grain." These

considerations suggest that originally he had intended to discuss all the activities of the third day of creation in a single sermon, which would have been the sermon of the previous evening, and that after abbreviating that sermon he was now simply continuing where he had left off.[28]

This fifth sermon was also the most practical so far. In his previous sermons Basil had discussed more speculative ideas about the creation of heaven and earth, and he had been able to connect those ideas with ordinary experiences only through metaphors and everyday examples. In contrast, a sermon about plants, trees, and farming was directly relevant to many of his listeners, who were landowners, farmers, and herdsmen. Basil included discussions of seeds and roots, germination, the usefulness of poisonous plants, different types of trees, and the importance of grape vines and olive trees. Although he may have gleaned some of this information from agricultural manuals or the remarks of earlier authors, it is quite possible that he, like the members of his audience, was familiar with details about the produce of the land. Some of the details seem particularly relevant to Cappadocia. When discussing the failure of crops, he mentioned the appearance of "black wheat," produced as the result of having been "burned by the extreme frost." When discussing different types of trees, he noted a technique for improving the taste of bitter almonds. The cultivation of almonds and other nuts was common in central Asia Minor. Since so many of his exegetical points involved aspects of common agrarian life that the listeners in his audience could readily confirm or dispute, in some respects this was perhaps the most difficult sermon to preach.[29]

Basil's contribution to these details about agrarian life was to superimpose a message about moral and religious expectations by including both warnings and recommendations. Already at the beginning of his sermon he had warned his listeners against thinking that the sun was responsible for the growth of plants and hence worshipping it as "the cause of life." The rebuttal in this case was the observation that God had commanded the generation of plants before He created the sun on the next day. Another warning stressed the transience of prosperity. Flowers bloomed only briefly; likewise even a vigorous man would soon succumb to old age or illness. In particular, Basil warned people who preened themselves for their wealth, offices, or entourages of supporters to remember that their good fortunes were as fleeting as the frailest of flowers. It is not readily apparent why he here suddenly criticized the successes of local notables and municipal magistrates; perhaps he was playing to the resentments of the ordinary farmers and workers in his audience. In contrast, an emphasis on good horticulture suggested an appropriate analogy for instruction about goodness. Later in the sermon Basil included a truly remarkable concession that people could learn proper behavior even from a non-Christian. In his discussion of the benefits for cultivated figs from cross-pollination with wild figs he argued that in a similar fashion it was possible to learn about good works from "those foreign to our faith," such as "a pagan or someone separated from the church because of some perverted heresy who is [nevertheless] cultivating an ascetic life and other order in his character."[30]

In a discussion about plants and trees the primary difficulty was to find cosmic meanings in such mundane aspects of agrarian life. In Basil's earlier discussions of the creation of heaven and earth the subject matter had been abstract and seemingly irrelevant to ordinary life; in this sermon the subject matter was instead almost too familiar. Centuries earlier, even Archelaus, the last king of Cappadocia, had written a treatise about agriculture and livestock. Most people probably thought of crops and produce not in terms of cosmogony and morality, but simply in terms of food and survival. So Basil's objective in this sermon was to stress God's role in agrarian life. "I want the marvel of creation to be so deeply impressed on you that wherever you are and whatever plants you discover, you may find an obvious reminder of the Creator." "Whenever you see cultivated plants or wild plants . . . , increase your love of the Creator." Like his listeners, Basil could hardly bring himself to stop talking about plants and trees. Even after he reminded himself that he was running out of time, he still slipped in a few more quick comments about the pine tree and the tamarisk.[31]

Common Sense: Sixth and Seventh Sermons

After five sermons (perhaps originally planned as four), Basil was halfway through the six days of creation. The fourth and fifth days of creation he covered in another pair of sermons on the next day of his preaching.

The topic for the morning sermon was the creation of the lights in the firmament, that is, the sun and the moon. This topic had the potential to influence Basil to abandon his direct engagement with his audience's interests and revert instead to his learned discussions about metaphysics and philosophy. In fact, he did include some erudite discussions that might not have been very understandable to his listeners. When he began his exegesis of the verse describing the creation of the lights, he first discussed a philological explanation. The account in Genesis had distinguished the creation of light on the first day from the illumination later offered by the sun on the fourth day of creation. The true son of a grammarian, Basil now was embarrassed that the Greek translation (in the Septuagint) had used a word for "illumination" that was not found in classical texts: "the peculiarity of the vocabulary should not make you laugh." He used the distinctions between fire and a lamp and between "whiteness by nature" and "something painted white" to make a similar distinction between "the actual nature of light" and "this solar body that has been prepared to be a form for that first-born light." Although he here resorted to an important philosophical distinction between essence and quality, the oddity is that he introduced this discussion as a consequence of his misgivings over a nicety of Greek vocabulary that most people in his audience probably would not have noticed without his highlighting. He then included a lengthy criticism of astrology and of the Chaldaeans, "who say that our life is attached to the movement of the stars." The purpose of this refutation was, of course, vital, since a concession to the determining power of fate would undermine "the great hopes of Christians" who stressed the importance of choice and merit in their behavior. But the interminable length of his list of counterexamples made the entire sermon very long, by far the longest of the whole series and about one-third as long as most of the other sermons. Even Basil finally admitted that his listeners needed no more of this excessive digression.[32]

Despite the potential for a sermon about the creation of the sun, moon, and stars to drift into an assessment of highly technical cosmogony, Basil finally turned most of this sixth sermon too into a very practical discussion. The introduction of the sermon made perfectly clear not just his regard for the concerns of his audience, but also his expectations of what they might contribute. Basil noted that the regulations for festivals required spectators to have uncovered heads in order to demonstrate that they too were somehow also participants in the athletic contests. Using that analogy he suggested that "a listener of truly important and inexpressible wisdom" should share responsibility with "the exegete of these great and immense marvels," that is, himself, but as a fellow competitor and not as a judge. This emphasis on sharing responsibility was of course a self-effacing means for deflecting criticism in advance, "lest my stumble should become a disaster for the listeners." It also defined as a prerequisite for listening to the sermon a qualification that was achievable by virtually everyone. Now it was not familiarity with Greek philosophy but simply looking at the stars and thinking about the Creator that made someone "a qualified listener, worthy of being in the crowd in this distinguished and delightful theater." With this comment

Basil had gone beyond being merely sensitive to his audience's concerns and was actually expecting them to become active participants.[33]

The topics of this sermon were the sun, the moon, and the stars, and Basil deftly connected them to the topics of the sermon of the previous day by comparing them to flowers that God had used to decorate heaven. By distinguishing between the command and the making of the heavenly lights he also made a quick doctrinal point about the "doubleness of the Persons" of God: "the teaching of theology is mystically interspersed everywhere in history."[34]

But Basil's primary concern was to interpret the sun, the moon, and the stars as "signs," not in the context of astrology, which he thoroughly rejected, but in the context of meteorology. Much of this sermon discussed the most common topic of ordinary chitchat, the weather. Basil offered several examples of how sailors, travelers, and farmers could predict the likelihood of storms, droughts, and heavy winds by noticing various aspects of the sun and moon. He also offered a series of remarks about the differences among the seasons, and then an explanation of the apparent smallness of the sun by comparing it to a team of oxen or a ship that seems tiny when viewed at a distance from the top of a mountain. Through analogies and rather commonplace observations he had now firmly connected the creation of the sun, the moon, and the stars with the everyday life, and especially agrarian life, of most of his listeners.[35]

In this case, though, Basil was not content with merely making this connection. Most of his comments in this sermon resembled those found in modern farmers' almanacs, a mixture of common sense, traditional wisdom, and sometimes just plain goofiness. In a discussion of the full moon, for instance, Basil claimed that "those who sleep [outside] under the moon have the cavities in their heads filled with excessive moisture." This lunatic observation, which was presumably some commonplace aphorism, is a poignant indication of how far he has modified his approach in these sermons. In his first sermon he had been prepared to joust with the philosophical ideas of "the wise men of the Greeks." In this sermon too he had included a long digression about the mistakes of astrology in order to dispute the Chaldaeans, but at the end, after all his comments about the sun, the moon, the seasons, and the weather, he was more concerned about issuing a warning against taking seriously "some ridiculous tales told by drunken old women" about the moon. For an elderly bishop who was spouting his own nonsense about the weather the most important rivals were now old wives' tales.[36]

At the conclusion of this sermon Basil suggested that "the meanness of my words" had all the nourishment of bread made from barley. This remark was certainly disingenuous, although if in fact he was delivering these sermons during a week of fasting, then it may have been intended to remind people that these words would be their only nourishment until they could eat again later in the day. As a way of stressing God's greatness, he also noted that "in comparison with the Creator the sun and the moon have the reason of a mosquito or an ant." This final remark was a preview of the sermon that evening in which he intended to discuss the appearance of sea creatures and birds on the fifth day of creation. In fact, in the opening remarks of his next sermon he mentioned that mosquitoes were some of the tiny creatures generated from the muddy slime.[37]

Because Basil then went on to talk almost entirely about sea fish and other sea creatures, this seventh sermon was perhaps somewhat remote to the concerns of people in a landlocked region. Cappadocians certainly ate freshwater fish that they caught in rivers and lakes, but Basil probably derived much of his knowledge of sea fish from books and supplemented it with hearsay. One source was "people who grew up along beaches and coasts," who had informed him about one fish that supposedly chewed its cud and about the prescience of the sea urchin in predicting the weather. Obviously neither he nor members of his audience knew much about the characteristics of sea fishes.[38]

So Basil instead emphasized the moral implications. The behavior of fish and other sea creatures was especially suitable for use as paradigms because, unlike plants and trees, they were the first of God's creatures to have souls and share in sensation. Some fishy behavior was reprehensible. Fish that fed on other fish resembled greedy men who swallowed up the weak: "beware lest the same fate as that of the fish ensnares you, somewhere a hook or a trap or a net." An octopus that changed its color to match its surroundings was similar to men who modified their standards in order to insinuate themselves to the ruling powers. In contrast, other examples from the lives of fishes were laudable. In his earlier sermons Basil had sometimes included warnings against the greediness of those with power. In this sermon he now suggested that people "who partition the land and join house to house and field to field so as to seize something from their neighbor" should instead follow the example of fish who stay and feed in their own particular bays.[39]

In addition, in this sermon he used an example from marine life to include some advice about marriage and family life. After discussing the sea urchin Basil suddenly, and rather unexpectedly, quoted the apostle Paul's recommendation that husbands were to love their wives. The example he selected to illustrate his point was the "marriage" of a viper, "the most dangerous of snakes," with a sea lamprey. Various learned commentators had already debunked this odd coupling as a fable. Basil nevertheless drew some rather disturbing conclusions about marriage from this legend. One was that a wife must put up with her husband even if he was rough, violent, and drunk, and she should not even consider splitting their marriage. Another was that a husband, just like the viper who spits out his venom out of respect for his marriage, should set aside any roughness or cruelty in his soul. These conclusions were consistent with Basil's recommendations elsewhere about the inherent unevenness of expectations about the behavior of husbands and wives in marriages. In those canons he had insisted that wives were to take back adulterous and violent husbands. But already then he had been discomfited at the absence of any logic behind this convention, and in this sermon too he apparently sensed that his analogies were a bit insensitive. As he drew one more analogy, he too seemed to question the reliability of the story about the marriage of the viper and the lamprey. Because their intercourse was "an adultery against nature," it was also a warning to men who were plotting against others' marriages. At this point Basil was clearly stretching for possible implications, literally improvising aloud and hoping that "this example would perhaps be of some other use to us."[40]

This sermon about fish and other sea creatures was hence a difficult one to make relevant and applicable to his listeners. Because of his listeners' apathy and his own ignorance, perhaps Basil felt compelled all the more to introduce recommendations about proper behavior, in particular about relationships within marriage, a topic that had not previously come up in this series of sermons. Delivering this sermon apparently took its toll, because by the end he complained about "the weakness of my body." This complaint is understandable, since his health had always been fragile and he had by now delivered seven sermons in four days. He also mentioned that the late hour compelled him to end his sermon. This is an odd excuse, since in fact this sermon had been comparatively brief, about one-third shorter than most of the others. It seems more plausible that his stamina was failing, and that he was simply running out of things to say about fishes. To fill out his conclusion he resorted to a series of puns about water and the sea that were perhaps the closest he came to using some humor in these sermons. "Somehow the marvels of creation, overtaking us one after another like waves, have left our sermon underwater." "Let us bring our sermon to an anchorage." At the end of this sermon Basil hoped that his listeners would discuss both his morning and his evening sermons over their meals.[41]

Nods and Murmurs: Eighth and Ninth Sermons

Some obviously did. On the next day Basil delivered another pair of sermons in which he apparently intended to conclude his preaching with a discussion of the climatic events of the sixth day of creation. The verse from Genesis with which he started his eighth sermon in the morning described the creation of land animals at the beginning of the sixth day, and his initial comments made it clear that he planned to proceed directly with analyzing the implications of the appearance of these animals. His first reaction to this verse was a refutation of the argument that, because God had commanded the earth to produce living creatures, the earth was therefore itself a source of life. Basil attributed this "disgusting opinion" to the Manichees, and insisted instead that God had bestowed the power of production through His "divine word." He then argued that land animals possessed more of this "power of life" than sea creatures, and as examples he cited a donkey's ability to recognize its owner's voice and a camel's capacity for harboring resentments. Yet there was still a difference between the soul of irrational animals and the soul of a man, since "the soul of animals is earth."[42]

These opening comments were a typical prelude to a consideration of land animals, and most of his audience probably anticipated that Basil would now follow the model of his discussion about fish by cataloguing various types of animals and deducing some moralizing applications. In his comments about different souls he furthermore mentioned that he would tell his audience about the formation of the human soul "a little later." This remark was presumably a preview of the subject matter for his final sermon that evening. But Basil soon went off in a different direction in this sermon, apparently as a result of watching his audience's reactions. "Many are perhaps wondering why, in the middle of my sermon [this morning], I was suddenly silent for a long time. The more diligent listeners surely know the reason for my silence. How so? By looking at one another and nodding they turned my attention to themselves and directed me to consideration of what had been passed over. For an entire category of creatures, an important category, had escaped us. My sermon [of last night], almost at its conclusion, ended by leaving this category completely unexamined."

In the conclusion to his comparatively short sermon of the previous evening Basil had conceded that his discussion had remained completely "underwater." But since at the beginning of that sermon he had cited the verse from Genesis that mentioned the creation of both fish and birds on the fifth day of creation, presumably he had originally intended to conclude his exegesis of fish with a discussion of birds. Fatigue and the lateness of the evening had cut that sermon short. On the next day, this morning, he originally must have decided to skip his discussion of birds and proceed with his original plan of devoting his final pair of sermons to the creation of land animals and man on the sixth day of creation. A discussion of the creation of animals and man certainly would have provided an appropriate culmination to his series of sermons. A few minutes into his sermon, however, some of his listeners indicated through their nods and murmurs that they still wanted to hear about birds. So Basil now halted his discussion of land animals and, apparently after a pause, restarted, first by citing again the verse from Genesis about the creation of fishes and birds and then by continuing with a discussion of birds and other flying creatures.[43]

This exegesis followed the format of his discussion of fishes. Some of Basil's comments, such as the argument that fishes and birds were related because of a similarity between swimming and flying and the list of different species of birds, represented the sort of learned information that he had certainly borrowed from others' writings. He also mentioned some of the practical, moral, and theological implications of the behavior of birds and flying insects. With their diligence and submission to a monarch, bees provided a model for life in a community. Cranes, storks, and crows provided examples of vigilance, affection, and hospitality, while the turtledove was a paradigm of a bird that preferred to remain alone after losing its first mate. In contrast, eagles that abandoned one of their nestlings were not worthy of imitation.[44]

In addition to these applications for everyday life Basil also claimed that the behavior of birds and insects reinforced his own theological doctrines. The doctrine of a virgin birth was apparent in the habits of vultures, which could lay eggs without coupling. The apostle Paul's description of the transformation of the human body at the moment of resurrection resembled the metamorphosis of the Indian silkworm from a caterpillar into a flying insect. Basil was then able to apply this example of the silkworm directly to the experiences of some of his listeners, the women who sewed at home or worked in the textile mills of Caesarea. "Women, when you sit and unwind the work of these caterpillars, that is, the threads that the silk merchants send to you for the fabrication of soft garments, remember the metamorphosis in this creature, formulate a clear idea of the resurrection, and do not doubt the transformation that Paul announces for everyone."[45]

Basil was so carried away by his discussion of birds that his first attempt to prevent "his oration from exceeding the limit" was unsuccessful, and he continued to list more facts about birds and insects. Finally, he heard the call of dry land and its creatures and prepared to stop. Even then he could not resist twitting his audience about the upcoming interlude before the evening's sermon. Because some of them might go off only to play at dice, detaining them was to their advantage; and because it was a day of fasting, his listeners had no banquets to anticipate. Until the evening's sermon they would have to be content with "this morning's feast."[46]

That evening Basil started his ninth sermon by asking whether his listeners had enjoyed "the morning's feast of words." As was usual by now, there clearly had been some critical discussion of his earlier sermon. Some of it had focused on the quality of his exegesis. Although Basil was prepared to concede that his comments were perhaps poor fare, he also insisted that people should not dismiss them. Other reactions had apparently expressed misgivings about the literalness of his interpretation. Basil replied, rather defensively, that he was indeed familiar with the "laws of allegory." But because other commentators had too often pushed their own ideas under the pretense of exegesis, he insisted that it was better to accept everything as it was written. Since he in fact had used allegorical interpretations in his earlier sermons, this was both an odd complaint and an equally odd denial.[47]

Basil now resumed his discussion of land animals that he had interrupted in his morning's sermon in order to discuss flying creatures instead. Since both land animals and man had been created on the sixth day, he first had to impose some distinctions. While land animals were earthy, with their necks bent toward the ground, man was heavenly, capable of looking up. More importantly, the most telling characteristic of the soul of animals was the absence of reason. Yet because animals were fundamentally irrational, their admirable behavior was all the more impressive as a model for human behavior. So, as usual, Basil mentioned examples of the qualities of animals that people should imitate. Some of his examples continued his recent emphasis on relationships within families, in particular between parents and children. He also twice stressed the gratitude and loyalty of dogs, and illustrated his point by mentioning "a recent misfortune" in which dogs had flushed out some murderers. This example suggests that he was here reminding people of a recent event with which they were all familiar.[48]

After providing these examples Basil decided to return to "contempla-
tion of creation," and hence began to provide many odd details about various animals. But his audience by now apparently wanted to hear not about
animals, but about themselves. "I realize that just recently I was asked about
the creation of man, and I all but seem to hear my listeners crying out in their
hearts, 'We have learned about the nature of our animals, but we do not
know about ourselves.'" In the morning's sermon the reactions of the audience had convinced him to interrupt his discussion of land animals in order
to discuss birds; in this sermon his audience had again convinced him to go
on to another subject. Since he perhaps had advertised earlier that this second sermon about the sixth day of creation, the final sermon of his series,
would discuss the creation of man, his listeners now seem to have insisted
that their interruption of the morning not deter him from his original plan.[49]

So Basil began to discuss the "image" and the "likeness" that people
shared with God, although primarily in a way that allowed him to criticize
some of his doctrinal rivals, in particular Jews, pagans, and Anomoeans, the
"Dissimilars" who supported the theology of Aetius and Eunomius. Most
of his comments concerned the Persons of God. He first noted that because
God had ordered the creation of man by saying "Let Us make man," he had
clearly not been talking with Himself. He illustrated this argument by citing
some everyday occupations that would have been familiar to his audience.
"What blacksmith, what carpenter, what shoemaker says to himself, when
no one is helping him, 'Let us make this sword, let us construct this plow,
let us make this boot?'" According to Basil, it was therefore impossible for
Jews to deny the existence of a Second Person. Nor was it possible for Jews
to suggest that God had been here addressing his angels, because people too,
when perfected, might be raised to the dignity of angels. "And what creature
could be the equal of the Creator?" So when God referred to "Our image"
as the model for the creation of man, He meant the image of the Father and
the Son. Basil then noted that the emphasis on God as the creator was a
prudent return to the singular, since even as it implied "the Son with the
Father," it prevented pagans, whom he referred to collectively as "Hellenism,"
from arguing in favor of polytheism. And finally he noted that since there
was only a single image, there could be no dissimilarity between the Persons. The Anomoeans, the Christians who argued for dissimilarity between
Father and Son, should hence be ashamed of themselves. In Basil's perspective, even though it was only in his own time that he and other theologians
were finally articulating correct theology, it had been inherent in God's
creation from the beginning.[50]

Although at the beginning of this sermon Basil had felt compelled to defend the quality of his exegesis, when he dismissed the people at the conclusion he again encouraged them to decorate their tables with the recollection of his words. Since this was his final sermon, he also wanted to emphasize the theological implications of the account of the six days of creation, and hence he ended with these warnings against Jews, pagans, and heterodox Christians, and with arguments in favor of his preferred doctrines. During this sermon, however, he seems to have decided that this conclusion was inadequate, since he twice mentioned "future discussions" in which he intended to analyze "how man is in the image of God and how he shares in His likeness." Because of his digressions, he had apparently not been able to fulfill his original plan of devoting all of his final sermon to an analysis of the creation of man, and so he seemed to be hinting at the possibility of more sermons later. It is still an open question whether Basil was ever able to deliver, or even draft, these later sermons.[51]

An Earthquake

"Even if he had ten thousand mouths and ten thousand tongues or even if he lived for ten thousand years," an earlier commentator on the story of creation in Genesis had conceded, "no one can properly reveal the entire exegesis and the entire plan of the six days." Basil's original plan seems to have been to discuss creation in eight sermons delivered over four days, with the first pair devoted to the first day of creation, the next pair to the second and third days, the next pair to the fourth and fifth days, and the final pair to the sixth day. In the end, because of illness, time constraints, and the insertion of various digressions, he had delivered nine sermons spread out over five days; and even then he had stopped short just as he was about to elaborate on the details of the creation of mankind and man's likeness to God.[52]

At the time his series of sermons had been an important public event, perhaps part of a festival at Caesarea. The sermons had also been part of a dialogue during which Basil too had learned from and responded to his audience. Sometimes he had blabbered on too long or cut his sermon short because of his own fatigue or his audience's restlessness. Sometimes he had responded to questions and grumbling or had tried to enlist the audience's support. After his first sermon he even had effectively modified his approach in midflight by increasing his allusions to and comparisons with aspects of ordinary life and decreasing his references to the learned ideas of Greek philosophers. Much of his success as a preacher came from his willingness and ability to adapt to the needs of his audience. Basil was an effective speaker because he was a careful listener.

After the publication of Basil's sermons, however, this immediacy and spontaneous dynamism were simply lost. First reactions were predictably mixed. Some readers considered some of his interpretations to be inadequate. Others were truly impressed. Gregory of Nazianzus enjoyed reading the sermons aloud and rolling the words on his tongue, since he then had the impression that he was standing right next to the Creator and actually understood creation. Gregory of Nyssa thought that his brother had been successful in reaching all the members of his audience: "most people understood him, and the more learned admired him." Gregory also used his brother's sermons as inspiration for some of his own treatises, since he compensated for Basil's failure to discuss the creation of man by composing a treatise on the subject, and he replied to some complaints about his brother's sermons by writing a long defense. In these books Gregory asserted the continuity of his thinking with his brother's pronouncements and insisted that he was not contradicting any of Basil's ideas even when the logic of his own discussion led him to a different interpretation.[53]

When Basil spoke, Gregory of Nazianzus claimed, his voice was comparable to an earthquake that would jolt the entire world. Earthquakes were terrifyingly common in Cappadocia. In order to describe the misfortunes of human souls ensnared by their cravings for worldly pleasures, Gregory of Nyssa once used a graphic comparison with the fates of people trapped in the ruins of an earthquake. "Their bodies are squeezed in the rubble. Not only are they buried in the wreckage, but they have been pierced with nails and wood splinters."[54]

Originally, Basil's series of sermons had had the seismic impact of a natural calamity. By initiating a dialogue with his audience he had been able to capture his listeners' attention. Once published, however, these sermons on the Hexaemeron became part of the exegetical tradition, yet another learned commentary that subsequent readers evaluated strictly in terms of its style or content and without regard for its context. These sermons, and others of Basil's sermons, instead became generic examples of moral teachings and good style, with no concern about the original circumstances. One abbot was able to recommend Basil's sermon about drunkenness simply as a demonstration of how to mold character according to the precepts of philosophy. A Byzantine reader could praise the clarity and persuasiveness of Basil's literary style in his sermons on the Hexaemeron without commenting at all on the actual content. Basil's sermons became a permanent and timeless landmark, towering over the intellectual landscape like Mount Argaeus over Caesarea. Just like those intrepid climbers who had made it to the summit of Mount Argaeus and claimed that on a clear day they could see both the Black Sea and the Mediterranean Sea, Basil's admirers too thought that his comments on creation allowed them to look further into the mysteries of nature.[55]

Even as they acknowledged their reverence for Basil's sermons, however, by treating them as a static commentary and as a starting point for their own reflections both Gregory of Nazianzus and Gregory of Nyssa had already dampened the original impact. The fire had gone out of these sermons. Already in Basil's day, Mount Argaeus too was no longer an active volcano but only a smoldering snow-capped peak. Subsequent readers studied Basil's sermons with the same mixture of apprehension and nonchalance that characterized their reactions to mountain ranges throughout central and eastern Asia Minor. Like these great peaks, Basil's sermons were both forbidding and inviting. While some explorers struggled to master the pinnacles, others enjoyed skiing and sledding on them.[56]

Chapter 7

Small Details:
The Cult of the Forty Martyrs

During late antiquity perhaps the most popular saints in eastern Asia Minor were the Forty Martyrs, a band of soldiers who had reputedly been left to die of exposure on an icy lake for refusing to perform pagan sacrifices. Already during the later fourth century many legends about their martyrdom were in circulation, among them those recorded in an anonymous *Passio* (an account of the martyrs' "suffering"), a sermon by Basil, and three sermons by Gregory of Nyssa. Most of these accounts reproduced the same basic narrative plot for the martyrdom. They also included many similar episodes, among them the refusal of the martyrs to sacrifice to pagan deities, their confession of allegiance to Christianity, their abandonment on a frozen lake, and the tempting offer of survival in a nearby warm bathhouse if they would only renounce their perseverance.

Despite similarities among the accounts in this collection of texts, the actual historicity of these forty saints and the events surrounding their deaths is certainly questionable, and the various extant versions clearly are not reliable sources for information about late Roman persecutions. Equally dubious is the assumption that it is possible to extract an original account of the suffering of the Forty Martyrs from the various versions that survive. Not only are the relationships among the extant written versions unclear and probably impossible to determine, and not only were there certainly even more oral versions in circulation; in addition, from the perspective of the audiences, whether listeners or readers, all of these versions were simultaneously correct. Ancient audiences certainly did not indulge in a higher criticism of resolving contradictions among texts. Basil claimed that the soldiers spent one night on the frozen lake, Gregory three nights. Basil tacked on a story about a woman who ensured that her son would be included among these martyrs as an afterthought at the end of his sermon, while Gregory featured the story in his narrative of the martyrs. Discrepancies such as these were essentially irrelevant. Since the meanings and the functions of these legends were contingent upon the needs and experiences of the preachers and their audiences, it is now misleading for modern scholars to insert notions of historicity or even plausibility into their analyses.[1]

Rather than offering merely an excuse for analyzing differences among texts, the survival of several versions presents an opportunity for comparing differences among contexts. Both the authors and the preachers were imagining an interpretive world, composing "a piece of social discourse" that conveyed to their readers and listeners important even if sometimes oblique meanings and significances. Since modern historians have little specific information about the audiences, the circumstances, or, in the case of the *Passio*, even the author, they must conjure up these interpretive worlds and this social discourse from the texts themselves and then add material that seems to be relevant for imagining larger contexts.[2]

In particular, both Basil and Gregory were using their sermons about the Forty Martyrs to clarify their own ideas and doctrines, to articulate concerns about their own reputations, and to criticize some of their rivals. "Meaning is added in the retelling." Even though the foundation for their sermons was of course the basic plot about the deaths of the Forty Martyrs, Basil and Gregory had no hesitation over tinkering with the narrative and modifying the conventional episodes. It is furthermore correct that even though this basic plot then served as the source of the "truths" they wished to convey, it was itself, not so paradoxically, a fiction and a myth from the beginning. The social discourse was true and meaningful, even though the history was false.[3]

The Martyrdom

One of the earliest accounts of the Forty Martyrs, perhaps the earliest, was the anonymous *Passio*. Although this text included the basic plot, it also indicates that early on modifications of the conventional episodes were in circulation.

One form of modification was through the provision of small details, in particular the addition of specific names for individuals and places. This *Passio* claimed that these forty men had earned their martyrdom during the reign of the emperor Licinius, and it named their primary opponents as Agricolaus, a *hegemon* (apparently a provincial governor), and Lysias, a *dux* (apparently a military commander). It identified the forty men as soldiers from Cappadocia and named three of their leaders, of whom the most important was Cyrion. It furthermore located the scene of their hearing before these magistrates and the place of their martyrdom on an icy lake in Sebasteia. A second form of modification was expansion, through the elaboration of the stories in the basic plot and through the inclusion of new episodes. Other information about the Forty Martyrs, including some additional written texts, was in circulation apparently independently of the *Passio*. One of these independent texts was a simple list of the names of the martyrs. The *Passio* too included its version of a list that named all forty men. It also seems to have expanded, and perhaps even invented, various episodes, such as those describing the extended confrontations between magistrates and martyrs, the desertion of one of the Forty, his replacement by the warden guarding them, the encouragement of a mother who wanted her young son to die with his comrades, and even some appearances by Satan himself.[4]

Some of these details might indeed have a connection to historical events. By the end of his reign in the early 320s the emperor Licinius had in fact become so intolerant toward Christians that he ordered soldiers and imperial administrators to offer sacrifices during pagan festivals or lose their ranks and offices, and he imposed various restrictions on Christian communities. Eventually provincial governors sanctioned the execution of some bishops in Pontus, and at Amaseia and other cities in Pontus churches were destroyed. This correlation does not necessarily imply that the *Passio* provided additional information about intolerance under Licinius, since it seems more likely that the author of the *Passio* mentioned this emperor because in central and eastern Asia Minor his reign had acquired a reputation for persecution. In fact, for most of the details and supplementary information no verification is possible. Nor was it necessary for an ancient audience. Rather than conveying exact historical information, the specific names instead provided a more immediate and convincing chronology and geography for the sufferings of the Forty Martyrs, while the expansion of the stories provided more nuanced and elaborate circumstances for the basic plot. These new details furthermore enhanced some of the meanings of this particular version of the martyrdom.[5]

The *Passio* seems to have had several purposes. One was to offer an appropriately stirring account. To heighten the drama the *Passio* used direct discourse, in particular in the exchanges between Cyrion, the spokesman for the Forty, and the "tyrants" Agricolaus and Lysias. Agricolaus threatened and postured and gave the Forty time to reconsider, and Lysias once ordered other soldiers to throw stones at the Forty. Despite this harassment, Cyrion was usually moderate and reflective in his responses. These exchanges, and in particular the dialogues that were almost antiphonal contrasts of good and evil, made the overall account attractively compelling. Christian readers would probably have appreciated the slapstick of the soldiers hitting only each other with their stones and the stirringly confrontational invective that Cyrion himself used against Agricolaus. The *Passio* also dramatized and personalized the martyrs' deaths with the stories of the deserter and the warden. The deserter may have left his frosty torment, but as soon as he stepped into the steaming bathhouse, he died. In contrast, when the warden saw crowns of victory coming down from heaven, he confessed that he was a Christian and immediately joined the others to keep their number at forty. At its conclusion the *Passio* tugged at its audience's emotions with the story about a mother who prayed that her son would persevere through these tortures. After the magistrates decided to burn the corpses of the martyrs, they left this young man's body because he was still breathing. The mother then carried her own son to the pyre. Details about confrontation, betrayal and redemption, and a mother's resolve could elevate even the most prosaic account into a rousing legend.

Presumably this *Passio*, like other accounts of saints and martyrs, was read during the celebration of the saints' festival. If so, then not only did it need an attractive story, it also had to be suitable for use in the liturgy. A second purpose of this *Passio* was to transform a straightforward story about confrontation and torture into a narrative grounded in biblical expectations and terminology. One of the common motifs in the *Passio* was the tendency of the Forty Martyrs to cite biblical verses, in particular passages from Psalms. At one point their leader Cyrion compared their current struggle to their previous military battles. "Whenever we began to fight, did we not always recite this Psalm?" The Forty and their leaders consistently used biblical citations to explain and comment on their predicament, and to encourage themselves. According to the *Passio*, when they were dispirited by the defection of one of their comrades, they called for the Lord's assistance by citing a litany of verses and by comparing themselves to notable figures from the Old Testament who had benefited from divine assistance in moments of tribulation.[6]

The *Passio* was hence a translation of the Bible, not into one of the many local languages still used throughout Asia Minor, but into a more updated and recognizable story that would presumably have had more relevance and immediacy for its audience. After hearing how these martyrs had acquired reassurance from reciting biblical verses and comparing themselves to various paradigmatic figures such as Jacob, Joseph, and Moses, listeners and readers could understand how they themselves might, or should, react to their own contemporary difficulties. As a component of the liturgy the *Passio* acquired its own didactic function as a way of conveying messages about biblical teachings. It was also a representation of the liturgy itself. The celebration of the liturgy was a moment of intense community, as people gathered in the same place at the same time to hear the same readings and even chant Psalms together. In this sense the experiences of the Forty Martyrs provided a model of the unanimity expected from an ecclesiastical community. When the Forty had recited biblical verses, they spoke "as if with one voice from one mouth."[7]

To be attractive the *Passio* had to provide a good yarn, and to be instructive it needed to highlight its biblical foundation. A final purpose was more practical. The *Passio* located this martyrdom at a specific city. "There is in Sebasteia a lake with much water. At the time when the holy men became martyrs the lake was covered with thick ice." In the early Roman empire cities had competed over status and prestige through sometimes extravagant claims about their pedigrees, reputations, and festivals. During the fourth century a new form of competition involved the possession of relics and the celebration of saints' cults. Another text about the Forty Martyrs also in circulation during the fourth century was their so-called *Testament*, an account in the guise of a will that reputedly described their final farewells and their last wishes. According to this *Testament*, the martyrs insisted that all of their relics should be collected and buried in a particular village near a particular city. Even though the identity of both towns is uncertain, this assertion in the *Testament*, put into the mouths of the martyrs themselves, was clearly an attempt to stake a claim to their relics and their subsequent cult.[8]

In contrast, the *Passio* provided a different cover story for the disposition of these martyrs' relics by identifying their suffering so directly with Sebasteia. The final section of the *Passio* reinforced this association. In order to prevent the collection of the martyrs' relics, the magistrates had had their bodies burned and the remains scattered in a river. But within a few days Peter, the bishop of Sebasteia, learned through a vision that the martyrs' relics were intact in the river. So he and his clerics retrieved the relics "that flashed in the water like stars" and deposited them in reliquaries. This account in the *Passio* hence provided an explanation for the survival and discovery of the saints' relics, and it reinforced the notion that Sebasteia was to be the center of the cult of the Forty Martyrs.[9]

Whatever the historical reliability of this account (and it was probably minimal at best), the *Passio* offered a gripping story, a set of readings for the liturgy, and a justification for the establishment of the cult at Sebasteia. This *Passio* would hence have been quite suitable for a festival of the Forty Martyrs specifically at Sebasteia. But the cult of course spread, and relics of the Forty Martyrs were circulated to other cities in the region. With this wider circulation the basic legends about the martyrdom required revisions in order to maintain their relevance for new circumstances and new locations. In addition, stories about martyrdoms were sometimes difficult to accommodate in a Christian empire. These stories had typically described confrontations with imperial magistrates from the early Roman empire when Christianity had been an insignificant religious movement. But because during the fourth century many magistrates and military commanders and almost all the emperors were themselves Christians, commemorating these earlier confrontations sometimes seemed inappropriate.

Because these legends seemed to be increasingly part of a bygone past, preachers had to adjust them to fit the times. Basil helped to introduce the cult of the Forty Martyrs to his episcopal see of Caesarea. Gregory of Nyssa later celebrated their cult both at Caesarea and at their original hometown of Sebasteia. In the process both modified the meanings of the cult to fit their own agendas.

Basil's Agenda

Basil delivered an oration about the Forty Martyrs to celebrate the dedication of a new shrine, apparently at Caesarea. Since he noted that his listeners would understand the tortures these martyrs had endured because they had themselves experienced a cold winter, and since he associated the martyrs with the forty days of Lent, he probably delivered this oration on a festival day for the Forty Martyrs at the beginning of March.[10]

His version of their martyrdom in many respects followed the usual plot, and Basil certainly could anticipate that his audience would be already familiar with the traditional legends about these martyrs from eastern Asia Minor. His listeners probably had been talking about these saints during the days leading up to the celebration of their festival. In addition, because the interior of the shrine seems to have been decorated with paintings of scenes from their martyrdom, his audience already was looking at one version of the story about their martyrdom. Gregory of Nyssa once described another shrine, most likely at Euchaita in Pontus, that was dedicated to St. Theodorus, another soldier who had become a martyr reputedly during the persecutions in the early fourth century. This shrine was magnificent, embellished with animals carved from wood and stone panels polished to a silver sheen. The decorations included paintings of scenes from the martyr's "cycle of heroism," such as the tortures, the savage faces of the tyrant emperors, and the martyr's death. "The artist depicted everything for us with his colors, as if in a book that could speak. He clearly outlined the martyr's struggles, and he decorated the church like a sunny meadow." With all these brilliant illustrations this shrine was itself a text, "a mute treatise," a picture book that even the illiterate could comprehend in order to learn about St. Theodorus.[11]

At the beginning of his sermon Basil seems to have acknowledged the presence of these paintings in this shrine to the Forty Martyrs by contrasting the different techniques of orators and painters. "Whatever a historical oration offers through listening, a painting, even though it is mute, reveals through imitation." Since orators were always quick to reinforce their comments by referring to or even gesturing at nearby objects or buildings, Basil could readily appreciate the corroboration for his oration from this cycle of paintings. As he preached, he probably pointed at the appropriate scenes on the walls. But even as these paintings assisted Basil's sermon, they also had the potential to become contradictory. In this shrine the audience was receiving two narratives simultaneously, one by looking at the paintings, the other by listening to the sermon. Basil had to be careful as he sometimes spoke in counterpoint. After his opening direct allusion to these paintings he proceeded to offer his own interpretation of the martyrdom of the Forty both by transforming and elaborating some of the traditional episodes and by making their message more directly relevant to his listeners.[12]

Basil modified the plot first by toning down the confrontation with the imperial magistrates that was such a prominent feature of the *Passio*. He mentioned an "edict of the emperor" that the governor displayed to the soldiers, and he noted that the governor tried to seduce them into complying with various offers and threats, but he did not highlight any confrontational dialogue. Instead he focused on the reactions and motives of the soldiers. At one point Basil even had them discuss the ethical and biblical implications of removing their clothes before being exposed on the frozen lake: "we are not removing our cloaks, but we are laying aside the 'old man' that is corrupted through the desire of sin." In the *Passio* the conflict had been an external, public confrontation between stubborn magistrates and equally stubborn soldiers. In his oration Basil instead emphasized private internal conflicts, the sort of interior dilemmas that all Christians faced. Even though Basil tended to view his own world in terms of conflict and persecution and to identify with the era of the martyrs, in this oration he stressed private ethical dilemmas rather than public confrontations. By transforming the Forty Martyrs into exemplars of the sort of personal decisions about commitment that all Christians were to make, he made martyrs and martyrdom relevant in a Christian empire. Each individual choice of denial and obedience was the equivalent of a martyrdom: "praise a martyr sincerely, so that you become a martyr by choice and proceed to value the same rewards as they, but without persecution, without fire, and without whips." In Basil's estimation this story provided paradigms for everyone, since young men could imitate these young soldiers and fathers could pray to have such sons. Even mothers had an exemplar in the mother who placed her own son on the wagon for burning.[13]

Basil also transformed the plot about the Forty Martyrs by turning it into a more timeless and universal story that was unencumbered by references to specific people and specific places. In his oration he mentioned no names at all, leaving the emperor, the governor, and all the martyrs anonymous. Although he noted that the lake on which they had been exposed was in the middle of a city, he did not name the city as Sebasteia.

Ignoring all these details, and in particular the name of the city, presumably allowed Basil to accomplish several goals. One was to associate these martyrs more closely to his audience in Caesarea. Basil conceded that encomiastic orations typically praised the homelands, native cities, and families of their subjects. But in this case he went out of his way to stress that he was not going to mention the homeland or the native city of the Forty Martyrs, because their spiritual heritage was more important: "the city of the martyrs is the city of God, . . . the Jerusalem above." Basil likewise announced that he was going to ignore their families, because "God is their common father." In part these comments represented some rhetorical posturing, a polite way for Basil to cover up his ignorance about these martyrs. But by highlighting their spiritual heritage and pedigrees he also opened the possibility that his listeners too could become spiritual relatives of the Forty. As their relics had circulated, the martyrs had continually adopted new homelands: "these are the men who have embraced our region, like a series of towers offering protection from enemies' attacks, not enclosing themselves in one place but already migrating to many regions and adorning many fatherlands." Because Basil had transformed these martyrs into anonymous abstractions, they could be adopted by his audience in Caesarea as members of their city and their own patrons.[14]

Another consequence of anonymity was to highlight instead the oneness that these Forty Martyrs represented. In Basil's account the martyrs had always acted as a unified brotherhood by submerging their own identities. Their collective martyrdom was a forceful symbol of unity and harmony. Each of the martyrs had identified himself not by name, but simply as a Christian; and because they shared one vow, they had suffered together and shared a single crown of righteousness. Even when one deserted for the warm bathhouse, one of the guards joined the martyrs as a substitute, "in imitation of men in battle who immediately fill the phalanx when someone in the first line falls." Likewise the intermingling of their remains after their ashes were thrown into a river implied that the power of all the Forty Martyrs was present even in the smallest of relics. In life and in death the Forty had merged their individual identities in the interests of a common commitment. As a result, they offered a powerful image of the sort of harmony that Basil presumably hoped for in his community. According to his pithy summation of the outcome of their martyrdom, "mixed together they dance as one."[15]

The absence of specific names and locations hence made it easier for people at Caesarea to claim these martyrs as their own and to acknowledge them as suitable models. But Basil also had perhaps another reason, this time personal, for leaving the martyrs anonymous and rootless. During his episcopacy his own relationship with the Christian community at Sebasteia was distinctly frosty. For almost twenty years Basil had considered bishop Eustathius of Sebasteia his mentor. By the early 370s, however, their relationship was beginning to deteriorate over suspicions about Eustathius' theology, and soon these former friends had become opponents. Another city with which Basil had a confrontational relationship was his own hometown of Neocaesarea. While growing up in Pontus, Basil had heard the legends about Gregory Thaumaturgus, the patron saint of Neocaesarea, and he still referred to some of those stories later in his life. Yet during his episcopacy, perhaps because of his animosity toward bishop Atarbius of Neocaesarea, Basil seems not to have introduced a shrine or a festival in honor of Gregory Thaumaturgus at Caesarea. Such a shrine would have implied a humbling acknowledgment of the influential role of Neocaesarea in preserving the memory of Gregory Thaumaturgus.[16]

Basil now faced a similar problem with the Forty Martyrs. They were too popular to ignore entirely, but too tainted through their association with Sebasteia to be acceptable to Basil. His solution was to depersonalize them. By turning the Forty into anonymous, rootless, generic martyrs Basil could introduce their cult to his own episcopal see without awarding any honor to the see of a rival. Caesarea was now doing the Forty Martyrs a favor by giving them a home.

Gregory of Nyssa's Agenda at Caesarea

After Basil's death Gregory of Nyssa delivered two sets of orations about the Forty Martyrs. Since he delivered his sermons before different audiences in different cities and regions, he had to negotiate many disparate expectations and concerns, both his own and those of his listeners.[17]

Gregory delivered one pair of sermons at Caesarea during a celebration of the martyrs' festival. After having memorialized the memory of the martyrs themselves in his first sermon (no longer extant), he used his second sermon on the next day to draw out the implications of their zeal "in the competitions" and to exhort his listeners to imitate their behavior and motivations. Gregory mentioned some of the usual episodes about their martyrdom, including the emperor's edict to perform pagan libations, the resistance of the Christian soldiers, their tortures on the frozen lake, the replacement of the deserter by one of the guards, and the burning of their corpses. But he also filled out this minimal narrative with all sorts of asides and digressions, including a discussion of the cold weather in Armenia, comparisons with biblical figures (among them, as an example of the connections between apparent opposites, Daniel's three friends whom the Babylonian king had had placed in a fiery furnace), a truly odd disquisition on the difference between "warmer" and "colder" animals, and a charming vignette of stonecutters using their tools to chop ice during the long winters. In his treatises Gregory had a tendency to flit about among various interests and topics, and he had always been much more adept than Basil at using images and analogies. In this sermon, however, his objective was to present the Forty Martyrs as paradigms of moral behavior: "if they did not enter the arena, they would not have revealed their courage as athletes." "With their hope let a Christian be bold."[18]

Lurking behind Gregory's comments, however, was the legacy of his brother Basil's episcopacy. At the beginning of his sermon Gregory had praised "the great Basil" and noted that his brother had previously "crowned" these martyrs with his own oration. With these comments he was presumably acknowledging Basil's role in the establishment of this cult at Caesarea.[19]

But two other concerns were also important. One involved his own relationship with Basil. Gregory had always been somewhat estranged from his older brother. Although he had consistently supported Basil, in particular by becoming bishop of Nyssa, Basil in turn had been suspicious of his brother's maturity and suitability and had kept him at arm's length. So Gregory now used this sermon at Caesarea to demonstrate his ties with his otherwise aloof brother. In his own earlier sermon about the Forty Martyrs Basil had offered an austere and anonymous account. In contrast, Gregory now included a series of deeply revealing personal reminiscences. After mentioning the scattering of the martyrs' ashes Gregory confessed that he had his own relic of the Forty. He noted that his parents were buried in a shrine dedicated with relics of the Forty Martyrs. He told a story about a miracle that he had heard directly from a soldier whose lameness had been healed at this shrine. And finally he mentioned a rather intimate, almost embarrassing, episode from his own youth that described his sullen reluctance to heed his mother's insistence that he attend the martyrs' festival. He had pouted, until in a dream he had seen soldiers, the Forty themselves, threatening him with a beating. "I wept for my folly with many laments."[20]

The village in which Gregory's parents had built their family shrine was near Ibora. Since Gregory noted that he now "owned" this village, it was perhaps the settlement for the people who worked on some of his family's estates. His description of this shrine hinted at the association of particular cults with particular families and individuals that would become an increasingly common feature of society in both the medieval West and the Byzantine East. In his own sermon Basil had never alluded to any association between his family and the cult of the Forty Martyrs. Nor did he hint at such an association in any of his letters, even when he might have welcomed the martyrs' support in the face of opposition and hostility. In contrast, in front of Basil's former congregation, Gregory now indulged in true confessions about himself and his family. In the years following Basil's death Gregory had been diligent in claiming his brother's legacy, for example by taking up his controversy with Eunomius and by supplementing his sermons about the Hexaemeron. In this sermon about the Forty Martyrs he used these personal revelations to create another link with his brother. Although Basil had participated in establishing the cult at Caesarea a few years previously, Gregory now revealed that he and his family had a longstanding connection with the cult. By implication he and Basil had had this cult and their reverence for these martyrs in common. Gregory had to expose his deepest feelings about the Forty Martyrs in order to claim a true emotional attachment with his brother.[21]

A second concern for Gregory was his relationship with Caesarea, its congregation, and its new bishop. Basil had had a long association with Caesarea, first as a young student, then, after his return from his studies in Athens and his ascetic isolation in Pontus, as a priest and metropolitan bishop. In contrast, Gregory had not studied in Caesarea and had not served as a cleric there. In fact, he could not claim many ties with the entire region of Cappadocia. Gregory may have become bishop at Nyssa, but he had been away from his see for a few years in exile, had served briefly as bishop at Sebasteia, and had spent much time at Constantinople and elsewhere attending councils and delivering orations. He seems to have been much more aware of his and his family's connections with Pontus, where he and his brother Peter still owned property. So Gregory now had to establish his credentials at Caesarea.

Just as Basil had once tried to obscure the connection of the Forty Martyrs with Sebasteia and Pontus, so Gregory had to obscure his own standing as an outsider. His personal reminiscences in this sermon would have enhanced his reputation before his brother's old congregation at Caesarea by highlighting his links with Basil. This close linkage with Basil also offered Gregory the opportunity for implicit criticism of a new rival, someone else who may also have been trying to associate himself with Basil's legacy, the new bishop of Caesarea. Basil's successor was Helladius, and he and Gregory would have their disagreements. In this sermon Gregory was unfailingly discreet, but still never polite enough to mention the current bishop and make some appropriately complimentary remarks about him. Instead he noted that the true "paradigm of bishops" was still Basil himself. By highlighting Basil and his episcopacy again, Gregory could also divert some attention from the current bishop of Caesarea to Basil's brother, himself.[22]

Gregory's overt goal in this sermon had been to encourage and exhort his listeners to follow the example of the Forty Martyrs and be comforted by their assistance. He even argued that he had included the personal stories about himself and his family to advance this public objective: "I related these [stories] so that we might believe that the martyrs are alive and are God's soldiers and helpers who today assist and ornament our church." But in the process Gregory had also contributed to his own personal agenda of linking himself with Basil, establishing his credentials before the congregation at Caesarea, and taking pot shots at the current bishop of Caesarea.[23]

Gregory of Nyssa's Agenda at Sebasteia

A few years later Gregory delivered another set of sermons about the Forty Martyrs, this time at their hometown of Sebasteia. Unlike his brother Basil, who had had a chilly and remote relationship with Sebasteia, Gregory by now had a close association with the city, even if it had not always been a pleasant one. After bishop Eustathius' death a delegation from Sebasteia had eventually requested his assistance in selecting a new bishop. While meeting with the other bishops to vote, Gregory himself ended up being selected. His episcopacy at Sebasteia was difficult. Some people mocked his voice, his clothes, even his gait. His opponents spread rumors that his doctrines did not correspond to orthodox Nicene theology. A local military officer convinced the provincial governor to harass him. Gregory prayed for deliverance. "The prophet Jonah was confined in the whale for [only] three days, but by then he was discouraged. In contrast, I have spent so much more time imprisoned in the bowels of a beast, and I still cannot be disgorged from this vast gullet!" After serving for a few months, Gregory left. His replacement as bishop at Sebasteia was presumably one of his opponents.[24]

But by the time Gregory returned to deliver these sermons, his younger brother Peter was bishop of Sebasteia. Both Gregory and Peter had attended the ecumenical council at Constantinople in 381. After the council an imperial edict had named Gregory as one of the arbiters of orthodoxy, and it had expelled opponents from their churches. Gregory was still in the process of reestablishing himself at his see of Nyssa, and Peter now became the new bishop of Sebasteia. To consolidate their authority both used their connections with the cult of the Forty Martyrs. At Nyssa Gregory funded the construction of a new shrine in honor of martyrs, who may well have been the Forty Martyrs. At Sebasteia Peter first established a cult in honor of "the most blessed Peter," who was most likely the Peter who during his own episcopacy at Sebasteia had retrieved the relics of the Forty Martyrs. The opportunity now for the new bishop to found a cult in honor of the homonymous predecessor who had founded the cult of the Forty Martyrs was simply too propitious to miss. Peter then invited his brother Gregory, another former bishop at Sebasteia, to join in the inaugural celebration of this new cult. He also invited Gregory to deliver the sermons at the festival of the Forty Martyrs.[25]

As at Caesarea, so now at Sebasteia Gregory was preaching to an audience familiar with his family. But whereas at Caesarea he had had to resort to personal stories to highlight his relationships with a cult that had been established at the city only recently and with an older brother who often had been somewhat aloof, here at Sebasteia he did not have to introduce himself. Instead, he could presuppose familiarity with the cult, and he already had a close relationship with his younger brother. At the beginning of his first sermon Gregory even seems to have included a glancing allusion to his brother, because as he acknowledged the large crowd, he cited the apostle Peter's concern about the crowds that had once pressed around Jesus. Perhaps it is possible to guess that his brother Peter had expressed his own apprehension about the crowd that milled around his brother, and that Gregory was now establishing his rapport with his audience by making a gentle joke at his host's expense. "For many it is unpleasant to be squeezed against others, but for me this is the highest happiness."[26]

To celebrate the festival of the Forty Martyrs this large audience had gathered apparently at their shrine. As Gregory thought aloud about the potential subject of his sermon, he noted that "some of the readings" might provide an appropriate starting point. Since he then mentioned Job, Proverbs, the apostle Paul and his letter to the Ephesians, and Psalms, these prefatory readings may well have included selections from both the Old Testament and the New Testament. Another possibility is that these prefatory readings had included selections from the *Passio* of the Forty Martyrs. Since this *Passio* was itself filled with various biblical citations, in particular from Psalms, Gregory may have been following up on some of its citations. Readings from a *Passio*, and especially from the extant *Passio* that stressed the importance of Sebasteia as the site of the martyrdom, would be particularly appropriate for the celebration of the martyrs' festival at their shrine in Sebasteia. Such readings would also help explain a peculiar oddity of this sermon, the almost complete absence of any discussion of the martyrs and their martyrdom. If readings from the *Passio* had already outlined the story of their martyrdom, then Gregory could instead go on to discuss another subject, his listeners themselves.[27]

Rather than being a sermon to his audience, this was a sermon about his audience. Gregory still had to earn the good graces of a congregation that a few years earlier had failed to support him as bishop. He talked about his audience in various ways. He first claimed that his listeners were all his ancestors. Since his own parents had died long ago, he needed to honor other parents: "you are my parents, you who are the parents of my parents." He furthermore noted that it was most appropriate for an affectionate son to care for his aged parents. This comment was not so much a rationale for his own sermon, as rather perhaps an oblique compliment for his brother

Peter, who by serving as bishop of Sebasteia was now caring for the members of his ecclesiastical family. Another way that Gregory discussed his audience was by describing their home region. Since in his estimation this region was bountifully endowed with natural amenities and fertility, the greatest honor he could offer was a verbal portrait of these features. For conjuring up this portrait he took advantage of the fact that the celebration was apparently meeting in the open air by gesturing at various landmarks that were also important memorials in the legends about the suffering of the Forty Martyrs, such as the river that divided the city and the nearby lake: "it is possible not only to talk about [them] but also to show [them]." The most distinguished of the region's products were its martyrs, "fertile offspring that have contributed more than thirty to the multitude of fruit."[28]

By now Gregory had embraced his listeners as his parents and complimented them for the productivity of their region. The final way in which he focused on his audience was by letting them tell their own stories about the Forty Martyrs. Rather than narrating or interpreting the narrative of the martyrdom for them, he invited them to imagine their own recollections. The cues to assist their memories would be this specific place and this particular time. "Look at this holy field. Here are the sheaves of martyrs. If you wish to know what field I am talking about, do not look far from this one. What is the place that embraces the crowd? . . . What sort of stories does the commemoration of this day recall and relate to you? . . . If you look at the place, it says that it is the stadium of the martyrs. If you consider the day, like a herald with a loud voice it proclaims the crown of the martyrs." For a guest preacher Gregory was surprisingly modest, and he simply dismissed himself as someone with a weak voice and a monotone, unable to match the rowdy clamor of the festival itself. He also claimed that he anyway could not compete with the memories associated with this shrine and this festival: "what narratives of this sort do I have?" In this sermon Gregory hence had neatly reversed the expected roles, since the audience was to provide the narrative and he, the speaker, would become the listener. And in fact, he ended this sermon because shouts from the crowd were interrupting and becoming obtrusive. The audience had obviously taken up his invitation and was compelling him to listen to their stories.[29]

On the next day Gregory delivered another sermon. This time the setting was different, since the people met in a church where, in contrast to the previous day, they were the hosts and the martyrs were the guests. Gregory too had different objectives, since he now intended "to recite all the deeds of the martyrs in order, as if enacting their struggle before your eyes in this theater." Unlike the sermon of the previous day in which he had barely mentioned the Forty Martyrs and had allowed his audience to take over the storytelling, this sermon would focus on the saints' martyrdom.[30]

At the beginning of his account Gregory gave every indication that he was planning to follow the basic narrative. "Once upon a time there was a detachment of soldiers in a neighboring city that was a garrison for all the people against barbarian attacks." But almost immediately he introduced a new story about these soldiers. According to his account, when an attack by barbarians led to a shortage of water, the prayers of these Christian soldiers generated a heavy thunderstorm that provided water and devastated the enemy camp. As a result, the same "adversary of human life" who had envied the prosperity of Job advised the military commander that he could not claim credit for the victory over the barbarians until he had sacrificed the Christians. Not only had Gregory here included a new story about the background of the martyrs, but he had explained their subsequent tortures in terms of diabolical envy and completely eliminated the role of the emperor. He then took his time describing the threats, the various tortures, and the disdainful reactions of the soldiers, with an almost masochistic shiver of anticipation: "this oration lingers fondly at the beauty of the moment."[31]

After this long buildup Gregory accelerated through the climax of their martyrdom. In fact, he suddenly became distracted, as if he no longer wanted to continue with the narrative, and he even apologized for "telling you your own miracles." He noted that the men were brought out to the frozen lake, and he described their sufferings. He mentioned the episodes of the guard who replaced the defector and the cavalcade bringing their bodies to the fire only in passing, one sentence for each episode. And he described the mother who encouraged her son to become a martyr.[32]

As an account of the sufferings of the Forty Martyrs this sermon was distinctly peculiar, especially since Gregory had begun by promising to re-create their struggle. Gregory seemed more interested in their piety, their training, and their subsequent suffering than in the details of their martyrdom. The parallel he seems to have found most appropriate for his interpretation was the sufferings of Job. The soldiers had been brought to the tribunal for a hearing because of envy over their successes, "just as we learned from those passages now read to us from the history of Job." In the *Passio* the anonymous author had had the soldiers comfort themselves by chanting passages from Psalms; in Gregory's version the soldiers resigned themselves to their fate by quoting Job.[33]

Several reasons perhaps influenced Gregory to ignore much of the basic narrative. One was the proximity of Lent, which he could readily connect to the trials of the Forty Martyrs: "this is the beginning of Lent, the mystery of the holy forty. The forty days of supplication are with us, a number equal to the crowns of the saints." By stressing the tribulations of the Forty Martyrs Gregory seems to have been preparing his listeners for the fasting that they were now expected to undertake. A second reason was his interest in other topics. When he noted that "we too are running with the saints to the conclusion of their suffering," he was not so much introducing the climax of his account, as simply trying to get through it as quickly as possible. In fact, toward the end of his sermon he decided to skim over the usual stories and comparisons in favor of another, more pressing issue. "My oration desires to run over these topics as if they are already known, and now to examine one of those relevant topics analyzed recently." Gregory reminded his listeners of some earlier questions and his responses. Even though he did not have the time to recapitulate, he raised one question in particular about the flaming sword that guarded access to Paradise. Although he tried to make this question relevant to the Forty Martyrs by asking whether such "athletes" would be excluded from Paradise, he was clearly using this sermon to expand his response in an earlier discussion: "under these circumstances the question has this answer." For all his good intentions of discussing the sufferings of the Forty Martyrs, Gregory ended with clarification of a small exegetical point that had apparently been nibbling at the corner of his mind.[34]

A Common Language

Sermons about saints were essentially long, extended epitaphs. Tombstones from Pontus memorialized loved ones by celebrating their virtues. Outside Amaseia one man even had his tombstone speak on his behalf. "[I am] Severus, a very cunning man. Since the earth has enclosed my dead body, it allows me to speak only from this tombstone. When I was alive, men praised me extravagantly. Now that I have died, this stone marker is my advocate. It preserves my voice, the voice of a dead man. As my replacement it presents men with my immortal voice." Sermons were likewise commemorations, and the speakers often preached at the saints' tombs. Like an epitaph, each sermon was a "memory" or "memorial."[35]

But sermons differed from epitaphs in one important aspect. Epitaphs were engraved on stone markers, indelibly permanent. Each epitaph was the singularly exclusive and final version of a person's life. In contrast, sermons were malleable, capable of responding to current concerns and new situations. In his sermon about the Forty Martyrs Basil had wanted to promote the cult at Caesarea, but without giving any credit to their hometown of Sebasteia. When speaking at Caesarea Gregory of Nyssa had wanted to establish his links to both the cult and his older brother. When speaking at Sebasteia he had wanted to ingratiate himself to a city where he had failed as a bishop and where his younger brother was now starting as bishop. Since Basil and Gregory could never be sure how far their audiences shared their personal agendas, legends about the Forty Martyrs provided a common starting point. These legends were perhaps better known even than biblical stories. In central and eastern Asia Minor most Christians could hum the tune of these legends, even if they did not know or understand all the lyrics. As a result, these legends provided a repertoire of stock characters and episodes that Basil and Gregory could reassemble into new and relevant performances. The legends were a common language.

When investigating the legends and traditions about saints and their cults modern historians tend to be suspicious of differences in details, as if those discrepancies have undermined the accuracy and validity of these stories. For them, tiny discrepancies are indications of fabrication and invention, proofs that these stories possess, at best, only a central core of historical material. Ancient audiences heard these stories differently. For them, the central episodes in saints' legends were probably already familiar enough to be taken for granted, while the small details guaranteed the realism, the authenticity, and therefore the relevance of those episodes. The discrepancies in incidental details that lead modern historians to conclude that these stories have little historical basis were precisely the anchors that grounded these stories most firmly in the experiences and concerns of the audiences. The telling of these episodes marked not a simple recounting of historical traditions, as rather a shared exuberance and intimacy. And for this feeling of community the small details that could vary from place to place were more satisfying than the basic narrative that usually remained the same.

Gestures and Words

The cult of the Forty Martyrs continued to flourish and spread, even far beyond central Asia Minor. When Gaudentius traveled through Cappadocia in the later fourth century on his way to Jerusalem, he acquired relics of the saints. After he became bishop of Brescia, in northern Italy, he deposited these relics in a new church that was subsequently known as "The Assembly of Saints." At Constantinople, Pulcheria, the spinster sister of the emperor Theodosius II, had a vision of the Forty Martyrs. They directed her to discover some of their relics that had been inadvertently buried beneath another shrine in the capital. Back in eastern Asia Minor the reputation of the cult of the Forty Martyrs seems to have set off a bidding frenzy on group cults. At Melitene there was a shrine in honor of the Thirty-Three Martyrs, and at Nicopolis a shrine in honor of the Forty-Five Martyrs.[36]

The Cappadocian Fathers made much of their reputations by talking, preaching about doctrinal controversies, the creation of the world, saints' cults, or significant current topics. Even their commentaries and theological treatises were dictated first, and then often read aloud to other theologians. Basil once suggested that a correspondent should visit, "so that we might talk to each other about these issues in person." Before there were texts, there were conversations. Talking implied the presence of listeners, whether the secretaries taking dictation, the study groups of learned theologians, or the large audiences that gathered for festivals. The essence of Christian teaching was direct dialogue and personal negotiation.[37]

This emphasis on face-to-face interaction was so persuasive that it carried over to ideas about God. A bishop in western Asia Minor once proposed the startling doctrine that God could neither speak nor hear. He concluded that God could not hear because he did not want to accept that "ears had been fashioned for Him." This refusal to imagine any body parts for God also obligated his conclusion that God could not speak. But in this case, the body part this bishop could not imagine for God was not a mouth, but hands. Even God would have had to be seen to be heard; but by denying Him hands, this bishop had effectively silenced God.[38]

Bishops preached with their hands, and audiences watched their gestures as they pointed at the paintings on the church walls, at features in the landscape, or at their listeners. Like a panegyrist, a preacher acted out his ideas by using "the pitch of his voice, the movement of a hand, and those other techniques that often make silly comments seem attractive." Without these visual and aural cues, however, the surviving sermons can easily seem to have been lifeless, drab monologues, usually with few indications of a specific moment or place or context. Ancient audiences listened to verbal inflections and watched the body language, while we modern historians can only read texts. For understanding the dialogues between preachers and audiences we are at a disadvantage. All we have are the words. They had performances.[39]

The Life to Come

In the Byzantine empire people knew exactly what the Cappadocian Fathers looked like, and they could readily recognize them in frescoes on the walls of their churches.

Gregory of Nazianzus was not a big man. He was somewhat sallow along with his elegance, and his nose was flat. His eyebrows were placed in a straight line and his gaze was gentle and soft, with more gloominess in his right eye which a scar had pinched in the corner. His beard was not thick, but it was sufficiently shaggy. He was balding with white hair, and the tips of his beard peeked out as if blackened by smoke.

Basil the Cappadocian was a tall man. The posture of his body was erect, and he was austere, with a dark complexion but mixed with paleness in his face. He had a long nose, with his eyebrows curled into a circle and his forehead squeezed together. His gaze was piercing, similar to that of a thinker, and his face wrinkled with a few creases. His cheeks were somewhat long, his temples were hollow, and his hair was clipped rather close. His beard reached down far enough and was partly gray.

Gregory of Nyssa was similar to Basil in all respects except for the grayness, and he had more elegance.

One intriguing feature of these descriptions is the blending of physical characteristics with details of their personalities. Gregory of Nazianzus was gentle, while Basil looked stern and piercing. Gregory of Nyssa may have been more graceful than his peers, but in iconography as in life he was still just a reflection of his domineering older brother.[1]

One reason later Byzantines deduced personalities from appearances was the absence of other information. Even when they recognized the Cappadocian Fathers, they did not know much about them. During their lifetimes the Cappadocian Fathers had had ambivalent relationships with their own pasts. By declining to discuss his many years as a student and rhetorician, Basil had simply ignored the entire first half of his life. Gregory of Nyssa was always aware of his junior standing within his own family, in part because his big sister Macrina and his big brother Basil kept belittling his talents. After their deaths he finally had the opportunity to tell his own story by writing a biography of Macrina and delivering a panegyric about Basil. Gregory of Nazianzus simply wallowed in his past. Since his father lived to be almost a centenarian, he had direct access to memories that stretched back to the dark ages of pagan emperors and persecutions. He himself constantly rewrote his own life's story in various autobiographical poems. Basil was silent about his past, Gregory of Nyssa was both defensive and custodial, and Gregory of Nazianzus was compulsively loquacious. None would have been a very good historian.[2]

The best historian from Cappadocia was their younger contemporary Philostorgius. He too was interested in appearances. One hero of his history was Eunomius, the Cappadocian theologian who had been an opponent of Basil and Gregory of Nyssa. Philostorgius wrote his history in part to rehabilitate Eunomius' reputation. In the process, he also decided to defend Eunomius' appearance. During the theological disputes with his rivals Eunomius had had to endure intensely personal ridicule, which had perhaps included comments about his disfigured face. Philostorgius too had carefully noted Eunomius' appearance, in particular "the white spots that scourged and flecked his face." But behind this pockmarked face he saw only an admirable man. Philostorgius now characterized these blemishes as "marks of physical beauty."[3]

The chapters in this section discuss the images of illustrious Cappadocians, both attempts at self-portrayal in their own writings and the evaluations of later generations in the form of reputations, legacies, and afterlives.

Philostorgius would find an understanding of himself by writing a historical narrative. He seemed to sense he was a misfit. In Cappadocia he was a heterodox Christian, and at Constantinople he was a Cappadocian. But rather than obsessing about his personal detachment, Philostorgius focused on larger themes, such as the interaction between capital and province and the interplay between orthodoxy and heresy, and he proceeded to write a more general history of the Greek East during the fourth century.

In contrast, Basil had literally sailed right by Constantinople. He passed up the high life overseas to return to Pontus and Cappadocia, and he had a sense of rightness about his theology that blinkered any interest in historical vagaries. Since he already knew the future, he no longer needed a past, including his own past.

Gregory of Nazianzus was certainly interested in his own past, and he certainly liked to write. He once described himself as "a man whose nature it is to write, just as it is the nature of water to flow and of fire to become hot." He combined his two interests and composed poems about his own life. In the process he tried to teach himself how to write autobiography.[4]

For all three, Constantinople represented an important transition. Once Philostorgius moved to the capital he was able to resolve his parochial anxieties by locating them in a wider imperial context. Constantinople expanded his personal and cultural horizons. Basil's avoidance of the capital was symbolic of his rejection of secular honors in favor of an ascetic perspective. He was furthermore more interested in connections with the Near East than with the Greek Roman empire that Constantinople portended. Constantinople was outside his ecclesiastical horizons. Gregory had served briefly as bishop at Constantinople. After he returned to Nazianzus, he constantly replayed his failures at the capital, and in his autobiographical poems he defended his actions and criticized other bishops. Venting his disappointments in these poems then had an oddly split effect. Even as recording these experiences helped him forget his misfortunes, the people in his small hometown were reminded that he had once been a big-city bishop. Because Gregory seemed so obsessively mindful of his experiences at the capital, perhaps they could no longer count on him to be interested in their local concerns. His experiences at Constantinople seemingly had disqualified him from serving again as a small-town bishop.

Chapter 8

"I Saw a Parrot":
Philostorgius at Constantinople

In the later 380s a young man left his home village in Cappadocia and traveled to Constantinople. Philostorgius was only following the lead of many young men from the Greek provinces who, in their late teens or early twenties, would go to a larger city such as Antioch, Alexandria, Athens, or Constantinople to continue their education and expand their personal contacts. From Cappadocia alone his predecessors in going off to study at the big city had included the future heresiarch Eunomius, the future emperor Julian, and of course Gregory of Nazianzus, his brother Caesarius, and Basil. In Cappadocia Philostorgius' family was apparently not very prominent or distinguished. His grandfather Anysius had served as a priest at Borissus, a village located in a dead-end gorge near Nazianzus. Anysius' children had included four sons and a daughter named Eulampion. These siblings were contemporaries of Eunomius, Julian, and the Cappadocian Fathers, as well as of a doctor named Philostorgius. If this Philostorgius was a relative (as his name might suggest), then at least one member of the extended family had improved his reputation through familiarity with culture and science.[1]

Another means for transforming a family's standing was a decision about theological doctrines. In this case the catalyst was Eulampion's marriage. In Cappadocia her family lived in the shadows of the nearby family of Gregory of Nazianzus, whose father was the local bishop, and of Basil, a prominent churchman at Caesarea. Although previously Eulampion's family had accepted Basil's trinitarian theology, her new husband, Carterius, supported the teachings of Eunomius and proceeded to convince his wife and her entire family to embrace his doctrinal preferences. During the 360s Eunomius had been collecting an impressive lineup of opponents who included the emperor Valens and the future metropolitan bishop Basil. Despite this revilement even in their homeland, this couple and their relatives opted to support Eunomius' doctrines. Carterius and Eulampion gave their son the delightful name of Philostorgius, "fond of affection." Because Philostorgius seems to have been raised as a living memorial to Eunomius and his teachings, it is no surprise that the most memorable moment from his years in Cappadocia was a visit to his aged hero himself, then living in exile near Caesarea.[2]

Already in Cappadocia Philostorgius began to acquire a comprehensive education in Greek literature, philosophy, astronomy, cosmography, and medicine. This familiarity with classical culture seems never to have interfered with his Christian beliefs, however. Even though his and his family's preference for heterodox doctrines may have made them religious outcasts, Philostorgius was a devout Christian, ready to defend his religion against nonbelievers. Ever since his brief but unsettling reign the pagan emperor Julian had become a favorite target of Christian polemicists. Within Cappadocia, Gregory of Nazianzus had once attacked Julian and his ideas about classical culture and Christianity in two caustic treatises. Philippus of Side, an historian who was an exact contemporary of Philostorgius, would continue the tradition by composing yet another reply to Julian's writings against the Christians, and in the early fifth century Cyril, bishop of Alexandria, would weigh in with another immense refutation. But since Julian had favored Aetius, who in turn had been a mentor of Eunomius, Philostorgius was not about to adopt the emperor as a generic adversary for an assault on paganism.[3]

Instead, he focused on an earlier antagonist, the Neoplatonist philosopher Porphyry. During the later third century Porphyry had posed a powerful intellectual attack on Christianity, and after he had tried to contradict some of the claims of Christianity through the use of historical and theological criticism, various Christian scholars had responded to his arguments. Philostorgius was familiar enough with earlier refutations by some bishops to evaluate their effectiveness, and he now decided to continue this tradition of rebuttals by composing his own "on behalf of the Christians." Even though Julian had had direct contact with Cappadocia, and even though the emperor had a reputation for having been "wiser" than Porphyry in his refutation of Christian teachings, Philostorgius nevertheless decided to write a rejoinder to the philosopher's arguments. Philostorgius wanted to define himself as a true Christian intellectual, and with this selection of an appropriate pagan opponent he had located himself in impressive company, not just among past Christian apologists, but also among his contemporaries. In the early fifth century two of the greatest of Christian scholars, Jerome and Augustine of Hippo, would also struggle with Porphyry's arguments.[4]

Even as he situated himself among these eminent intellectuals, Philostorgius nevertheless seems to have sensed that his obscure background might become a handicap for achieving his ambitions. At about the same time other young men who were about the same age as Philostorgius would also realize the limitations of growing up in central Asia Minor. Palladius, a future bishop, was born and educated in Galatia. Hypatius, a future monk, was educated in both classical culture and Christian teachings in Phrygia. But as he became more interested in a life of asceticism, he could discover only "one or two pious men" to serve as models in his home region. Philostorgius' uneasiness likewise appeared as he thought about his fellow Cappadocians. One telling indication of his unspoken ambivalence was his pointed awareness of various churchmen from Cappadocia who had come from small villages and unassuming cities but still achieved prominence. When he later set out to write a history of his times, Philostorgius consistently noted the humble hometowns of such notable fellow countrymen, even those who may have disagreed with his own doctrinal preferences. These renowned Cappadocians who had risen above their obscure backgrounds included Ulfilas, the bishop who had converted the Goths; Eudoxius, another disciple of Aetius who had become bishop successively of Antioch and Constantinople; Meletius, bishop successively of Sebasteia and Antioch; and, of course, Eunomius. Philostorgius' interest in classical culture, religious disputations, and successful careers seems to suggest that already as a young man he had concluded that he too might achieve intellectual eminence despite his family's heterodox theological preferences and his modest background. To do so, however, he had to follow the example of those other successful Cappadocians and leave his native province.[5]

In the mid- and later 380s Palladius, Hypatius, and Philostorgius all left their home regions in central Asia Minor. Constantinople would be their ultimate destination. Palladius left Galatia in order to adopt an ascetic lifestyle in Palestine and Egypt. He finally returned to Asia Minor to become bishop of Helenopolis, a city in Bithynia on the Sea of Marmara opposite Constantinople. He also became an active participant in the controversies over John Chrysostom, the beleaguered bishop of Constantinople. Hypatius left Phrygia likewise to pursue his ascetic ambitions. He finally became a monk in a monastery that was outside Chalcedon, but still near "the radiance of Constantinople." Philostorgius seems to have gone directly to the capital in order to expand both his prospects and his intellectual horizons. Not only did he find there a large community of fellow "Eunomians." Eventually almost everyone and everything showed up in Constantinople.[6]

In the later fourth century the capital was a boomtown, flush from the patronage and new building projects recently initiated by the emperor Theodosius. Many provincials had moved there to serve in the senate, to hold offices in the palatine ministries, or to take advantage of the handouts of grain. Dominating the city were emperors, past and present. Constantine, the city's founder, was still a revered presence, and Philostorgius made a point of commenting on how Christians offered prayers to a giant statue of the emperor perched high on a porphyry column. He visited the mausoleum that contained the tombs of Constantine and his son Constantius, as well as the adjacent Church of the Holy Apostles that contained the tombs of St. Andrew, St. Luke, and St. Timothy, three apostles whose remains Constantius had appropriated for the capital. He glimpsed some of the powerful palatine officials and watched imperial ceremonies closely enough that he could comment on personal characteristics, such as the sparkling intelligence in the eyes of the prefect Rufinus and the tendency of the emperor Arcadius to nod off in public. The capital also offered other, more outlandish exhibits that were all reminders of its growing prominence in the Greek world and the Near East, and Philostorgius had obviously not missed the opportunity to gawk at them all. These wonders included the head of a renegade Gothic general carefully preserved in salt, a relief of a unicorn, the embalmed body of a monstrous ape that had been a gift from the ruler of India, and exotic birds with resplendent plumage. "I saw a parrot, which is the most loquacious of birds and most closely mimics a human voice."[7]

For a young man from smallville the extravagant sights at a metropolis were certainly memorable, and Philostorgius was curious enough and intrigued enough to be delighted by them all. Living in Constantinople was a transforming experience that gave him contact with other Christians who shared his heterodox doctrines, and it reinforced his sense of grievance about the treatment of Eunomius. His residence there was also an advantage, and perhaps a powerful catalyst, for the writing of the historical narrative that he was to compose in the early fifth century, since he was able to speckle his account with comments about his own observations and experiences in the eastern capital. In place of the small-town provincial, Philostorgius had become a cosmopolitan resident of the big city. He knew about the capital's earlier traditions. He could write learned digressions about the flow of rivers. He even knew the original location of Paradise.[8]

Philostorgius would find himself in the writing of history, and he literally inscribed himself in his historical account. The greatest of the classical Greek historians, Herodotus and Thucydides, had rather grandiosely introduced themselves to their readers by placing their own names as the first words of their narratives. Philostorgius was no less proud, but a bit more subtle. He now made sure that each successive book in his narrative started with a letter from his name. "He signed his name in the first letter of the books." Philostorgius' personal identity was inside his history, and his historical narrative had become his strategy for examining and presenting not only his times, but also himself. Like an acrostic poem, his historical narrative could be read simultaneously in various ways. As a result, reading his history was a form of gradual disclosure, with each book divulging a bit more of the author's identity. By the end, Philostorgius, signature and author, had been revealed.[9]

Writing a history was furthermore a means of sustaining his new confidence and ensuring that he supervised the broadcasting of his own convictions. Philostorgius had already seen the consequences of losing control over the past. Eunomius, his hero, had likewise broken away from his village and made his way in the larger world. But after he ran into powerful opposition, others had rewritten his life's story, and he had ended up back in his home province as a pale specter of his former eminence. Philostorgius seems to have been successful in maintaining his standing in the capital, and he may never have returned to Cappadocia. Since the booming capital was open to both provincials and heterodox Christians, Constantinople had given him freedom from the religious oppression that had humbled Eunomius, and reassurance that he could rise above his provincial origins to become a learned historian. If a talking parrot could find success at the capital, so could a heterodox Cappadocian. History was the key. To maintain his independence and reputation Philostorgius had to get control of the past by composing his own history. Writing the past was essential to guaranteeing a future legacy for himself and his theology.

Chapter 9
A Blank Sheet of Paper:
The Apocryphal Basil

Forty years before Philostorgius had gone to Constantinople Basil had also visited the new capital as a young man. In the later 340s he had studied there briefly with "the most accomplished sophists and philosophers" before going on to Athens. Then, little more than a decade after Constantine's death, construction was proceeding or recently had been completed on extensive fortifications, a senate house, the imperial palace, the hippodrome, baths, a monumental forum to honor the city's founder, as well as several churches. When Basil eventually visited Constantinople again to participate in a council in early 360, he may have attended the consecration of the Church of Holy Wisdom. Since the city was still expanding rapidly, the construction of aqueducts and the remodeling of the docks were enlarging its capacity to supply water and import grain for the increasing population.[1]

Yet Basil, unlike Philostorgius and almost everyone else who visited Constantinople, seems to have been entirely unimpressed. In a letter from the later 350s he actually prided himself on having once passed up the city's allurements by not visiting. When he later mentioned the council at Constantinople, he did not even hint that he had been there himself. In all of his writings the only experience he mentioned that seems to have resulted from his visits to Constantinople was an acknowledgment that he had once personally witnessed the migration of schools of fish through the Sea of Marmara into the Black Sea. Without that glancing allusion a reader would hardly guess from Basil's extant writings that he too had visited the new capital.[2]

After Basil became an active priest and then bishop at Caesarea, he had adopted a public life in which he might have been expected to parade his family's and his own prominence. Yet in an odd reversal he seems not to have been much interested in his own past. In his extant writings he never mentioned his father, his brother Naucratius, his famous sister Macrina, or his other sisters, and he mentioned his mother only a few times in passing, most notably when he referred to her death. Nor did he mention events from his earlier career. He never described his years at Athens or any of his teachers there. In the letters he wrote during his episcopacy he did not discuss his earlier years in Cappadocia or neighboring regions, not even such formative events as his retreat to Pontus, his unsuccessful candidacy for the episcopacy of Caesarea in 362, or his tenacious uneasiness with his predecessor, bishop Eusebius. He even passed over some of the important events of his episcopacy, such as his confrontations with the emperor Valens and the prefect Modestus and the consecration of his friend Gregory as bishop of Sasima.

Once Basil had passed through the transition from rhetorician to ascetic and cleric, he never looked back, and he acknowledged no further changes in himself and his life. Thereafter he insisted only that he had always been consistent in his theology and his friendships. In his presentation of himself Basil was virtually a man with no past, no great changes of mind to explain, no regrets that he had to face again, no memories that he wanted to share with others. He also had no future to speak of, since he would still be tomorrow what he was today. With such a perspective, a history, even in the form of an autobiography, was both unnecessary and impossible: there could be no history of the unchanging.

Legends

Reticence was both a disadvantage and an opportunity for subsequent historians. The primary source of information about Basil's life, then as well as now, was the lengthy panegyric by Gregory of Nazianzus. Copies of Gregory's panegyric seem to have circulated widely in cities from Constantinople to Antioch. This panegyric provided the basic biographical framework for Basil's life, and without it Basil's own writings, including his letters, would certainly be much more opaque. But because Basil had clearly become an important figure in Cappadocia and throughout the Greek world, people wanted to know more about him. Those without access to Gregory's oration had to rely upon other sources.[3]

The most common seem to have been oral traditions, sometimes based on or supplemented by creative imagination. For later authors Basil's reserve about himself became an advantage, since there were no uncongenial historical details to get in the way. They now had an open license to mold Basil's life to fit new agendas. Eventually, various accounts collected some of these oral traditions and new stories. Among the extant accounts are an epic history from Armenia, an anonymous homily, and an anonymous *Life* that also included some miracle stories. Just as Basil's interests and correspondence had linked him with the Near East, so many of these later traditions associated him in particular with Armenia and Syria.

The *Epic Histories* provided a perspective on the fourth century from Armenia. This anonymous historical account was compiled from earlier sources most likely during the later fifth century, about a century after Basil's episcopacy. Some of its episodes included stories about or allusions to Basil. In one, Nerses went to Caesarea to be consecrated as primate of the kingdom of Armenia. The bishop at Caesarea was Eusebius, and one of his priests was Basil. During the ceremony a dove first hovered over Basil's head, and then over Nerses' head. In another story Nerses went as an ambassador to the court of Valens, and during his visit he prayed for the recovery of the emperor's ill son. When his prayers were unsuccessful, Valens sent him into exile. This account then praised Basil for his reputation as "an apostle of Christ," and described the animosity between Basil and Eusebius. It also described Basil's assistance for his bishop when he participated in an argument against the emperor and some "Arian pseudobishops." Another story described Basil's own consecration, when a dove settled over his head again. And yet another story described Valens' death, here attributed to some martyrs who had emerged from the shrine of St. Thecla to restrain the emperor. As a result of the emperor's death Basil could offer to return to the people the taxes he had been holding in escrow.[4]

These stories have little if any historical value. Nerses in fact had become primate in the early 350s or earlier, well before Basil had become a priest and Eusebius the bishop of Caesarea, and he was killed a few years after Basil became bishop. The legends were instead more important as affirmations of the ongoing links between Cappadocia and Armenia. These two regions had shared close ecclesiastical ties since the career of Gregory the Illuminator, the founder of Christianity in Armenia and the first primate after his consecration at Caesarea in the early fourth century. Basil had once been commissioned to provide bishops for the kingdom of Armenia, and he may have known Nerses. These legends about the connections between the two churchmen during the later fourth century were a confirmation, in miniature, of the lingering bonds between the two regions a century later. Not only had the dove explicitly linked Basil and Nerses. In the story about Valens' ill son Nerses was outright substituted for Basil, whom Greek historians had associated with the son's illness, and Nerses then became the champion of orthodoxy against the heterodox emperor. In the kingdom of Armenia the model of Basil the bishop and champion of orthodoxy was too influential to pass over. Not only did this historical account make the primate similar to the bishop. It also appropriated some of the stories about Basil and attributed them to Nerses.[5]

An anonymous homily in Syriac of uncertain date provided another interpretation of Basil's life. This homily was an encomium full of platitudes, mistakes, and vague descriptions of Basil's life. At the beginning the author mentioned in passing Basil's youth, his studies at Athens and, supposedly, at Alexandria, his return to his homeland, his retreat, and his priesthood at Caesarea. This account was obviously cursory, and the author added some bulk by including a few charming details, such as the claim that during his priesthood Basil had read so much that he used a book as his pillow. The author also transformed some episodes into good drama by distorting the facts. At the moment of Basil's selection as bishop, for instance, the author neatly reversed the actual historical situation by having everyone, including Jews, give him their support, while Basil himself was oddly reluctant. As bishop, Basil converted some Jews, used the church plate to assist the poor, established an atmosphere of virtue in his city, and debated a philosopher. Since the author then announced that he wanted to accelerate his presentation, he skimmed over the communities of deacons and deaconesses, and mentioned how Basil was the personification of various virtues.

Before concluding his panegyric with a brief account of Basil's death and funeral, the author finally discussed a specific episode, Basil's confrontation with the emperor Valens. In his telling Valens stopped at Caesarea and decided to attend a service on Sunday. At the church no one said anything to him. When they did speak, Basil explained that the celebration of the liturgy was more important than talking with the emperor. The emperor's advisers then suggested that he send Basil into exile. Initially Valens was eager to do so, until he thought again about the reactions of the local notables and about Basil's virtues. When his son became ill, Valens appealed to Basil for assistance, but the boy died. Valens then left the city. He issued orders that sent various bishops into exile, and he had them replaced with new Arian clerics. During this persecution Basil was the embodiment of more virtues.[6]

This particular story about Basil and Valens clearly had a special resonance for the author and his audience. Of all Basil's remarkable contemporaries Valens was the only one whom the author mentioned, and in fact almost the only other person he mentioned by name in the entire panegyric.

This was furthermore the only episode from Basil's career about which the author knew any details, perhaps because he was familiar with an account from one of the earlier church historians. Without more information about the specific context and date for this panegyric, the precise significance of this story remains a mystery, of course, but it certainly carried within itself the possibility of many interpretations. This story gave the author an opportunity to highlight Basil's many virtues, and in particular his fortitude in the face of persecution. It also revived memories of the long-standing tension between capital and province by stressing the opposition of Cappadocians to an emperor's commands. In this case, when Valens was trying to send Basil into exile, the author claimed that the people of Caesarea had refused to abandon their bishop: "we have a better refuge in him than in your power and the walls of your city."[7]

The confrontation between Basil and Valens reappeared, in a much different version, in a Greek *Life* of Basil. This long account had some sense of the outlines of Basil's career, and the author sometimes mentioned his sources. But since the *Life* also contained so many historically implausible or just wrong stories about Basil, its author most likely had no knowledge of Gregory of Nazianzus' panegyric (despite seeming to refer to it), and little, if any, familiarity with Basil's own writings. Instead, the author spliced together a series of episodes into a biographical narrative of sorts and then added some stories about Basil's subsequent miracles.

The first set of episodes highlighted Basil's early education. According to this narrative, Basil did go to Athens, but he then interrupted his studies to visit a monk in Egypt and to pray in Jerusalem. Upon returning to Athens he converted his teacher, and they traveled together to Antioch, where Basil impressed the noted sophist Libanius with his learning, then to Jerusalem, where he was baptized in the Jordan River, and then again to Antioch, where he became a deacon under bishop Meletius. A second set of episodes discussed Basil's return to Cappadocia. Bishop Leontius welcomed him, and Basil soon succeeded him as bishop of Caesarea. During the celebration of the eucharist Basil once converted a Jew, and he also assisted a woman with her appeal to a provincial governor. He then exchanged polite insults with the emperor Julian, who vowed to plow Caesarea under upon his return from his campaign against the Persians. In order to appease the emperor Basil began to collect precious gifts from the people, and he led them in praying at a shrine of Mary the Mother of God on a mountain. After Julian's death Basil used much of this wealth instead to decorate the church at Caesarea. The next episode highlighted Basil and the emperor Valens. According to this version, Valens summoned Basil to Antioch upon hearing that the bishop supported the doctrine that the Son was "identical in essence" with God the Father. At Antioch Basil confronted an (unnamed) prefect, and tried to alleviate the illness of the emperor's son. After Valens' death the emperor Valentinian donated funds to help Basil provide assistance for the poor and the ill.

The next set of episodes consisted of stories that the author claimed to have heard from Helladius, Basil's successor as bishop of Caesarea, or from Ephraem, a famous Syrian exegete. In one story Basil was able to redeem a young man who had made a deal with a sorcerer to win the love of a senator's daughter. In another he shared some adventures with one of his priests, which ended with Basil's curing a disfigured man. In another story Ephraem traveled to Caesarea to hear Basil preach. Ephraem in fact had been a deacon in Edessa until his death in 373, and he had been noted for the hymns he had composed in Syriac. In this story, after Basil ordained him as a priest Ephraem was suddenly able to speak in Greek. The next episode again highlighted Basil and the emperor Valens. At Nicaea, the Arians convinced Valens to turn over a church to them. Basil then visited the emperor at Constantinople and proposed a contest to see which congregation, the Arians or the orthodox, could open the sealed church with their prayers and vigils. Basil's supporters were of course successful, although Valens still refused to convert. A final collection of episodes included stories about Basil's miraculous powers. Basil was able to help his brother Peter, the bishop of Sebasteia, prove that he lived in celibacy with his wife by demonstrating that burning coals could not singe either Peter's or his wife's cloak. He was also able to remit a woman's sins, even after his death. Initially he sent her to consult with Ephraem in the desert. Upon her return, she tossed a paper listing her greatest sin on Basil's funeral bier, and it was erased. In another story Basil was able to convert a Jewish doctor by demonstrating that he could postpone his imminent death for another day. The final story in the *Life* mentioned Basil's funeral, the eulogy by Gregory of Nazianzus, and his burial with the earlier bishops of Caesarea.[8]

Some of the stories in this *Life* projected an air of familiarity, in particular the stories that emphasized Basil's period of study at Athens, his youthful travels, and his confrontations with the emperor Valens and his prefect. The author tried to enhance the veracity of his narrative by including detailed stories about Basil's interactions with other notable contemporaries. Yet these stories were almost entirely fanciful, and hence are thoroughly suspect as historical sources. The author had Basil succeed Leontius, who in fact had been bishop of Caesarea when Basil was born. The author was confused about the sequence of Basil's early travels; wrongly presented him as the primary antagonist of Julian, an emperor with whom he had little firsthand contact; described some trips to Antioch and Constantinople even though during his episcopacy Basil had barely traveled beyond Cappadocia and eastern Asia Minor; and attributed the generosity that assisted Basil's plans for the poor and needy not to the emperor Valens, but to an emperor named Valentinian. The author may have been thinking about Valens' brother or his homonymous nephew, but both of them had been emperors in the western empire. The confrontation at Nicaea was an epitome of the clash between orthodoxy and heresy in a single symbolic episode. The ecumenical council at Nicaea in 325 had established the foundational creed; Basil and Valens had subsequently represented Nicene orthodoxy and Arian heresy; so Nicaea was an appropriate battleground for a decisive contest between orthodox bishop and heretical emperor. And then there were the inherently dubious stories. These implausible episodes included the account of the meeting between Basil and Ephraem, and the stories that demonstrated Basil's miraculous powers.[9]

The author of this *Life* had employed the usual tactics to enhance the impression of historical veracity. He attributed some of the stories to named informants, and he carefully linked Basil with other prominent contemporaries, such as bishop Meletius, the sophist Libanius, the hymnist Ephraem, and the emperors Julian and Valens. He then tried to combine these discrete episodes into a reassuring biography by providing a continuous life story. As a result, however unsatisfactory this narrative was as a proper biography, the *Life* seems to have become popular in the middle Byzantine period. In particular, a biography consisting of discrete episodes could readily switch media to become a series of discrete, episodic frescoes. Scenes from this *Life* became the basis for iconographic representations of Basil's life.

"The Abyss of Forgetfulness"

History abhors a vacuum. Since Basil had been so reticent about himself, apocryphal stories could easily substitute. The oddity is that these apocryphal stories became popular in Cappadocia itself. During the middle Byzantine period many churches were excavated directly in the soft volcanic cliffs and the freestanding stone cones in Cappadocia. One of these rock-cut churches was Tokalı Kilise, "Buckle Church," in the Göreme valley west of

Caesarea. This church was in fact a complex that consisted of three sanctuaries, known as the Lower Church, the Old Church, excavated in the early tenth century, and the New Church, excavated in the mid-tenth century. Because Tokalı Kilise was apparently dedicated to St. Basil, the walls of the New Church were decorated with frescoes depicting scenes from the life of Basil, or rather, from the *Life* of Basil. In many cases these frescoes are now in such a dilapidated state that all that survives are a few fragmentary images and the accompanying inscriptions that served as captions for the scenes. In Tokalı Kilise the frescoes highlighted Basil's interactions with three contemporaries: the emperor Valens, the ascetic Ephraem, and a penitent woman.

One tableau of five scenes formed an iconographic narrative of the confrontation between Basil and Valens over possession of the church at Nicaea. The first scene showed Basil before the emperor and was accompanied by an inscription that belittled Valens. "Emperor Valens, what evil have you done that you should give the church to the heretical Arians?" A second scene showed the Arians praying before the church. An inscription noted that even though "the Arians, because they desired the church, prayed for three days," they were nevertheless unsuccessful: "the church was not opened for them." A third scene depicted the Arians as they departed: "because the church of God did not open for them, the heretics obeyed and turned back empty-handed." A fourth scene showed the orthodox praying under Basil's guidance: "Holy Basil gathered the Christians and cried out, 'Lord, have mercy.' The doors of the church opened." A final scene depicted Basil and a group of people, perhaps celebrating their success; the inscription is too fragmentary to be read.

Another tableau of scenes depicted the meeting between Basil and Ephraem. Because of their degradation, these scenes are now essentially lost. An inscription accompanying one described their meeting. "Lord Ephraem, the metropolitan bishop summons you. Approach the altar."

A final tableau of scenes depicted the woman whose sins were forgiven through Basil's intercession. Most of the scenes in this iconographic narrative are now lost, but a final scene showed Basil's body on his funeral bier and a deacon looking at a blank scroll that had once listed the woman's greatest sin. One inscription noted the woman's initial despair. "The woman was crying and said, 'Holy man of God, [I have found] you too late.'" Another inscription stressed her redemption, as conceded by a deacon. "He took the sheet of paper and threw it away. He said, 'Woman, why are you weeping? Your sheet of paper is blank.'"[10]

The scenes in this church commemorated three apocryphal moments from Basil's life. This iconographic cycle preserved images of Basil as a defender of orthodoxy against a heterodox emperor, a friend of a famous Syrian ascetic, and an intercessor for people's sins. These were powerful images, even if historically the details were all wrong. Basil had not argued with Valens over a church at Nicaea, and he had not met Ephraem. According to Gregory of Nazianzus, Basil's burial procession had in fact turned into a virtual riot, and some people had become "funeral sacrifices," crushed in the pushing and shoving. Like the later textual narratives, these iconographic scenes were interpretive representations of Basil's life.[11]

Because of his single-minded devotion to his theology, his ascetic principles, and his pastoral care, Basil had himself simply erased all aspects of his life that might have been in conflict. In a sacrament of absolution by oblivion he had rinsed away most of his own past. Baptism was meant to transform Christians by scrubbing away their past sins; Basil had recreated himself by transcending and declining to talk about his entire past. He had pushed much of his life into what Gregory of Nazianzus would call "the abyss of forgetfulness." Because he had been so hesitant to talk about his own experiences and feelings, Basil had essentially left his life as a blank sheet of paper. Others would be free to fill it in for him. As a result, an Armenian history, a sermon, a *Life*, and the scenes in this church in Cappadocia all memorialized an apocryphal Basil.[12]

Chapter 10

"Trail of Sorrows":
The Autobiographies of Gregory of Nazianzus

Unlike Basil, Gregory of Nazianzus seemingly could not get enough of his past life, and as he incessantly rewrote and revised earlier episodes, he became a man with many, almost too many, pasts. To find a consistent trajectory in his life and activities, Gregory constantly examined and reinterpreted his earlier thinking and behavior. Since his uncertainties and anxieties had often prompted him toward extravagant reactions, he had much to examine. For subsequent historians, if Basil was problematic by having been tightlipped, Gregory was sometimes overwhelming by having been so voluble and garrulous.

Self-Pity

Writing about himself was not easy. Since autobiography can appear in different guises, such as recollections, memoirs and diaries, quotations and commentaries, even wills and novels, Gregory had to decide upon an appropriate format. He also had to determine how to link his subjective self with his objective actions and ideas. As an autobiographer he had to be both author and subject, observer and actor, artist and model.

His first attempt was not very successful. Probably the earliest example of his reflections on himself was a poem that he wrote shortly after his brother Caesarius' death in the late 360s. To make his grief quite clear Gregory immediately compared himself with biblical figures who had likewise faced potential disasters, such as Moses in battle, Daniel in the lion's den, Jonah in the whale, the three young men in the furnace, and Jesus' disciples on the stormy sea. Having located his own predicament among these biblical symbols of affliction he then asked God for a similar miraculous deliverance: "you have rescued the souls and bodies of many from calamities." Gregory had loved his brother, and he was certainly dismayed at his untimely death. But the oddity of his complaints in this poem is that rather than highlighting his sorrow, he instead bemoaned the inconvenience. In addition to continuing to care for his elderly father and mother he now had to assume responsibility for the administration of property and slaves. This participation in practical management not only exposed him to the vagaries of dealing with courts and tax collectors. It also subjected his soul to the "furious passions" and temptations that he thought he had once overcome.[1]

This poem hence revealed an unexpected sediment of peevish annoyance. Gregory was clearly using this poem as a sort of bibliotherapy to come to terms with an unexpected reversal, as his elderly parents lived on while his younger brother had died. Yet in describing his misfortune he showed himself to be priggish and rigidly small-minded, a middle-aged cleric who was so set in his ways that he felt harassed when faced with having to care for his parents and administer the family's property. His preference, as he himself conceded, would have been to flee to the mountains, as in fact he had done a few years earlier after his consecration as a priest at Nazianzus. This time, however, his love for his parents restrained him, "dragging me down to the ground just like a weight." As a result, by assuming responsibility for his parents he now found himself in what he thought was an untenable predicament. In his perspective, "my misfortune was a result of doing good."[2]

To underline the seriousness of his current misfortune Gregory mentioned some of his own earlier brushes with danger that no longer seemed so fearful, such as a storm at sea when he was sailing from Egypt to Greece, an earthquake in Greece, and the accident that had bloodied one of his eyes with a thorn. Nothing could compare: "whoever sees me should tremble with dread." To clarify his affliction further Gregory included some unexpectedly self-serving interpretations, one of a popular biblical parable, another of an episode highlighting his mother's pious devotion. When he mentioned Jesus' parable about the generosity of the Good Samaritan, rather than comparing himself to a guardian who was prepared to tend to his parents and the family's properties, he identified himself with the traveler who had been robbed, stripped, and abandoned for dead. When he mentioned his mother, he noted that she had dedicated him at birth as a "new Samuel," consecrated to serve God's altar. Although Gregory had fulfilled her vow by developing an intense love for "divine wisdom and the monastic life," he now was upset that his involvement in worldly affairs would divert him from his calling, as if loyalty to his mother's vow was somehow justification for his reluctance to accept responsibility for his parents' well-being. In Gregory's interpretations, his brother's death had left him as another victim on the road, unable to fulfill his own mother's vow for his life. This perspective presented a Gregory who seems to have been concerned much more about his own solace than about the welfare of his parents or the administration of his family's estates, and who seems almost to have resented, and not just regretted, his brother's death. At the end of this poem he hoped only for the restoration of his earlier tranquillity: "disperse all my burdens in the boisterous winds."[3]

These self-pitying sentiments can easily seem pathetically self-indulgent, especially in such circumstances of despair for both Gregory and his parents. They also indicate that Gregory seems to have instinctively sensed that in order to evoke sympathy for himself and try to achieve his own, rather selfish goals he had to manipulate the presentation of his own past. Reinterpreting events such as his mother's vow was one technique; another was the failure to mention other episodes. Even if he had not always gotten his way, Gregory had so far lived a charmed life, defined by his joyful years of study in Athens, the loving support of parents whom he might not have expected to live so long, and even his bold reaction to the emperor Julian. Yet he never mentioned these happy and successful episodes from his earlier life that would have tempered a reader's sympathy. Most notably, he never hinted either at any support from his influential friend Basil, who did in fact attempt to assist by sending letters to important imperial magistrates. In this poem Gregory had highlighted only his aloneness, deprived of the help of siblings, isolated without the assistance of relatives, and abandoned by his companion monks who were distracted by internal feuding.[4]

This early poem was hence too maudlin and full of self-pity to be a convincing interpretation of his early life. But Gregory seems to have absorbed two important lessons. One was a sense of a preordained trajectory to his life. Caesarius' death had been upsetting because it had momentarily diverted him from fulfilling the destiny to which his mother had committed him at birth, and because he could not quite see how to restore his earlier trajectory. Autobiography was the answer. "The narrative is conscious, and since the narrator's consciousness directs the narrative, it seems to him incontestable that it has also directed his life." In this poem Gregory's response to his feeling of helplessness was to highlight the tranquillity of his earlier life, as if he could revive it by simply describing it. Writing his earlier life gave him direction for living his current life.[5]

The other lesson concerned the connection between his life and his

poetry. Reviewing his life in poetry seemed to provide a sense of empower-
ment, because not only was he reinterpreting his life, he was also fitting it
into the demands of correct meter and proper vocabulary. The sense of
mastery that he acquired from writing a technically complex poem would
serve as a substitute for the uncertainty and awkwardness he had sometimes
experienced in his actions. Metrics shaped this poem about his life, and
therefore his representation of his life too. In a poem his life would finally
scan properly.[6]

Caesarius' death was the first in a series of personal misfortunes that
challenged Gregory's sense of destiny. These subsequent calamities included
his unwanted consecration as bishop at Sasima, the collapse of his friendship with Basil, and the deaths of his parents. His brief service as bishop at
Constantinople was perhaps most distressing. Because he had agreed to
go to the capital and eventually had allowed himself to become bishop, he
could not avoid accepting some responsibility for events there. Upon his
return to Cappadocia in 381, he again had a lot of explaining to do, to others and to himself. Most of his longer poems about himself and his earlier
career dated to this final decade or so of his life.

Poetry remained his preferred format for writing about his life, for several reasons. Some were practical. About a year after his return he became
concerned about the presence in his native region of supporters of Apollinarius, the bishop of Laodicea. Apollinarius' doctrines had already been
condemned as heterodox. Yet he and his ideas remained attractive, in part
because of his literary skills. Apollinarius had been trained as a rhetorician,
and two decades earlier, as a reaction to the emperor Julian's attempt to
separate Christian teachers from classical literature, he had rewritten biblical books in the style of various classical authors. His rewriting of the
Psalms as classical poems had been so seductive that Gregory noted that
some people considered those "new Psalms" to be a "third Testament." He
now decided to provide a balance to "the charm of those verses" by writing
poems of his own. Apollinarius may have composed paraphrases of the
Psalms in verse, but Gregory would now transform sophisticated theology
into heroic verse. In the process of composing these poems he could also
achieve other objectives, one to demonstrate yet again that pagans had no
greater claim than Christians on the heritage of classical Greek poetry, and
another to make his ideas more accessible and appealing to young readers
who preferred verse over prose.[7]

Versifying theology was difficult, however, not least because the man-
dates of the vocabulary of orthodoxy sometimes did not coincide with the

rules of poetical meter. In "laboring over the meter" in his theological poems Gregory hence ended up resorting to false quantities, coining nonce words, and stretching the meanings of words. Yet the discipline that he needed to write poems about orthodox theology perhaps reinforced the possibility of analyzing his own life in verse. Just as a long poem had helped him cope with his brother's death, so a series of new autobiographical poems might help him come to terms with his experiences at Constantinople. Gregory decided that he would again "present some of my own toils in meter." If he could versify orthodox theology, then perhaps he could versify an orthodox version of his life too.[8]

Reticence

Gregory also now looked to restore his sense of a consistent trajectory to his life. Since going to Constantinople had been his choice, he could not simply complain about the outcome, as he had after Caesarius' death. Instead, he adopted various approaches to his life's story that were less petulant and pitying about himself. In some poems he hardly mentioned his own past experiences, in others he was nostalgic, and in still others he carefully re-viewed aspects of his entire life. Gregory ignored his past, sentimentalized his past, and scrutinized his past. These poems were hence the equivalents of different drafts of his life's story. Finding a consistent theology had been easy compared with finding a consistent self, and in these poems Gregory seemingly "stuttered" as he tried out different approaches and searched for a definitive reading of his experiences. At the very least he showed that he had learned how to use his life's story to create sympathy for his current positions.[9]

Soon after his departure from Constantinople, Gregory composed several poems in which he mentioned his candid evaluations of recent events and other bishops. At the time he was full of opinions, many of them angry and resentful. In one poem he proposed to "strike back at my assas-sins with a short discussion." In order to "unload his pain," however, he decided that he had to begin his story a bit earlier. But in this case, rather than recounting his own earlier life, he began only with his departure for Constantinople a few years before. According to this account, initially he had been successful in building up the congregation of orthodox Christians at the capital, until some bishops turned against him. Gregory then took the opportunity to discuss at length the qualities of good and bad bishops.

Good bishops were similar to the apostles and spoke plainly and directly: "articulate your philosophy in simple language, and even if you speak without refinement, you will satisfy us." Bad bishops indulged in extravagance and luxury and were unable to conceal their inadequacies and disdain. As he put it in a striking even if rather inept comparison, a cat dressed like a bride was still a cat and would prefer to chase mice.[10]

Because it seemed hardly autobiographical, this poem was remarkably subtle and understated. Only once did Gregory even allude to an event from his early life, when he noted that in his current retirement he now again had the opportunity to fulfill his mother's vow by turning to God. Nor did he explicitly classify himself among the good bishops whom he praised. Yet his discussion was certainly exculpatory, and at the end of the poem he hinted that the best model for a new bishop at Constantinople was in fact himself. Even this hint turned into an admonition, since he hoped that the new bishop, if he were "another Gregory," would be treated better.[11]

In other poems in which he was critical of bishops Gregory was similarly reluctant to discuss specific episodes. In one poem he mentioned how he had lost his see at Constantinople after he declined to become "an intrepid warrior for a single faction." Rather than elaborating on that suggestive hint, however, he then noted only how happy he was to have dropped his anchor in the calm port of Cappadocia. In another long poem he criticized the bishops who had turned against him by discussing various laudable ideals, but without mentioning his own circumstances. The purpose of this poem was simply therapeutic: "one remedy for distress is to relate a story even in the mist." In other poems he again confronted his hostile critics by praising his own firmness and constancy. In his own estimation, he now remained "as the unmoved guardian of the truth," who would "stand among the shifting powers without turning." And in yet another poem he criticized the lives of unscrupulous bishops while complimenting himself for being content with a quiet life.[12]

For all of Gregory's dismay, and even anger, over his treatment at Constantinople he was markedly discreet in these poems. Although he highlighted his own consistency and composure, he did not demonstrate how his actions had developed from his earlier life. And although he railed against his opponents, he never mentioned any by name. In this case his preference for anonymity might have arisen from his own uneasiness over talking about the qualifications of good bishops, since he himself had never been keen to assume episcopal service. Because a man who had never wanted to be a bishop could not justifiably evaluate other bishops by referring to his own behavior and attitudes, Gregory now matched reticence about his own earlier life with discretion about the bishops who had become his opponents. Criticism of other bishops was not an appropriate framework for providing details about his own past.

Nostalgia

During this same period Gregory further reflected upon his experiences at Constantinople by adopting another perspective that likewise did not require inclusion of events from his past. In one poem he recounted a dream about the Anastasia ("Resurrection"), the private home that he had used as a small church when he had first arrived in the capital. Gregory obviously missed this church, in part because it represented his own success as an ecclesiastical leader, "the work of my careful hand," "the fruit of my labors." There, in his dream, he could imagine himself presiding over his clergy and delivering sermons that his congregation admired. Yet the recollection of this moment of pride was merely a prelude to his current sadness and nostalgia. "This is what I had. But the crowing of roosters shook this dream from my eyes, and along with it the Anastasia. For a time I retained the image of the image, but then it faded and slowly left my heart. Only sorrow remained for me, and troublesome old age."[13]

Thinking about his short tenure as the leader of this small church obviously still left Gregory distraught and even resentful. "This is the groaning of Gregory as he longs for the Anastasia, from which lazy jealousy once expelled him." So he now managed his current pain by transforming his earlier experiences into a dream world. In addition, in contrast to his means of coping with his despair a decade earlier over his brother's death, he did not indulge in a litany of earlier misfortunes or hysterical complaints. Not only did he not mention his past life, but he had transformed his tenure at Constantinople into an idealized dream.[14]

Short tenures had been a consistent feature of Gregory's sporadic episcopal career. He had refused to serve at Sasima, had been acting bishop at Nazianzus for less than a year after his father's death, and had led the Nicene congregation at Constantinople for about three years and served as official bishop for only a few months. His intermittent service as a bishop had become perhaps the most imposing obstacle to finding a consistent trajectory to his life's story. Gregory was certainly aware of his spotty record, and his uneasiness over his apparent fickleness seems to have been another catalyst behind the composition of some of his autobiographical poems after his return to Cappadocia. When he had remembered his service in the church of the Anastasia, he had not only been expressing his sense of loss and distress. He had also been trying to explain and justify his departure. Even though the Anastasia had been "my throne," the intrigues of others had compelled him to leave. He had been powerless, and all he could do now was grieve over "this church that another possesses."[15]

With these interpretations Gregory was trying to explain away an apparent contradiction in his behavior at Constantinople, the contrast between his proprietary claim on the Anastasia and his sudden abandonment of his episcopal service. Even though his tenure had been so brief, his love for his congregation had never wavered, and back in Cappadocia he had continued to dream about his own church in the capital.

Reluctance

Gregory provided another explanation for his short tenures that placed his departure from the capital in the longer context of "his trail of sorrows." In this lengthy poem he highlighted his consistent lack of ambition. Gregory addressed this poem to his former congregation at Constantinople, and again claimed them as his own by describing them as "once mine, but now another's." In this case, however, he was asserting more of an emotional and personal attachment to the people than an ecclesiastical and official title to the see. When he mentioned his "trail of sorrows," he added an ironic concession, "or rather, of successes." In his perspective, although others might consider his tenures as bishop as successes, he thought of them as his misfortunes. The whole purpose of this retrospective poem was to demonstrate that he had never wanted to be a bishop, or even a lesser cleric.[16]

The consistent feature of his behavior had always been his reluctance to assume ecclesiastical office. When he mentioned again his mother's vow already before his birth, he stressed how as a result he had been offered to God. In Gregory's telling in this poem, this dedication had defined a consistent pattern of passiveness regarding ecclesiastical service. Already in this sacrifice by his parents he had had no say. In his early life Gregory had taken the initiative only twice, once by acknowledging his "burning passion for culture" and going to study at Alexandria and Athens, and then by deciding upon a life that combined solitude and practical involvement. "The sanctuary of a church was holy for me, but only when I was standing at a distance, just as the light of the sun [overpowers] weak eyes." Both preferences, one for classical culture and the other for a life of disengagement, would have inhibited him from becoming a cleric.[17]

But because of pressure from others, for decades Gregory had been unable to fulfill his own preferences. His father "tyrannized" him into becoming a cleric, and then begged him to return from his self-imposed exile. His friend Basil, with the support of Gregory's father, compelled him to become bishop of Sasima, and his father then asked him to assist as auxiliary bishop of Nazianzus. After his father's death some pious people insisted that he remain as bishop, until finally he fled again. A few years later when he went to Constantinople, it was "at the summons of many pastors and their lambs." "And so I arrived, not of my own will but kidnapped by forceful men." After his confrontation with his rival Maximus over the leadership of the Nicene community in the capital, Gregory was so depressed that he hinted at leaving. The people in his community responded by posting a watch on his movements, and they begged him to stay. He agreed, but only until the expected arrival of other bishops. "They thought that they were keeping me, but I thought that I would be staying for only a short time." After the emperor Theodosius arrived in the capital, people shouted that Gregory should become bishop. Gregory demurred by explaining that the timing was inappropriate. He finally allowed the bishops at the general council in 381 to consecrate him as bishop, but only because he hoped to mediate the various disputes. Once the arguments spun out of control, he had one goal only, "departure, which would bring relief from all these evils." After two decades of bowing to the wishes of others, he again had the opportunity to follow his own dictates: "I now leave willingly." He had chosen his devotion to classical culture; he had chosen a life of seclusion; the third choice Gregory had ever made in his life was his decision to leave the capital.[18]

Gregory had left Constantinople following objections from other bishops that his consecration as bishop of the capital was improper and noncanonical. In this poem, by demonstrating that he had never accepted his consecration as bishop at Sasima and that he had served only as acting bishop at Nazianzus, he was not suggesting that he could therefore legitimately become bishop at Constantinople or that he still had a claim on the see. Instead, he was arguing that he had never wanted to become bishop anywhere. Although he did hope to contradict some of his opponents' accusations, this poem was not a special plea for the rightness of his consecration as bishop of Constantinople, and he did not care about the "long-obsolete canons" that had been cited against his consecration. Gregory claimed that he was disengaged from the burdensome values of Greek aristocrats that compelled them to compete over prestige and status. He now presented himself as a man with no ambitions. All he had ever wanted was "a life without a [bishop's] throne, a life without distinction but also without danger." In the end, he was grateful for the opportunity to leave Constantinople, since it finally allowed him to resume the life of solitude and occasional engagement that he, and not someone else, had decided upon twenty-five years earlier. Gregory may have been bitter about the carping, but he was relieved to have left. "I will shroud myself in God."[19]

Gregory's interpretation of his life in this poem is, yet again, certainly suspect, since it would otherwise be difficult to understand why people were so insistent on the leadership of a man who repeatedly declined public exposure, and why he himself so passively, but equally repeatedly, acquiesced. But in this poem, as in the others that he wrote after his return to Cappadocia, he had found another way of explaining his past behavior even as he justified it. His reticence about his earlier life seemed to lift him above the fray. His nostalgia implied that he had been forced to leave Constantinople despite his love for his beloved church there. His professed reluctance to advance his own career by serving as a bishop seemingly made him into a completely objective observer, whose evaluations reflected the disinterested opinions of an outsider rather than the partisan judgments of a participant. Whatever the inadequacies of these later poems as historical interpretations, they provided him with a very effective apologetic and critical stance. As a man with no ambition Gregory could now sniffle at any complaints about his actions at Constantinople, explain his departure from the Anastasia while professing his lasting love for the congregation, and criticize his opponents as bad bishops.[20]

A Big-City Bishop

In these poems Gregory had highlighted a constant trajectory in his life by emphasizing his discretion, nostalgia, and sorrow. By creating a consistent literary characterization he had wanted to imply a lifelong consistency in his own character. But however effective these apologies may have been for readers at the capital, back in Cappadocia Gregory had become a misfit. In order to accommodate his experiences at Constantinople, he had created an image of himself that was no longer attractive at Nazianzus. He had most likely not anticipated that at his hometown these sorts of explanations would become more evidence of his shortcomings. A few months after writing this poem about his reluctance to serve as a bishop and his relief for the opportunity to resume a life of solitude, he again began serving as acting bishop of Nazianzus. Because this became a difficult tenure, he wrote more poems about his new misfortunes.[21]

In one poem he seemed to be responding to various complaints from locals. Some apparently had criticized him for exposing his litany of misfortunes so often. "Many grumbled and did not believe in my sufferings, and they either said or thought that in my arrogance I was belittling the people who were in God's image." Others had wondered why he had not resumed his service as bishop of Nazianzus more quickly. Gregory's response was that he never had accepted the see in the first place. "I have not rejected the beloved throne of my great father. It is not possible, nor is it proper, to contest the laws of God. The law had given [the throne] to him." In another poem he responded to resistance to his attempt to find an appropriate full-time bishop for Nazianzus. Again there were critics, including leading clerics. "Foremost were those who hold the second thrones, the leaders of the people and the elders, a distinguished council, who were not favorable to us. Who expected that? Some . . . were two-faced and two-colored like some cloaks, with [one color] on the outside in our presence but steadfastly evil on the inside. . . . Others were not secretly hostile but completely open, embarrassed if they seemed reluctantly evil."[22]

Not surprisingly, Gregory's term as acting bishop at Nazianzus was brief, only about another year, before a relative took over as permanent bishop. This time there were perhaps few regrets about his departure. Soon after resuming episcopal duties at Nazianzus, he had defined himself again in terms of his suffering. "My reputation is in my misfortunes." "I am a new Job." For all his protests about his lack of ambition, Gregory had always remained concerned about his local standing, as resolute about his personal prestige as Basil and Gregory of Nyssa had been during their hounding of Eunomius and his theology. After his return to Cappadocia he had developed a more or less consistent viewpoint for narrating the trajectory of his past. Highlighting his misfortunes and presenting himself as a victim had given him a stance from which he could criticize other bishops and justify his own intermittent service as a bishop. But at Nazianzus people were more concerned about the immediate issue of episcopal leadership, especially after so many years of enduring an empty see. And they seem to have held Gregory responsible for their predicament.[23]

In an ironic twist that Gregory himself would have ruefully appreciated, although at Constantinople he had been criticized for his small-town background, at Nazianzus people were wary because he had once been a big-city bishop. "Some say that because I accepted a great throne such as the one I left, I despise the poor and insignificant." A life story that highlighted his escapades at the capital had become a liability back in Cappadocia. Gregory had repeatedly analyzed his experiences at Constantinople in order to understand and manage them to his own satisfaction. But by reviewing them so often, he became suspect to people at Nazianzus, who seemed to think he was obsessed with his tenure at the capital. Local citizens, and eventually he himself, concluded that he was no longer fit to be a small-town bishop. So he retired to his estates.[24]

His brother Caesarius' service at the imperial court at Constantinople had been deeply disturbing for Gregory's parents, since it had taken their son away from their family and their province. Gregory's service as bishop at Constantinople would be a similarly upsetting experience, difficult to explain to people back in Cappadocia, equally difficult to incorporate into a consistent life story. To serve at the capital, whether as court official or bishop, a local notable had to have ambition and a desire to rise above his hometown and his native province. Caesarius had been aggressively ambitious; so too, even if belatedly, was Gregory. Although he did not want to admit it, Gregory could sense that his service at the capital seemingly had left him tainted in the eyes of his fellow Cappadocians. Despite his continued involvement in local affairs, he now seemed to be more interested in cosmopolitan concerns than in provincial issues, more a Constantinopolitan than a Cappadocian. In the long run, even his burial in Cappadocia seemed inappropriate.[25]

In the mid-tenth century the emperor Constantine VII Porphyrogenitus was dismayed to learn that Gregory's remains were still buried in Cappadocia. He had himself carefully studied Gregory's orations, and he attributed his growth as a Christian and an emperor to their influence: "I was nourished by the milk of your theological treatises." From his perspective in Constantinople it was an embarrassing oversight that Gregory seemed to have been discarded as a "foreigner, lying exposed to the open air," when he should have remained with "the flock he had tended" at the capital. "The land of the Cappadocians kept his body as if [he were] their guardian and founder, but it was neglected and deprived of its proper honor." In fact, when the emperor's envoys arrived in Cappadocia, they were unable to find Gregory's tomb and had to pray for a divine revelation. They finally found his remains by tracking down the "ineffable fragrance" that seeped from his bones. As they then returned with Gregory's remains through Asia Minor, angels were thought to have escorted the cortege.[26]

Constantine joined the procession in the suburbs and greeted the arrival of Gregory's remains with a festival at the capital. In his laudatory panegyric he welcomed Gregory back first to the imperial palace, then to the Church of the Holy Apostles, where his body was placed in a "fiery red sarcophagus." One later commentator thought the brilliant color of his tomb was certainly appropriate, because during his tenure at the capital Gregory himself had "glowed red with spiritual beauty" as he incinerated heresies. Constantine and subsequent emperors soon joined with the bishops of Constantinople to incorporate veneration of this champion of orthodoxy into their public rituals, since on the Monday after Easter emperor and patriarch would pray together and light candles before his sarcophagus before processing to the tombs of earlier emperors and patriarchs. In Cappadocia, Gregory had been honored simply as a local founder; at Constantinople, Constantine now suggested that he should become the "protector and defender of the empire."[27]

The translation of Gregory's relics had hence marked another rewriting of the meaning of his life. Because his despair over the circumstances of his departure had always tainted his memories of Constantinople, Gregory had been relieved to go home to Cappadocia. In contrast, Constantine now stressed Gregory's wish to serve again at the capital, and he highlighted instead his triumphant return. "Then we were instructed about his separation from us, but now we learn from his return." In this new perspective Gregory's relationship with the capital had been reversed, and he was now a successful resident rather than a failed outsider. "The Church [of the Holy Apostles] was an image of heaven. It sparkled and gleamed from its own glory, and from the glory of the Theologian." With the transfer of his body from Cappadocia to Constantinople, Gregory of Nazianzus had become Gregory the Theologian.[28]

Snow was falling as his remains arrived at the Church of the Holy Apostles. These flurries would have been a gentle reminder of the kingdom of snow that he had left behind in Cappadocia. Gregory himself might have been a bit reluctant to regain his standing as an honored former bishop of the capital, since the price he would have to pay was the loss of his homeland and the abandonment of his beloved parents. According to Constantine, in his revived zeal to restore the doctrine of the Trinity at the capital Gregory had now indeed done the unthinkable by "forgetting about his home and his father." But perhaps he would not have been completely dismayed, because

in addition to his tomb in the Church of the Holy Apostles, some of his remains were placed in his former church, the Anastasia. At Nazianzus, Gregory
had served as an interim bishop in a church built by his father, and at Constantinople he had acquired control of the major churches entirely through
the intervention of the emperor Theodosius. Only in the Anastasia had he
been able to develop and nuture his own community. The veneration of his
relics at the Anastasia was therefore a much more appropriate, and satisfying,
coda to his relationship with the capital. In the end, Gregory would be returned to the one church that had been his own, the church of his dreams.[29]

Vital Truths

Gregory once thought that the vicissitudes of his life would become the
stuff of legends: "a narrator of my misfortunes will remember Gregory."
Although later authors did write accounts of Gregory's life, they added few
if any apocryphal stories. Probably the first to compose such a *Life* was
Gregory the Priest, who lived most likely in the late sixth or the early seventh century and served as a cleric perhaps at Caesarea in Cappadocia. In
comparison to the great Theologian, Gregory the Priest saw himself merely
as a journeyman mason, "collecting information about him here and there
from his writings," then assembling these "bricks" into a single structure.
His most important sources were the long autobiographical poems that
Gregory had composed in his final retirement, "in which I found most of
the information for this account." Occasionally he added a few details that
he had gleaned from some of Gregory's orations and letters, or he deviated
a bit from Gregory's accounts. He also inserted a few details that were not
attested in Gregory's own writings, such as the observations that Gregory
had been baptized after his return to Cappadocia from Athens, that he had
himself baptized his rival Maximus at Constantinople, and that he had celebrated the arrival of the emperor Theodosius at the capital with a series
of panegyrics. But overall Gregory the Priest was quite reluctant to add new
bits of information or even comments of his own. Even his one significantly
new claim, the clearly mistaken assertion that Gregory had lived in Constantinople for twelve years, he seems already to have sensed was dubious,
since he attributed it to "rumor." Gregory the Priest was remarkably true
to Gregory's own narratives. Such fidelity came with a price, however, because at least one reader soon complained that the *Life* was unworthy of its
subject's life. But perhaps in this case Gregory the Priest had been only too
aware of the responsibility imposed by his own name. At the end of the *Life*

he asked his readers to "remember your Gregory, who composed this brief account for you." As Gregory's homonymous proxy, the best he could do, and the most he should do, was to abbreviate Gregory's poems. Gregory the Priest's biography was essentially a prose version of Gregory's autobiographical poems.[30]

In the early tenth century Nicetas the Paphlagonian composed an encomium on Gregory. Although his primary sources were Gregory's own writings, he was not much interested in Gregory's actual life. Not only did Nicetas likewise not add any new information, but he barely touched on the details of Gregory's life. He was more interested in eulogizing theology, not necessarily Gregory's theology, but simply theology in general. "I am speaking about Gregory, who was named after the most divine theology or, to be more precise, who is theology itself." For Nicetas, Gregory had been both the Theologian and the embodiment of theology. Unlike the historians and biographers who had fleshed out Basil's life with additional specific episodes, Nicetas compressed the specific details about Gregory's life into a series of general truths. Nicetas transformed Gregory into an abstraction.[31]

In subsequent centuries new apocryphal stories about Gregory were rare. Later Byzantine authors who wrote about his life consistently used the same sources, usually the autobiographical passages from Gregory's long panegyric about Basil, his lengthy poem about his own life, and Gregory the Priest's *Life*, and at most elaborated this information with their own rhetorical flourishes or personal observations. By repeatedly rewriting the narrative of his life and reinterpreting its meaning, Gregory had already blurred the distinction between autobiography and fiction. As he had reconstructed his life's story in his metrical autobiographies, he had transformed his memoirs into the equivalents of novels. "Autobiographers rely mainly on artifices of selection; novelists, on those of invention. But both communicate vital truths through falsifications."[32]

Gregory had seized control of his afterlife both by highlighting selected episodes from his life and by constantly inventing new interpretations. His experiences at Constantinople had been a powerful catalyst to his search for a stable, unwavering identity by compelling him to fit his episcopal tenure there into a consistent trajectory for his entire life. But in this search for an orthodox self, Gregory had also constructed an array of apocryphal identities. By composing a series of autobiographical poems he had already created a series of possible selves that were all retrospective falsifications of his life. Later biographers could make up little about Gregory that he had not already made up about himself.

Epilogue:
A Different Late Antiquity

Cappadocia might well have had a different late antiquity. Gregory Thaumaturgus had originally left Pontus to study Latin and Roman law at Beirut. While there, he might have been seduced from his legal studies not by biblical studies with the Christian teacher Origen, but by the delights of classical Greek culture. During the mid-third century, perhaps already when Gregory would have been a student there, one grammarian at Beirut was Lupercus, who made his reputation by composing a volume on the rules of grammar, another on Attic dialects, another on the Greek word for "peacock," and no fewer than thirteen volumes on linguistic genders and three more on a single adverbial particle. Lupercus was obviously a fastidious scholar. To demonstrate the breadth of his knowledge he also wrote a book about . . . shrimp.[1]

Such painstaking scholarship might have been irresistibly attractive, and Gregory too might have become a grammarian or a rhetorician, perhaps at one of the great centers of higher education around the eastern Mediterranean, perhaps back in his homeland. There he might have become a model for other local teachers, such as Basil the Elder at Neocaesarea. Basil the Elder's family, and in particular his enterprising sons, might still have adopted Gregory Thaumaturgus as a patron saint, but in this alternative history it would have been as a secular holy man, an exemplar of classical Greek culture in an otherwise backward region.

Instead, Gregory Thaumaturgus had returned to his homeland to become the apostle of Christianity in Pontus and an inspiration as a model of a Christian life for Basil the Elder's sons. The Cappadocian Fathers became Fathers of the Church in Pontus and Cappadocia, not rhetoricians, municipal councilors, or husbands and fathers. They furthermore reflected on the past, each in his own way, Basil by evoking an earlier period of persecution and martyrdom, Gregory of Nyssa by composing biographies of Gregory Thaumaturgus and his sister Macrina, Gregory of Nazianzus by writing autobiographical poems. Their letters, orations, and poems are of course the primary sources of information for my trilogy about Cappadocia. They are also the models and inspiration. The Cappadocian Fathers were already offering an analysis of Cappadocia in late antiquity. My three volumes are all sequels, the latest in the long line of studies about late Roman Cappadocia that extends back to their writings, to Eustochius' encyclopedia of Cappadocian antiquities, to Eutychianus' chronicle of the emperor Julian's campaigns, and to Philostorgius' ecclesiastical history.

If Cappadocia's late antiquity might have turned out differently, it also ran the risk of being forgotten entirely. Cappadocia had always been a liminal zone. In the distant past it had been on the edge of the Persian empire, and even after being included within the Roman empire it had remained an outlying region, on the margin of the world of Greek culture, midway between Constantinople and Antioch, not quite a frontier district but still a borderland. With the retreat of Roman rule Cappadocia was suspended between the Byzantine empire and various Muslim caliphates, and the region gradually became a nether world of romantic fantasy and heroic myths. One Byzantine legend claimed that Alexander the Great had asked to be buried at "the mountain with twin peaks near Caesarea," where he had already stockpiled gold, pearls, and valuable gems. The warrior Digenes Akrites lived on in the legends about his celebrated exploits, over and over strangling a lion, fighting bandits, and romancing an Amazon princess. Other legends commemorated the epic of St. Georgius, who rescued a king's daughter and saved his homeland from a fearsome dragon. Night after sleepless night Scheherazade would keep the sultan entranced, and herself alive, with amusing tales about a beautiful princess from "Caesarea of Armenia." These days tourists go to Cappadocia primarily to see the exotic landscape, the "lion-coloured uplands," and the canyons filled with stone monoliths, tufa pyramids, and towering cones that from a distance resemble "a barrier of sharks' teeth." These modern pilgrims can then visit the wonderful cave churches and monasteries that later Byzantine churchmen, monks, and local dynasts carved in the soft volcanic cliffs and the rock cones. Ancient Cappadocia had gone underground: "The whole world seemed inside-out."[2]

Legends, myths, and a fairytale landscape have likewise upended many memories of the flourishing of Cappadocia in late antiquity. The arrival of the conquering Turks, the spread of Islam, and various natural disasters have also contributed to this process of forgetting. In the later eleventh century, two Byzantine generals initiated a campaign against the

Turks in central Asia Minor. "When they arrived at the metropolitan city of Cappadocia, that is, the celebrated Caesarea, they set up camp in the old city and fortified themselves within the ruins of its wall in place of a trench and a palisade. Long ago an earthquake had reduced almost everything to rubble. The few towers that remained were evidence, I think, of the city's earlier prosperity." This historian had good instincts, because during late antiquity Cappadocia had indeed been a dynamic and influential region, important to the eastern empire as a source of horses, armor, and clothing for emperors' campaigns against the Persian empire, important to ecclesiastical affairs for the theological and pastoral initiatives of its church leaders.[3]

The three great Cappadocian Fathers, their parents, and their siblings were not the only notable figures from or associated with the region during the fourth century. The emperor Julian, the heresiarch Eunomius, bishop Amphilochius of Iconium, and the historian Philostorgius all had direct personal ties, and teachers like Himerius and Libanius, orators like Themistius, and historians like Ammianus Marcellinus were all familiar with Cappadocia and Cappadocians. This book, together with *Families and Friends* and *Kingdom of Snow*, has tried to reveal some of the majestic historical riches that lie beneath the surface of their texts. The writings of the Cappadocian Fathers, especially when combined with the histories, orations, and letters of their contemporaries or near contemporaries, offer beguiling additional possibilities for studying the social and cultural history of the region, and of the later Roman empire in general. These extensive writings, both ecclesiastical and secular, have bequeathed wonderful stories and characters, and modern historians can now provide the plots, the themes, and the characterizations. There are still more than enough stories to fill another thousand and one sleepless Cappadocian nights with all the primary ingredients of historical narrative: precise analysis, creative interpretations, interesting personalities, and tall tales.

Abbreviations

Budé	Collection des Universités de France publiée sous le patronage de l'Association Guillaume Budé (Paris)
CChr.	Corpus christianorum (Turnhout)
CPG	*Clavis patrum graecorum.* CChr. (Turnhout). Vols. 1–5, ed. M. Geerard (1974–1987); Supplementum, ed. M. Geerard and J. Noret (1998)
CSEL	Corpus scriptorum ecclesiasticorum latinorum (Vienna)
Families and Friends	R. Van Dam, *Families and Friends in Late Roman Cappadocia* (University of Pennsylvania Press, 2003)
FC	Fathers of the Church (Washington, D.C.)
GCS	Die griechischen christlichen Schriftsteller der ersten Jahrhunderte (Berlin)
GNO	Gregorii Nysseni opera (Leiden)
IGR	*Inscriptiones graecae ad res romanas pertinentes*, Vols. 1, 3–4, ed. R. Cagnat et al. (Paris, 1906–1927)
Kingdom of Snow	R. Van Dam, *Kingdom of Snow: Roman Rule and Greek Culture in Cappadocia* (University of Pennsylvania Press, 2002)
LCL	Loeb Classical Library (Cambridge, Mass., and London)
NPNF	A Select Library of Nicene and Post-Nicene Fathers of the Christian Church (reprint, Grand Rapids, Mich.)
PG	*Patrologia graeca* (Paris)
PLRE	*The Prosopography of the Later Roman Empire* (Cambridge). Vol. 1, *A.D. 260–395*, ed. A. H. M. Jones, J. R. Martindale, and J. Morris (1971). Vol. 2, *A.D. 395–527*, ed. J. R. Martindale (1980)
SChr.	Sources chrétiennes (Paris)
Studia Pontica 3.1	*Studia Pontica III: Recueil des inscriptions grecques et latines du Pont et de l'Arménie*, Fascicule 1, ed. J. G. C. Anderson, F. Cumont, and H. Grégoire (Brussels, 1910)
Teubner	Bibliotheca scriptorum graecorum et romanorum Teubneriana (Leipzig and Stuttgart)
TTH	Translated Texts for Historians (Liverpool)

In the notes, B = Basil of Caesarea, GNaz = Gregory of Nazianzus, and GNys = Gregory of Nyssa.

Notes

Introduction

1. Pentecost: Acts of the Apostles 2:9. Cappadocian martyrs in 310: Eusebius, *De martyribus Palaestinae* 11.1c, 21–23, 25–27.

2. Compliment: Sozomen, *HE* 6.34, with the comprehensive survey of early Christianity in central and eastern Asia Minor in Mitchell (1993) 2:37–67. Council of Nicaea: Eusebius, *Vita Constantini* 3.7–8, with the comparison to Pentecost.

3. Otis (1958), provides an excellent short introduction to their theology.

4. Air: Eustratius, *Vita Eutychii patriarchae Constantinopolitani* 89, *PG* 86.2.2373D, with Maraval (1986).

Orthodoxy and Heresy Introduction

1. Arrows: GNaz, *Orat.* 43.43. Horse races: GNaz, *Orat.* 21.5. Stadium: GNys, *In inscriptiones psalmorum* 2.2, *PG* 44.492B.

2. Hanson (1988) 824–75, provides a perceptive account of the trinitarian controversy of the fourth century; other sympathetic readings of Arius and Arianism include Gregg and Groh (1981), Williams (1987), and Wiles (1996) 9–26. For the use of classical philosophy by Christian theologians, see Stead (1994).

3. Eunomius' teachings: Socrates, *HE* 4.7, with the discussion of Vaggione (1987) 167–70, (2000) 253–57. Walkers in heaven: Philostorgius, *HE* 9.3. GNys, *Contra Eunomium* 2.67, no power, 79–80, children, with Mosshammer (1990), for Gregory's theory of language. Quotation about an adequate analogy from Pelikan (1993) 45.

4. For surveys of interpretations of heresy, see Van Dam (1985a) 78–92, Clark (1992) 11–42, and Burrus (1995) 1–24.

5. Libanius: GNys, *Ep.* 13.2, τῆς μονογενοῦς σου παιδεύσεως. Riddle: *Anthologia Latina* 1.1.281.261–63, on *conditum*, with Gowers (1993) 48n.214.

6. Arius' songs: Philostorgius, *HE* 2.2. For Gregory's poems about theology, see Chapter 10, and *Families and Friends*, Chapter 10. Art and theology: Mathews (1993) 52, "The images of the fourth century played an important role in this struggle to define who Christ was." Gestures: Sozomen, *HE* 4.28, Theodoret, *HE* 2.31, describing a sermon by bishop Meletius, with Spoerl (1993), and Drecoll (1996) 10–15. Aetius' flatulence: see the fragments of the lost *Contra Eunomium* by Theodore of Mopsuestia, in Vaggione (1980) 413–19. Vaggione (2000) 14, suggests that Aetius may have been a native of Cilicia. If so, then his heritage may have contributed to his

choice of an expressive medium, since in the early Roman empire the people of Tarsus were noted for their "snorting": see Jones (1978) 73–74.

7. Aetius the Groaner: Vaggione (1980) 419n.2. Eudoxius: Socrates, *HE* 2.43, Sozomen, *HE* 4.26. Sisinius' quips: Socrates, *HE* 6.22, Sozomen, *HE* 8.1. Council of Constantinople: GNaz, *Carm.* II.1.11.1720–32.

8. Eunomius: GNys, *Contra Eunomium* 1.608–10. For an attempt to interpret Basil's puns, insults, and irony as a sense of humor, see Tsananas (1980).

9. For the nature of friendship, see *Families and Friends*, Chapter 8; for Gregory of Nazianzus and Julian, *Kingdom of Snow*, Chapter 11.

Chapter 1. Eunomius as a Cappadocian Father

1. Hermogenes: B, *Ep.* 81, "the man who wrote the great unassailable creed at the great council"; *Ep.* 244.9, "the Nicene Creed originally pronounced by that man"; *Ep.* 263.3, "bishop Hermogenes of Caesarea." Asterius the Cappadocian: Athanasius, *De synodis* 18, ed. Opitz (1935–1941) 245, Socrates, *HE* 1.36, Sozomen, *HE* 2.33. For excellent discussions of Asterius, see Grillmeier (1975) 206–14, Wiles and Gregg (1985), and Hanson (1988) 32–41. Dianius: *Synodicon vetus* 42. Euphronius: Eusebius, *Vita Constantini* 3.62.2, Sozomen, *HE* 2.19; Theodoret, *HE* 1.22.2, claimed he had supported "Arius' secret disease." For Gregorius, see *Kingdom of Snow*, Chapter 3; for Georgius and Eudoxius, see below. Another Cappadocian who acquired ecclesiastical prominence was Auxentius, who was a priest at Alexandria when in 355 the emperor Constantius selected him to become bishop of Milan: see McLynn (1994) 20–44. Ulfilas: Philostorgius, *HE* 2.5, ancestors; Sozomen, *HE* 6.37.6, bishop; with the excellent discussions in Wolfram (1988) 75–85, and Heather and Matthews (1991) 133–53.

2. Pearls: Philostorgius, *HE* 10.6. Verbosity: Socrates, *HE* 4.7. Descriptions of the lost *Contra Eunomium* by Theodore of Mopsuestia: Photius, *Bibliotheca* 4, with Vaggione (1980) 403, 406. Opponents: Jerome, *De viris illustribus* 120, with the list in Vaggione (1987) XIII. The treatises against Eunomius include [Basil,] *Adversus Eunomium* 4–5. Although later writers and many manuscripts attributed these two books to Basil, he was almost certainly not the author: see Cavalcanti (1976) 47–66, and Risch (1992) 3–12. Böhm (2001), suggests that Basil used these two books as sources for his *Adversus Eunomium* 1–3. Churchmen also wrote treatises against Anomoeans ("Dissimilars"), the insulting name sometimes applied to supporters of Eunomius' doctrines; for one such treatise by Gelasius, bishop of Caesarea in Palestine during the later fourth century, see Photius, *Bibliotheca* 102.

3. Quotation about quarrels from Gleason (1995) 28, in an excellent discussion of the feuds among sophists during the second century. For friendship and self-representation, see *Families and Friends*, Chapter 8.

4. As Eunomius' date of birth, Sesboüé, de Durand, and Doutreleau (1982–1983) 1:19, suggests ca. 335, Vaggione (1987) XIV, (2000) 2n.9, more plausibly, the mid- or late 320s. Villages: GNys, *Contra Eunomium* 1.34, "this native of Oltiseris," 105, 109; 3.10.50, "another [orator] from Oltiseris." Sozomen, *HE* 7.17, mistakenly confused Dakora, the place of Eunomius' later exile in Cappadocia, with his birthplace. For the locations of Oltiseris and Corniaspa, see Ramsay (1890) 264, 270, 302, and Hild

and Restle (1981) 215; the reference in GNys, *Contra Eunomium* 1.35, to Eunomius' "inheritance in Canaan" is perhaps an oblique allusion to Chamanene, a pre-Roman administrative district in northwestern Cappadocia mentioned by Strabo, *Geographia* 12.1.4, 12.2.10. Sasima: GNaz, *Carm.* II.1.11.439–45. Description of Basilica Therma from Jones (1971) 186; see also Hild and Restle (1981) 156–57, mentioning the ruins of the facade of a Roman fountain there.

5. GNys, *Contra Eunomium* 1.34, a sarcastic description of "that famous man with the surname of Priscus, the father of this man's father." Gregory seems to have quoted Eunomius himself in describing the family's assets to have included "the mill and the leather [= a tannery?] and the income from slaves." This passage does not imply that Priscus had himself been a slave, as suggested by Kopecek (1979) 146, even though Theodore of Mopsuestia, a later critic of Eunomius, claimed that his ancestors had once been slaves belonging to Basil's family: see Vaggione (1980) 420, 424. For the role of way stations in supplying the army, see Mitchell (1993) 1:250–53. Eunomius' father: GNys, *Contra Eunomium* 1.49, with *Families and Friends*, Chapter 4.

6. Loss of reputation: GNys, *Contra Eunomium* 1.34. Grandnephews: GNaz, *Ep.* 157.2, with *Families and Friends*, Chapter 3. On Procopius' usurpation and Sophronius' career, see *Kingdom of Snow*, Chapter 6; for the prominence of *notarii* in general, see Petit (1955) 363–69, Jones (1964) 572–75, and Mudd (1989) 58–62. Shorthand and early life: GNys, *Contra Eunomium* 1.50. For the possibility that Eunomius initially tried to make a career at Constantinople, see GNys, *Contra Eunomium* 1.50, 102, and Theodore of Mopsuestia, *Contra Eunomium*, tr. Vaggione (1980) 424–25, with Kopecek (1979) 146–50, and Vaggione (2000) 8–11.

7. GNys, *Contra Eunomium* 1.36, patron and guide, 37–45, Aetius' career. Philostorgius, *HE* 3.15, Aetius' career, 3.20, recommendation at Antioch from bishop Secundus of Ptolemais. Aetius' father: *Suda* A.571, although note that some manuscript readings make his father a conscript in, rather than a supplier of, the army. For arguments over the date of Aetius' birth and surveys of his career, see Kopecek (1979) 61–75, 101–32, dating his birth to ca. 313, and Vaggione (2000) 14–29, suggesting, implausibly, that his father had died in the 290s.

8. Tip of tongue: Philostorgius, *HE* 8.18. Geometry: Epiphanius, *Panarion* 76.2.2. Echoes: GNys, *Contra Eunomium* 1.46. Excellent discussions of Aetius' complicated ideas include Wickham (1968), Kopecek (1979) 227–97, and Hanson (1988) 365–71.

9. Gallus at Antioch: Ammianus Marcellinus, *Res gestae* 14.1, 7, 9, 11, with Downey (1961) 362–68. Plot, teacher: Philostorgius, *HE* 3.27. For Gallus' reputation as a leg breaker, see Ammianus Marcellinus, *Res gestae* 14.9.8.

10. Domitianus: Ammianus Marcellinus, *Res gestae* 14.7.9–19, with *PLRE* 1:262, "Domitianus 3." Sesboüé, de Durand, and Doutreleau (1982–1983) 1:19, and Hanson (1988) 612, presumably following the sequence of events in GNys, *Contra Eunomium* 1.47–51, suggest that Eunomius joined Aetius after Gallus' downfall; Kopecek (1979) 106, 145, Hanson (1988) 599–600, and Vaggione (2000) 148, are more plausible in suggesting that Eunomius joined Aetius before he went to Gallus' court.

11. Gallus as lion: Ammianus Marcellinus, *Res gestae* 14.9.9. GNys, *Contra Eunomium* 1.47, admission that Aetius was judged but did not share the same fate as Gallus' other supporters, 48, Aetius and Georgius. Letters: Socrates, *HE* 2.35. Aetius as deacon: Epiphanius, *Panarion* 76.1.1, with Haas (1997) 280–95, on Georgius'

tumultuous episcopacy. Philostorgius, *HE* 4.4, hometown of Eudoxius was Arabissus (then in Cappadocia, later included in the new province of Armenia Secunda), 4.5, 8, ordination of Eunomius and exiles; Philostorgius placed these events before the earthquake that shattered Nicomedia in August 358 (cf. *HE* 4.10). Appeal to Constantius and his letter against Eudoxius: Sozomen, *HE* 4.13–14.

12. Recall of exiles: Philostorgius, *HE* 4.10. Boot: GNaz, *Orat.* 21.22. Aetius later collected his doctrines in his *Syntagmation*, a revised version of an earlier "short treatise" published before 360, according to Wickham (1968) 550, precisely in October 359, according to Kopecek (1979) 225–27. Constantius' investigation of Aetius' teachings: Sozomen, *HE* 4.23. Condemnation of Aetius: Philostorgius, *HE* 4.12, Theodoret, *HE* 2.27.22–28.8. For the centrality of this condemnation of Aetius at the council, see Giet (1955).

13. Innovations: Theodoret, *HE* 4.18.8, mentioning a priest "trained in the letters of Eunomius and skilled in writing rapidly." Parmentier (1909), defends this reading; but note also Mark the Deacon, *Vita Porphyrii* 88, for a stenographer who knew "the symbols of Ennomus," with the discussion of Grégoire and Kugener (1930) 136. Reputation: Philostorgius, *HE* 4.9, claimed that bishop Macedonius of Constantinople had once been favorably inclined toward "the [teachings] of Eunomius," although note that Hanson (1988) 357n.43, suggests that this may have been a mistake for the teachings of Eudoxius.

14. Philostorgius, *HE* 4.12, debates at Constantinople and deposition of Aetius, 5.1–2, exiles, 5.3, consecration of Eunomius, for which Eudoxius also had the support of bishop Maris of Chalcedon. Eudoxius and Eunomius: Theodoret, *HE* 2.29, with Brennecke (1988) 63–64. Deposition and theology of Eleusis: Socrates, *HE* 2.42, Philostorgius, *HE* 5.3, 8.17, 9.13.

15. Eunomius at Cyzicus and Constantinople: Philostorgius, *HE* 6.1. His teachings: Theodoret, *HE* 2.29.7.

16. Sermons and departure: Philostorgius, *HE* 6.2–3.

17. Acacius and Eunomius: Philostorgius, *HE* 6.4–5, with Brennecke (1988) 75–76. For a council at Antioch in 361 that Constantius attended, see Athanasius, *De synodis* 31.1–3, ed. Opitz (1935–1941) 259–60, and Socrates, *HE* 2.45.

18. Philostorgius, *HE* 6.7, recall, 7.5–6, Eudoxius and Constantinople, 8.2–4, 6–7, appointment of bishops, 9.4, Lesbos and Chalcedon, with Cavalcanti (1976) 14n.33, and Brennecke (1988) 169n.73, on these new bishops. Invitation: Julian, *Ep.* 15, with *Kingdom of Snow*, Chapter 9.

19. Jovian's relatives: Philostorgius, *HE* 8.6.

20. Opponents: Eunomius, *Apologia* 1, 27. For Aetius' influence on Eunomius' theology, note that Eunomius annotated Aetius' *Syntagmation*: see Vaggione (1987) 165–67. Wickham (1969), and Vaggione (1987) 5–9, (2000) 227, argue that Eunomius originally delivered his apology, or at least a first version of it, at the council at Constantinople in January 360, Kopecek (1979) 303–6, at a council at Constantinople in December 359. By far the best introduction to Eunomius' doctrines is Vaggione (2000); for other discussions, see Kopecek (1979) 306–46, Hanson (1988) 617–36, Uthemann (1993), and M. R. Barnes (1993). For analysis of the philosophical influences on his ideas, see Daniélou (1956), who discusses the importance of Platonic mysticism, theurgy, and Aristotelian logic, and Rist (1981) 185–88.

21. Aetius and Eunomius: Philostorgius, *HE* 8.18. Note also Theodoret, *Haereticarum fabularum compendium* 4.3, *PG* 83.420B, "Eunomius transformed theology into mere logical technique," with Vandenbussche (1944–1945), on the validity of this hostile characterization.

22. Athanasius: Sozomen, *HE* 1.17.7. Decision not to publish: B, *Ep.* 9, dated to 362 by Pouchet (1992a) 120, to probably 364 by Hauschild (1990) 169n.76. Characterization of Basil: Philostorgius, *HE* 8.11.

Philostorgius, *HE* 4.12, described the council at Constantinople. After first mentioning Basil and Eustathius (the bishops of Ancyra and Sebasteia, respectively) as the leaders of those who endorsed the doctrine that the Son was "similar according to essence" to the Father, he described "another Basil," then only a deacon, who was clearly the future bishop of Caesarea. Philostorgius next mentioned a debate in which "Basil" was the leader of those endorsing "identical in essence" as a description of the Son, and Aetius and Eunomius, who were then both deacons, of those endorsing "different in essence." This debate ended when Aetius defeated Basil and his supporters. Since Philostorgius clearly stated that Basil and his supporters had previously tried to stop this debate by claiming that bishops should not argue about doctrine with deacons, this Basil who participated in the debate and who then accused Aetius before the emperor Constantius was certainly bishop Basil of Ancyra, not Basil of Caesarea as assumed by Hanson (1988) 381. Even though Basil of Caesarea did later become a champion of the formulation "identical in essence," Philostorgius was often quite cavalier in misrepresenting theological formulations. At the council at Constantinople in 360, it is more likely the debate was over "similar in essence," a formulation endorsed by Basil of Ancyra: see Kopecek (1979) 299–302. Vaggione (2000) 222n.136, suggests that this confrontation between Basil of Ancyra and Aetius took place at the earlier council at Seleucia.

23. Philostorgius, *HE* 8.2, appointment of Euphronius as bishop for "Cappadocia and Galatia next to Pontus," 9.4, common fathers; Theodoret, *HE* 2.29.12, "the man who had been stripped of episcopal rank consecrated bishops and priests." Philostorgius placed these appointments immediately after the emperor Julian's death (*HE* 7.15, 8.1). For Basil's ascetic writings, see Rousseau (1994) 354–59.

24. Contests: Philostorgius, *HE* 9.3. For the role of dialectical prowess in agonistic confrontations involving Eunomius, see Lim (1995) 109–48.

25. Philostorgius, *HE* 9.5, Procopius at Eunomius' villa (although note that Philostorgius excused Eunomius by claiming he was away at the time), 9.6, Cyzicus and Lesbos. Procopius' pardon of Cyzicus: Ammianus Marcellinus, *Res gestae* 26.8.6–11, with *Kingdom of Snow*, Chapter 6, for additional discussion of Procopius' usurpation and Valens' isolation. Socrates, *HE* 4.7, and Sozomen, *HE* 6.8, incorrectly placed Eunomius' episcopacy during the reign of Valens after the end of Procopius' revolt in 366, although Vaggione (2000) 292–94, suggests that Eunomius had been briefly restored to Cyzicus in 365 before Procopius' revolt.

26. For the maneuvering over Valens' religious preferences in 364–365, see Socrates, *HE* 4.1–2, 6, Sozomen, *HE* 6.7, 10–12, with Brennecke (1988) 183–86.

27. B, *Ep.* 223.5, a recollection of earlier meetings with Eustathius; *Ep.* 9, discussion of theology; with Lipatov (2001), for a possible preview of Basil's doctrines. This council at Lampsacus met in early summer 364: see T. D. Barnes (1993) 161; its

decisions: Sozomen, *HE* 6.7. For the probable participation by Eleusius, bishop of Cyzicus, see Socrates, *HE* 4.4, 6, Sozomen, *HE* 6.8. Despite the claim by Philostorgius, *HE* 9.13, that the see of Cyzicus remained empty after Eunomius' departure, Eleusius seems to have returned and served at least until the early 380s: see Socrates, *HE* 5.8, 10, Sozomen, *HE* 5.5, 14–15, 7.7. Gribomont (1981) 35–38, suggests that Basil completed his *Adversus Eunomium* in 364, Sesboüé, de Durand, and Doutreleau (1982–1983) 1:42–45, before 366, possibly in 364, and Hauschild (1990) 17, before autumn 365; Drecoll (1996) 45–46, 145–46, argues that he completed the first two books in 364, and added the third in 365

28. B, *Adversus Eunomium* 1.1, falsehood. For summaries of and comments on Basil's arguments in the *Adversus Eunomium*, see Cavalcanti (1976) 27–46, Kopecek (1979) 372–92, and Anastos (1981); Rousseau (1994) 93–132, analyzes it in the context of Basil's formation as a churchman, and Drecoll (1996) 43–146, as an early formulation of his Trinitarian theology.

29. B, *Adversus Eunomium* 1.1, Galatian, love of honor, 2, "guise of an apology," 3, boasting, 5, babbling and logic. Georgius: GNaz, *Orat.* 21.14, 16. Gregory was apparently unaware that although Georgius had lived in Cappadocia, he had been born at Epiphania in Cilicia: see Ammianus Marcellinus, *Res gestae* 22.11.4.

30. Later reading: Photius, *Bibliotheca* 137. For the employment of verbal abuse to reinforce social hierarchy, see Peachin (2001).

31. Sophist: B, *Ep.* 20, dated to 365 after Basil's return to Caesarea by Hauschild (1990) 174n.121; Leontius, the recipient, may have been a sophist in Galatia, or even the governor of Galatia in 364–365: see *PLRE* 1:500–501, "Leontius 9" and "Leontius 10," and Pouchet (1992a) 141–43. Fire at Sodom: GNaz, *Orat.* 43.67.

32. Conversation: GNys, *Contra Eunomium* 1.98, "I remember his holy voice when he spoke about Eunomius." Amphilochius: B, *Ep.* 232–36; reference to Anomoeans ("Dissimilars") in *Ep.* 236.1, dated to early 375 or perhaps 376 by Hauschild (1993) 204nn.181, 186, to spring 376 by Pouchet (1992a) 349. Eunomius: B, *Ep.* 244.9, dated to autumn 375 by Hauschild (1993) 214n.302.

33. Philostorgius, *HE* 9.6, Aetius' death, 7, Eunomius' expulsion (with the correction in the critical apparatus of Bidez' edition), 8, exile by Auxonius, who was prefect of the East from 367 to 369 (*PLRE* 1:142–43, "Auxonius 1"), 11, Modestus, 13, Demophilus, who succeeded as bishop of Constantinople in 370.

34. Julian's body: Philostorgius, *HE* 9.18. Although overlooking this reference from Philostorgius, Grierson (1962) 40–41, dated the transfer of Julian's body to the Church of the Holy Apostles in Constantinople to Theodosius' reign. In 382 Theodosius presided over the burial of Valentinian I at Constantinople: see *Consularia Constantinopolitana* s.a. 382, with Johnson (1991) 502; so perhaps Eunomius thought he could earn the emperor's favor by retrieving Julian's body and providing another opportunity for a public funeral. Di Maio (1978), argues that Julian's body was not brought to Constantinople until the sixth century or later. Commentary: Socrates, *HE* 4.7. Letters: Philostorgius, *HE* 10.6, Photius, *Bibliotheca* 138. Soul: Nemesius of Emesa, *De natura hominis* 2.104–5, ed. Morani (1987) 32–33. For Eunomius' other works, see Vaggione (1987) 165–90. It is not obvious why Jerome mentioned Eunomius' reputation in his *Chronica* under the year 373, when Eunomius was in exile.

35. Since it is no longer extant, Eunomius' *Apologia apologiae* must be reconstructed from citations in the responses by Gregory of Nyssa and other authors; the best reconstruction is Vaggione (1987) 99–127. GNys, *Ep.* 29.8, characterized the two goals of Eunomius' treatise as "invective against us" and "refutation of healthy doctrine." For the possibility that Eunomius was familiar with Basil's sermons about the Hexaemeron, see van Esbroeck (1988), with Chapter 6.

36. Eunomius' dream: GNys, *Contra Eunomium* 1.24, with Daniélou (1956) 430, "il a aussi des allures de mystagogue." Aetius' dream: Philostorgius, *HE* 3.15. GNys, *Contra Eunomium* 1.25, labors and trials, 29, tragedy, 35, reputation.

37. GNys, *Contra Eunomium* 1.74, liar, 78, competition, 79, Basil's flight and cowardice, 111–12, Cyzicus, 119, cowardice. Eunomius' accusation that Basil was a παρέγγραπτος, a "pretender," "improper intruder," or even "carpetbagger," was perhaps a sly comment on his opponent's own origins, since Basil had made his ecclesiastical career in Cappadocia even though he had been born most likely in Pontus: see *Families and Friends*, Chapter 1.

38. GNys, *Contra Eunomium* 1.22, hatred, 74, madness, 537, judgment.

39. Philostorgius, *HE* 3.15, Aetius' impact, 8.12, Basil's depression. In *Ep.* 29.2 Gregory noted that because someone had loaned him a copy for only seventeen days, he had hardly had time to study or take notes on the two books.

40. Inheritance: GNys, *Contra Eunomium* 1.10, with May (1966) 128, on the importance of this debate for establishing Gregory's reputation as a theologian, and Bannon (1997) 158–73, on the tension between fraternity and fratricide in the legends of Romulus and Remus.

41. Peter's encouragement: [GNys,] *Ep.* 30.4. GNys, *Contra Eunomium* 1.13, Olympiads, 2.127, *Iliad.*

42. GNys, *Contra Eunomium* 1.28, fussiness, 29, falling asleep. Readings at Constantinople: Jerome, *De viris illustribus* 128. For the immoderate thoroughness of Gregory's refutation, see Photius, *Bibliotheca* 6: "His use of arguments and examples was excessive." For summations and evaluations of Gregory's doctrines, see Cavalcanti (1976) 70–105, and the essays in Mateo-Seco and Bastero (1988).

43. Mendacity: GNys, *Contra Eunomium* 1.105, "So if Basil called a man who had his residence on the border of [two] fatherlands in an unnamed remote corner of Corniaspa a Galatian rather than a native of Oltiseris . . . , for this he is called a liar?," 109, "[Basil,] the man of God, allowed a falsehood when he by chance mentioned the neighboring region because of ignorance or oversight of the name of that place." For confusion over the boundary between Cappadocia and Galatia, see Ramsay (1890) 315: "The bounds of Cappadocia on the north must have varied at different times." Wrestling: GNys, *Contra Eunomium* 1.82; for Basil and the imperial court, see *Kingdom of Snow*, Chapters 6–7.

44. GNys, *Contra Eunomium* 1.7, childish treatise, 14, vocabulary, 480–81, style, 549, syllogisms, 568, child; similar criticism of Eunomius' style in Photius, *Bibliotheca* 138. For a concise summation of Gregory's unspoken evaluation of the quality of Eunomius' education, note Kopecek (1979) 507: "the ancient equivalent of a correspondence course." For criticism of Gregory's criticism, note Meredith (1976) 318: "although he overtly criticizes the rhetoric and philosophy and newness of Eunomius, there is not a little of these elements to be found in him."

45. GNys, *Contra Eunomium* 1.245, leather worker, 601, millstone, 2.537, shorthand. GNys, *Contra Eunomium* 1.50, 3.7.25, again mentioned "the skill of Prunicus"; for Προύνικος as a "swift stenographer," see *Suda* Π.2904, and Lampe (1961) 1191.

46. Ignorance: GNys, *Contra Eunomium* 3.10.54, with the evaluation of Burrus (2000) 109: "this self-consciously naughty text."

47. Philostorgius, *HE* 9.18, new bishop, 19, Theodosius, 10.1, Antioch, 6, imperial court. Constantinople: Socrates, *HE* 5.20, Sozomen, *HE* 7.6, 17. After Valens' death the emperor Gratian visited the Balkans and apparently expelled "Eunomians" from their churches: see John of Antioch, *Frag.* 185 = *Suda* Γ.427, with *Kingdom of Snow*, Chapter 8, for Gregory of Nazianzus at Constantinople. The fundamental reconstruction of the sequence of publication of the books in Eunomius' *Apologia apologiae* and Gregory of Nyssa's *Contra Eunomium* is still Jaeger (1960); see also Vaggione (1987) 79–98.

48. Sozomen, *HE* 7.6: Flaccilla dissuaded her husband Theodosius from seeing Eunomius. Anathema: Council of Constantinople, *Canon* 1. Creed: Hanson (1988) 805–20. Edict of July 30, 381: *CTh* 16.1.3; restrictions on Eunomians: *CTh* 16.5.11–13, 17, 23. For the context of Eunomius' *Expositio fidei* in 383, see Socrates, *HE* 5.10, Sozomen, *HE* 7.12, with Wallraff (1997), and Vaggione (2000) 326–29, for discussion of this "council of all heresies." Conversion of Eunomians: Sozomen, *HE* 8.1.6. Philostorgius, *HE* 10.6, named Eunomius' estate in Cappadocia as Dakoroenoi; Sozomen, *HE* 7.17, called it Dakora and identified it as a village in the territory of Caesarea. Dakora is perhaps to be identified with Sadakora, mentioned by Strabo, *Geographia* 14.2.29: see Hild and Restle (1981) 192.

49. Gregory's opposition: Jerome, *De viris illustribus* 117, "adversum Eunomium libri duo." These two books were probably some of Gregory's sermons; for his disputes with Eunomians at Constantinople, see Gallay and Jourjon (1978) 29–34, Norris (1985), (1991) 53–68, and Lim (1995) 160–62. Poems: GNaz, *Carm.* I.1.2, with Moreschini and Sykes (1997) 67, 93–104. Evil: GNaz, *Ep.* 202.6, dated to ca. 387 by Gallay and Jourjon (1974) 26–27, to 383 by McLynn (1997) 304–8.

50. Bread: GNys, *Refutatio confessionis Eunomii* 115, with Jaeger (1960) XI, on the composition of the treatise. Story: GNys, *Contra Eunomium* 1.101.

51. GNys, *Contra Eunomium* 1.40, bracelet, 43, doctor, 103, Eunomius' fees. Sources: GNys, *Contra Eunomium* 1.37, mentioned that he had learned about Aetius from bishop Athanasius of Ancyra, who had also showed him a letter from bishop Georgius of Laodicea.

52. GNys, *Contra Eunomium* 1.103, Basil's generosity, 156–57, Ephesus.

53. Consultation: Sozomen, *HE* 7.17, with Vaggione (2000) 342–46, on disagreements among Eunomius' supporters. Nephew: Philostorgius, *HE* 12.11. Village in Syria: Theodoret, *Ep.* 81, ed. Azéma (1964) 196. Emperor Anastasius: *Anonymus Valesianus*, Pars posterior 13.78; for Eunomians in Thrace during the sixth century, see Procopius, *Anecdota* 1.15.

54. Theophronius: Socrates, *HE* 5.24, Sozomen, *HE* 7.17. Philostorgius, *HE* 3.21, encomium, 9.9, Philostorgius' family, 10.6, visit. Basil's presumptuousness: Photius, *Bibliotheca* 40.

55. Epigram: *Anthologia Graeca* 9.193, with Bidez (1913) XCIX–CI. Photius,

Bibliotheca 40, Philostorgius as liar and mythmaker. The most complete discussion of Philostorgius' life and history is still Bidez (1913) CVI–CXLIII; see also Emmett Nobbs (1990), and Chapters 5, 8.

56. Muddle: Sozomen, *HE* 6.25.7. Hatred at Caesarea: Philostorgius, *HE* 10.6. Book burning: *CTh* 16.5.34, dated to 398, with Philostorgius, *HE* 11.5.

57. Evaluation of Philostorgius: Photius, *Bibliotheca* 40, with Bidez (1913) XII–XVII, on Photius' excerpts. Although in *Bibliotheca* 138 Photius reviewed Eunomius' second apology, he did not have a copy and derived his information from the response of Gregory of Nyssa: see Vaggione (1987) 80. False name: Epiphanius, *Panarion* 76.54.32. Aetius the atheist: Socrates, *HE* 2.35. Eunomius the dissimilar: Philostorgius, *HE* 9.13. Puns on "Philostorgius": Philostorgius, *HE* 2.1, 11. For the rhetoric of vituperation used against Aetius and Eunomius, see Vaggione (1993) 181–89, (2000) 181–97.

58. Disputation and reputation: GNys, *Contra Eunomium* 1.56, 58. Wrestling: GNys, *In inscriptiones psalmorum* 2.13, *PG* 44.572B.

59. Libanius' students: GNys, *Ep.* 15.

60. Christian: B, *Moralia* 59, *PG* 31.792C, with Rousseau (1994) 228–32, dating the *Moralia* to before 361. For a fine discussion of Eunomius' deep concerns about soteriology and worship, see Wiles (1989); for Eunomius' inability to defend himself, Vaggione (1993) 213, on his promotion of moderate asceticism: "It was this incautious espousal of moderation which left him open to the . . . brickbats of his opposition."

61. Philostorgius, *HE* 9.6, Aetius' funeral at Constantinople, 11.5, Tyana, Eunomius' body, teacher; Caesarius was prefect of the East from late 395 to mid-397: see *PLRE* 1:171, "Caesarius 6." For the rivalry between Caesarea and Tyana, see *Kingdom of Snow*, Chapter 1. Kopecek (1979) 528, suggests that Eunomius died in ca. 394, Vaggione (2000) 359n.280, in the winter of 396–397.

62. Statues in the Forum of Constantine: *Parastaseis syntomoi chronikai* 39, with Dagron (1984) 141–43.

63. Quotation from Gould (1989) 25, in an entertaining discussion of these examples and the notion of historical contingency.

64. B, *Ep.* 258.2, creed, 4, Magusaeans, with Hauschild (1993) 224n.408, dating this letter to autumn 376, and Pourkier (1992) 42–46, 92–93, on Epiphanius and Basil. Epiphanius identified the Magusaeans as descendants of Shem, a son of Noah: see Epiphanius, *Ancoratus* 113.2, with Trombley (1993) 2:122–26, for other possible connections. Innovation: B, *De spiritu sancto* 6.13, 7.16; also B, *Ep.* 226.3.

65. Epiphanius, *Panarion, Rescriptum ad Acacium et Paulum* 1.2, medicine chest; *Panarion* 17.1.2, Daily Baptists, 37.2.6, Ophites, 39.1.3, Sethians, 52.2, Adamians, 55.1.2, Melchizedekians, 58.1.6–7, Valesians, with Pourkier (1992) 47–51, on the date of the *Panarion*. Five hundred years later Epiphanius' tome was still considered to be "the most extensive and most useful" handbook about heresies: see Photius, *Bibliotheca* 122.

66. Epiphanius, *Panarion, Recapitulatio brevis* 1, mothers; *Panarion* 60.1.1, Angelics.

67. For contingencies in the development of orthodoxy, see Pagels (1979) 170, on the implications of Gnostic writings: "They suggest that Christianity might have

developed in very different directions"; and Le Boulluec (2000) 308: "L'orthodoxie devient le produit de processus historiques." Hanson (1988) xx, 873, begins and ends his excellent survey of the development of trinitarian doctrine by describing it as a process of "trial-and-error." This formulation still begs the question of how to set the criteria for determining error; note Wiles (1996) 180, on Hanson's approach: "he is able to present the controversy as one . . . apparently little affected by its immediate historical context."

Conversion Introduction

1. Julian's arguments: Libanius, *Orat.* 18.178.
2. Heresies: Epiphanius, *Panarion* 47.1.2–3, with the survey of Mitchell (1993) 2:96–108.

Chapter 2. Christianity and Local Traditions

1. Amphilochius' request: B, *De spiritu sancto* 1. Three letters: B, *Ep.* 188, 199, 217. Specific biblical texts: B, *Ep.* 188, Can. 15, interpretation of Psalms 8:8, Can. 16, question about Naaman.

2. Mitchell (1993) 2:100–108, suggests that Basil and Amphilochius were responding to challenges from the many heterodox Christian communities in Phrygia, eastern Pisidia, Lycaonia, and northern Isauria. Hence his wry conclusion: "The Christianity of fourth-century Phrygia and Lycaonia presents an artless individuality quite different from the dragooned Orthodoxy of Basil's Cappadocia" (p. 107).

3. B, *Ep.* 188, Can. 3, degradation of deacons; *Ep.* 199, Can. 27, priests and "illegal marriage," 32, degradation for clerics who commit "the sin unto death"; *Ep.* 217, Can. 51, "single penalty," 55, clerics and bandits, 69, penalties for readers, 70, priests and deacons. Priests and oaths: B, *Ep.* 188, Can. 10, *Ep.* 199, Can. 17.

4. Comana: Harper (1968) 102–4, no. 2.08, dated to late second or early third century. Sebastopolis: *IGR* 3:43–44, no. 115, with Anderson (1903) 35–36. See also Jones (1940) 174–75, 227–28, discussion of the tenure of magistracies and priesthoods, and Mitchell (1993) 1:100–17, discussion of priests and priesthoods in the imperial cult, especially in Galatia, 199–204, survey of municipal magistracies and priesthoods.

5. Look back: Libanius, *Orat.* 2.42, with the survey of senatorial careers in Heather (1998): "there was a substantial group among the élite of the eastern Mediterranean whose lives followed a pattern of occasional and brief tenures of high office" (p. 192).

6. For the careers of Symmachus, see *PLRE* 1:865–70, and Matthews (1975) 12–17; of Martinianus, Aburgius, and Sophronius, *Kingdom of Snow*, Chapter 3; of Petronius Probus, *PLRE* 1:736–40, and Cameron (1985) 178–82. Fish out of water: Ammianus Marcellinus, *Res gestae* 27.11.3.

7. Wife and children: GNys, *Ep.* 18.5, with Pasquali (1923) 78–82, for the interpretation. Widow: GNaz, *Orat.* 36.6. For the careers of the Cappadocian Fathers, see *Families and Friends*, Chapters 1–3.

8. GNys, *Ep.* 17.6, God's affairs, 10, wealth, shadow, 28, friends. Favors: B, *Ep.* 290. Bishop at Comana: GNys, *Vita Gregorii Thaumaturgii, PG* 46.933B–940B.

9. On Basil's failure to become bishop, see GNaz, *Ep.* 41.10: while commenting on the choice of a successor for Eusebius, Gregory the Elder seemed to hint at some of the factors that had been influential in Eusebius' promotion in 362 when he worried that a faction, family influence, or a turbulent crowd might sway the selection "again." Backgrounds of Cappadocian bishops: Kopecek (1973). This trend was not unique to Cappadocia, since throughout the Roman empire most of the bishops of the fourth century were from curial backgrounds: see Eck (1978). Sermon, philosophy: GNys, *Vita Gregorii Thaumaturgii, PG* 46.936C, 937C.

10. GNaz, *Ep.* 87.5, does not belong; *Ep.* 182.4, canons, 5, bishop. For additional discussion of the restrictions resulting from lifetime tenure, see Van Dam (1985a) 69–78, (1986) 62–68.

11. Fifty χωρεπίσκοποι: GNaz, *Carm.* II.1.11.447. Jurisdiction: B, *Ep.* 142, mentioning a rural bishop who administered a poorhouse in a συμμορία, a "region." Villages near Isaura, a city in Lycaonia: B, *Ep.* 190.1. Discipline: B, *Ep.* 53, 54. See *Kingdom of Snow*, Chapters 1, 5, for the division of Cappadocia; Gain (1985) 94–100, for a survey of rural bishops; and Pouchet (1992a) 709, for a list of Basil's references. For an excellent discussion of the testy relationship between Basil and the rural bishops in Cappadocia, in particular after the division of the province, see Scholten (1992): "Chorbischöfe in allem gewöhnliche Bischöfe sind" (p. 152).

12. GNaz, *Ep.* 246.3, Glycerius as patriarch; *Ep.* 247, threats to Glycerius; *Ep.* 248, chiding Basil. Glycerius was deacon at Venasa, which is probably to be identified with Vanota: see *Kingdom of Snow*, Chapter 1. Gallay (1964–1967) 2:135n.2, dates this incident to between 370 and 375; for the correct assignment of these letters to Gregory and not to Basil (as [B,] *Ep.* 169–71), see Cavallin (1944) 81–92, and Gallay (1964–1967) 2:170–71.

13. GNys, *Ep.* 1.4, misfortunes, 6, meeting at the "metropolis," that is, Caesarea, 9–10, reception, 13, silence, 21–22, conversation, 24, meal, 25, storm. The authorship of this letter has been contested. Honigmann (1961) 32–35, Devos (1961a), and Gallay (1964–1967) 2:139, 171–72, assign it to Gregory of Nazianzus as [GNaz,] *Ep.* 249. For its correct attribution to Gregory of Nyssa, see May (1966) 120–21, Wyss (1984), Maraval and Hanriot (1984), and Maraval (1990a) 53–55.

14. GNys, *Ep.* 1.16, leper, 17, equal rank, 18, sinners, 31, council, 32, similar qualities, 35, vanity.

15. Anger, pain: GNaz, *Ep.* 219–20.

16. Consecration of Gerontius: Sozomen, *HE* 8.6; for the suggestion that GNys, *Ep.* 17, was a reaction to the selection of Gerontius, see Maraval (1990a) 39–41.

17. Bishops as models: GNys, *Ep.* 17.22–26. Law of spiritual promotion: GNaz, *Orat.* 43.25.

18. B, *Ep.* 199, Can. 23, brothers and sisters, and brother's wife; *Ep.* 217, Can. 68, forbidden kin, 78, penalty.

19. Second marriages: B, *Ep.* 160; for the identification of the recipient as the Diodorus who was a priest at Antioch and later bishop of Tarsus, see Pouchet (1986) 254–59, (1992a) 356–59. For penalties on relationships between stepsiblings, see B, *Ep.* 217, Can. 75; between a man and his daughter-in-law, Can. 76.

20. For the contours of Republican families, see Bradley (1991) 156–76; for late Roman senators, Evans Grubbs (1995) 153–54. Penalties for "polygamy": B, *Ep.* 188, Can. 4, 12; *Ep.* 199, Can. 18, 24, 50; *Ep.* 217, Can. 53, 77, with Giet (1941) 42–70, for a general survey of Basil's ideas about marriage. Stepmothers and incest: B, *Ep.* 217, Can. 79, with Dixon (1992) 143–44, on the stereotypes.

21. Quotation about marriage strategies from Bourdieu (1976) 141.

22. For "welcome gifts" from a suitor to the father of his future wife, see GNys, *Vita Macrinae* 4, with Evans Grubbs (1995) 156–71, on prenuptial gifts. Remarried father: B, *Hom. in Hexaemeron* 9.4. Remarried widow: B, *Ep.* 300.

23. Justinian's marriage: *CJ* 5.4.23, with Honoré (1978) 9–11. For the commonness of marriages between cousins in the eastern empire, see Patlagean (1977) 118–28, Lee (1988), O'Roark (1996), and van Bremen (1996) 258–59; Shaw and Saller (1984), argue that close-kin marriages were not common in the western empire. Treggiari (1991) 107–19, provides an excellent discussion of *affinitas*, "relationship by marriage"; Dixon (1992) 71–83, 90–95, and Gardner (1993) 123–26, discuss concerns over rank and status; see also Evans Grubbs (1995) 306, on Constantine's attempts "to re-establish traditional Roman status distinctions."

24. B, *Ep.* 199, Can. 22, general regulations, 25, rape and marriage, 30, widows and penalties on abductors, 38, girls; *Ep.* 217, Can. 53, widow.

25. Mother: GNys, *Vita Macrinae* 2, with *Families and Friends*, Chapter 6. Widow: GNaz, *Orat.* 43.56, with Van Dam (1996) 39–40, for the identification of the vicar.

26. Young woman: Basil of Ancyra, *De virginitate* 39.

27. Assistance: B, *Ep.* 199, Can. 30. Village: B, *Ep.* 270.

28. Quotation from Arjava (1996) 38. Snake: B, *Ep.* 270. Evans Grubbs (1989), (1995) 183–93, provides an excellent survey of marriage by abduction in late antiquity; for the influence of Basil's canons on later Byzantine legislation, see Laiou (1993).

29. B, *Ep.* 188, Can. 8, general regulations, 11, severity of injuries; *Ep.* 217, Can. 56–57, penalties. In *Ep.* 188, Can. 13, Basil noted that "our fathers" had not considered killing in war as homicide.

30. Bandits and pursuers: Hopwood (1989), and Shaw (1993). Judicial savagery: MacMullen (1990) 204–17. For Christian violence, see Chapter 4. Brothers: GNys, *Vita Gregorii Thaumaturgi*, PG 46.925B–928A. Dogs: B, *Hom. in Hexaemeron* 9.4.

31. Tomb as οἶκος: *Studia Pontica* 3.1:93, no. 70b, from Neoclaudiopolis; as δόμος: GNaz, *Epigram.* 91.9 = *Anthologia Graeca* 8.225. Warning: *Studia Pontica* 3.1:44, no. 30. Penalty: Moraux (1959) 11 = Woodhead (1962) 186–87, no. 561, from Neocaesarea. Note also B, *Ep.* 217, Can. 66, for ecclesiastical penalties for grave robbers. Village: B, *Ep.* 288.

32. Quotation about the use of violence from the analysis of Sicilian *mafiosi* in Blok (1974) 172. Difficulty: Basil, *Ep.* 217, Can. 54. For Basil's misunderstandings of the dangerous situation in Lycaonia and Isauria, see Lenski (1999) 322: "Basil's attempts to regulate local policing were unrealistic."

33. GNaz, *Ep.* 144.3–4, tears, laws, *Ep.* 145.1, executioners, with Clark (1999) 235–37, on the contrast between Roman law on divorce and Christian exegesis, and Evans Grubbs (1995) 242–60, on the variety of attitudes among Christians about divorce.

34. Diocletian: *Mosaicarum et Romanarum legum collatio* 6.4, partially quoted in *CJ* 5.4.17, issued in 295, with Evans Grubbs (1995) 100–101. Constantine: *CTh* 9.24.1, issued "to the people" in 326, with Seeck (1919) 61, 63, for the date, and Evans Grubbs (1995) 350–52, for discussion. In 374 Valentinian and Valens issued an edict that limited the opportunity for prosecution in cases of abduction to five years: see *CTh* 9.24.3.

35. Law and Latin: Gregory Thaumaturgus, *Oratio panegyrica in Origenem* 1.7, with Dagron (1969), a stimulating discussion of the use of Latin in the Greek East, and Millar (1999) 105–8, on Greeks studying Roman law. Hardly any Greek churchmen knew Latin: see Rochette (1997) 150–54, 251–53. Roman laws: GNaz, *Ep.* 78.6, with Van Dam (1985b) 13–17, on the difficulties of enforcing imperial edicts.

Chapter 3. Christian Narratives of Conversion

1. Compliment: GNys, *Vita Gregorii Thaumaturgi*, PG 46.909B, 953D. On the interpretation of legends about Gregory Thaumaturgus, see Van Dam (1982), Lane Fox (1987) 517–42, Slusser (1998) 1–16, and Mitchell (1999).

In the early fifth century Rufinus translated and expanded Eusebius' *Ecclesiastical History*. Eusebius, *HE* 7.28, had mentioned Gregory Thaumaturgus; when Rufinus translated that chapter, he inserted a long digression that described some of Gregory Thaumaturgus' miracles: for the text of this digression, see Rufinus, *HE*, ed. Mommsen, vol. 2, pp. 953–56, to be inserted at p. 703. Rufinus included an odd series of three disparate miracles: the resolution of a feud between brothers by making a lake go dry, the movement of a boulder to make space for a new church, and a confrontation with Apollo that led to the conversion of a priest. He also quoted a confession of faith that he claimed to have found in Gregory Thaumaturgus' *Metaphrasis in Ecclesiasten*. Although some of his stories were similar in outline to stories in Gregory of Nyssa's *Life* of Gregory Thaumaturgus, many details differed. Rufinus' source for these stories is unknown. He certainly knew about the Cappadocian Fathers, since he translated some of the writings of Basil and Gregory of Nazianzus; but since he did not mention any of Gregory of Nyssa's writings, he had most likely not used his *Life*. When Rufinus introduced these stories, he referred only to oral traditions: "the deeds of such a man are celebrated in everyone's conversations." Whatever the source, Rufinus was certainly not above modifying the facts to suit his audience. By the time he translated Eusebius' *History*, he was living at Aquileia, and a desire to make Gregory Thaumaturgus relevant to an audience in northern Italy might explain one absurd detail. In one story Rufinus had Gregory Thaumaturgus enter a temple of Apollo as he was travelling through the Alps!

2. GNys, *Vita Gregorii Thaumaturgi*, PG 46.908D–909A, "Phaedimus, at that time leader of the church at Amaseia," 933B, Comana. Sayings: B, *Ep.* 204.6, with Van Dam (1982) 280–88, on these oral traditions. Liturgy, criticism: B, *Ep.* 207.2, 4. Characters, listen: GNys, *Vita Gregorii Thaumaturgi*, PG 46.913A; for the ongoing debate over the authenticity of this creed, see Froidevaux (1929), Abramowski (1976), who argues that it was a later fabrication, Riedinger (1981), Hanson (1988) 785–86,

and Mitchell (1999) 108–16, who suggests that Gregory of Nyssa himself composed the creed. GNys, *Vita Gregorii Thaumaturgi*, PG 46.956A, mentioned that Gregory Thaumaturgus had declined to use "the place reserved for his tomb"; but by the sixth century there was a tomb in the church: see John Diacrinomenus, *HE* frag. 2 = *Epitome* 555.

3. GNys, *Vita Gregorii Thaumaturgi*, PG 46.948C, two trees.

4. GNys, *Vita Gregorii Thaumaturgi*, PG 46.928A, marsh, 932B–C, staff.

5. Peter in Asia Minor: Eusebius, *HE* 3.1.2, 4.2. Apostles, centurion: GNys, *Ep.* 17.14–15. For the legends about Longinus, see Aubineau (1978–1980) 2:779–804, 846–68, and Berges and Nollé (2000) 2:411–13. For his shrine at "Sandralis" or "Andrales" near Tyana, see [Hesychius of Jerusalem,] *Martyrium Longini* 15, *Passio et capitis inventio Longini* 17, with Maraval (1985) 374.

6. GNys, *Ep.* 2.2, Jerusalem, 5–7, temptations, 9, presence of God, 15, Bethlehem, 18, travel, 19, believers, with Kötting (1962), on later readings of the letter. For similar hesitations to concede the spiritual importance of holy places in Palestine by the historian Eusebius of Caesarea, see Walker (1990) 51–92.

7. B, *Hom. in Hexaemeron* 8.4–6, birds, 8, silkworm; for additional discussion of Basil's sermons, see Chapter 6.

8. Sojourn and memory: GNys, *Vita Macrinae* 1, with *Families and Friends*, Chapter 6, on Macrina.

9. Musonius' hospitality: GNys, *Vita Gregorii Thaumaturgi*, PG 46.921B–C. Bishop Musonius: B, *Ep.* 28, 210.3.

10. Ancestors: see *Families and Friends*, Chapter 1. Portraits of Maximinus: GNaz, *Orat.* 4.96. Gregory's description of these icons is ambiguous. These portraits may have depicted Maximinus on his deathbed, wasting away after being struck by "God's whip," or they may themselves have been mutilated, "their faces blacked out with dark paint": see Eusebius, *HE* 9.10, final illness, 11, destruction of portraits, with Kurmann (1988) 324–35.

11. For the Forty Martyrs, see Chapter 7, and *Families and Friends*, Chapter 3.

12. Treatise by Gregory Thaumaturgus: B, *Ep.* 210.5, with *Families and Friends*, Chapter 1. Gregory Thaumaturgus, *Oratio panegyrica in Origenem* 1.7, 5.58, Latin, 5.59–71, Beirut. For the nature of Origen's school at Caesarea, see Knauber (1968), Crouzel (1970), and Slusser (1998) 19–21. In defense of Gregory of Nyssa's omission, Gregory Thaumaturgus' *Oratio panegyrica* was most likely not available in Cappadocia: see Van Dam (1982) 281–82. GNys, *Vita Gregorii Thaumaturgi*, PG 46.901C, student, 901D–905C, Alexandria.

13. GNys, *Vita Gregorii Thaumaturgi*, PG 46.909A, power of prophecy. Note that by the ninth century Gregory of Nyssa had been blurred with Gregory Thaumaturgus and Gregory of Nazianzus into a lineage of "three Gregories, I mean the Thaumaturgus, the Theologian, and the holy man from Nyssa": see Photius, *Bibliotheca* 162.

14. For Gregory's family, see *Families and Friends*, Chapter 2. Ancient city: GNaz, *Epigram.* 30.1–2.

15. Montanist account of St. Theodotus: Mitchell (1982). Novatians and St. Autonomus: Foss (1987), and Mitchell (1993) 2:99, "a charter myth."

16. Jerusalem: GNaz, *Orat.* 43.59, with *Families and Friends*, Chapter 10.

Chapter 4. Ancient Legends and Foundation Myths

1. Disrepair at Caesarea: B, *Hom.* 7.4. Gregory Thaumaturgus' church: GNys, *Vita Gregorii Thaumaturgi, PG* 46.924B–C. For an earthquake at Neocaesarea in the mid-fourth century, see Jerome, *Chron.* s.a. 344, "Neocaesarea in Pontus was overturned, except for the church."

2. Commiseration, expansion, splendor: GNys, *Ep.* 17.17. Diocletian at Nicomedia: Lactantius, *De mortibus persecutorum* 7.8–10. Description of earthquake: Ammianus Marcellinus, *Res gestae* 17.7.2–8, 22.9.3–5. For the emperor Julian's earlier attempt at reviving Nicomedia, see *Kingdom of Snow*, Chapter 9. Foss (1995), surveys the impact of the foundation of Constantinople on the standing of Nicomedia.

3. Autopsy of Cappadocia: Strabo, *Geographia* 12.2.3, "my visit" to Comana, 4, "I saw" the Pyramus River. Strabo the Cappadocian: Josephus, *Antiquitates Iudaicae* 13.286, 14.35, 104, 111, 138, 15.9, and Constantine VII Porphyrogentius, *De thematibus* II, ed. Pertusi (1952) 63; with Clarke (1999) 229–30, and Dueck (2000) 4–5.

4. Strabo, *Geographia* 12.3.26, Homer and Pontus, with Dueck (2000) 31–40, on Strabo's reverence for Homer.

5. Strabo, *Geographia* 11.2.10, etymology, 12.2.3, Orestes at Comana (*kome* is the Greek word for "hair"), 12.2.7, Orestes and Tyana, with Berges and Nollé (2000) 2:331, for local legends about Orestes, 14.5.27, "the poet did not mention Cappadocia," with the survey of Strabo's comments about Cappadocia in Panichi (2000).

6. Heraclea Pontica: Menander Rhetor, *Treatise* I.358, ed. Russell and Wilson (1981) 56, with Strubbe (1984–1986) 258, for Hercules in northern Asia Minor. Strabo, *Geographia* 11.2.18, myths about Jason, 11.4.8, 13.10, memorials, 11.5.4, 12.3.21, Amazons as founders, 12.3.11, Autolycus at Sinope. Heniochians: *Periplus Ponti Euxini* 9. For classical myths about the Black Sea and the Caucasus, see Braund (1986).

7. Myth and history: Strabo, *Geographia* 11.5.3.

8. Strabo, *Geographia* 11.5.4–5, legends about Alexander, 12.3.28, garrisons, 12.3.30, Mithridates and Cabeira, 12.3.39, Amaseia.

9. Coin from Amaseia: Price and Trell (1977) 90–93. Lucullus' gardens: Plutarch, *Lucullus* 39.2, with Clarke (1999) 236–37, on the significance of Lucullus' plundering. Strabo, *Geographia* 12.3.1, divisions, 12.3.30, Magnopolis, 12.3.31, Diospolis, treasures, 12.3.39, Amaseia, 12.4.6, Troad.

10. Tieium: Strabo, *Geographia* 12.3.8.

11. Imperial cult at Caesarea: Price (1984) 269. Festivals for Commodus and Septimius Severus' sons: Mitchell (1977) 75–77, (1993) 1:218, 221; for Gordianus: Bland (1991) 217; with Van Nijf (1999) 184–85 = (2001) 316, "agonistic festivals were an invented tradition." Names of Neocaesarea: Strabo, *Geographia* 12.3.30–31, with Magie (1950) 1071n.11. GNys, *Vita Gregorii Thaumaturgi, PG* 46.897D, distinguished emperor, 956B–D, festival. Imperial cult: Price and Trell (1977) 94–97, and Price (1984) 150–51, 267. Games: Lane Fox (1987) 538.

12. Epigram: *Anthologia Graeca* 11.436. Career of Pausanias, a student of Herodes Atticus: Philostratus, *Vitae sophistarum* 593–94. Funerary imprecation: Moraux (1959), who suggests that the author may have studied with Herodes Atticus.

13. For indigenous and oriental names, see Robert (1963) 492–93, 503–40, and

Mitchell (1993) 2:29, on Cappadocia, "where Persian cults and Persian nomenclature are a distinguishing characteristic, especially of the aristocracy."

14. Longinus: Cyril of Scythopolis, *Vita Theodosii* 1, mentioning Longinus, an elderly Cappadocian ascetic at Jerusalem in the mid-fifth century. Theodorus or Theodora: *Studia Pontica* 3.1:195, 209, 211, 215, nos. 200, 217, 223, 234. Gift of God: GNaz, *Orat.* 11.1, with *Families and Friends*, Chapters 1–3, for the families of the Cappadocian Fathers. Note that Gregory Thaumaturgus' original pagan name had been Theodorus, "gift of god": Eusebius, *HE* 6.30, Jerome, *De viris illustribus* 65.

15. Diogenes: GNys, *Ep.* 21.2. "Basil" as grand name: GNaz, *Orat.* 43.10, with Kurmann (1988) 85, for *basileus* as "emperor." For the increasing use of Christian names in Egypt during the fourth century, see Bagnall (1993) 280–81; more widely, Salway (1994) 139–40.

16. Rivers, shrines: Libanius, *Orat.* 30.9. On the destruction of pagan temples, see Fowden (1978) and Van Dam (1985b).

17. Churches at Comana: Procopius, *Bellum Persicum* 1.17.18. Gordius: B, *Hom.* 18, with Zgusta (1964) 137, and *Kingdom of Snow*, Chapter 3, on the commonness of the name. Mamas: B, *Hom.* 23, with Robert (1963) 527n.9, "un nom certainement épichorique," and Zgusta (1964) 282–83. For the commonness of the name in Cappadocia, see GNaz, *Ep.* 225, a petition on behalf of a reader named Mamas, who had become a cleric despite being the son of a soldier. In passing, note one irony of Basil's panegyric about St. Mamas. More than likely he was delivering this oration in a shrine constructed for the martyr by the future emperor Julian. During his exile in Cappadocia the young Julian had been a Christian, but as emperor, he was a pagan: see GNaz, *Orat.* 4.24–26, Sozomen, *HE* 5.2.12, with the commentary in Kurmann (1988) 94–100, and *Kingdom of Snow*, Chapter 6. Shrine of St. Orestes: GNaz, *Orat.* 43.58, with Maraval (1985) 373, "un saint local." Later legends claimed that Orestes had been a martyr during the reign of Diocletian: see *Martyrium Orestis*, PG 116.120–28, with Hild and Restle (1981) 259, on the possible location of his shrine, and Berges and Nollé (2000) 2:394–96, for other references.

18. Tragedy and comedy: GNys, *Vita Macrinae* 3.

19. Actors and theater: GNys, *Ep.* 9.1, with Easterling and Miles (1999), on dramatic performances in late antiquity.

20. Mithridatic ruins: see Cumont and Cumont (1906) 152–65, on the citadel and royal tombs, and Price and Trell (1977) 91–92, on the tombs. Strabo, *Geographia* 12.2.8, Ariarathes' lake, 12.3.30, Mithridates' watermill, with Horden and Purcell (2000) 250: "The management of ambient hydrology was indeed linked with power." Founder, lawgiver: GNys, *Vita Gregorii Thaumaturgi*, PG 46.908A.

21. GNaz, *Orat.* 43.4, Basil's piety, 22, Orestes and Pylades, 37, pious bishops.

Chapter 5. The Founder of the Cappadocians

1. Mosoch the Founder: Philostorgius, *HE* 9.12, ἀπὸ Μοσὸχ τοῦ Καππαδοκῶν γενάρχου; for additional discussion of Eunomius, see Chapter 1, of Philostorgius, Chapter 8. Equation with Meshech: Josephus, *Antiquitates Iudaicae* 1.125, referring to Genesis 10:2. In the seventh century the polymath Isidore in Spain

likewise identified Mosoch, "from whom the Cappadocians [descended]," as a grandson of Noah: see Isidore of Seville, *Etymologiae* 9.2.30.

2. Swerving: Philostorgius, *HE* 9.12, κατὰ παρέγκλισιν. To save Philostorgius from his befuddlement one seventeenth-century editor proposed changing the name of the city in this passage to "Mozoka": see the critical apparatus in Bidez' edition. Since in the tenth century the emperor Constantine VII viewed imperial administration through the lens of antiquarianism, he too mentioned Mosoch, with a slightly different spelling and description: see Constantine VII Porphyrogenitus, *De thematibus* II, ed. Pertusi (1952) 65, ἀπὸ Μουσὼχ τοῦ τῶν Καππαδοκῶν ἀρχεγόνου. For the loss of local traditions about another founder, note B, *Ep.* 258.4, on the Magusaeans, reputed to have been settlers in eastern Asia Minor from Babylon: "they claim a man named Zarnuas as the founder of their people." Trombley (1993) 2:123, suggests that Zarnuas was "perhaps an etymologically corrupted and shortened form of Zoroaster"; see also Chapter 1.

3. Second Sophistic: Philostratus, *Vitae sophistarum* 481. Quotation from Swain (1996) 410.

4. Volume of Demosthenes: GNaz, *Ep.* 31.7. Hours on end: Asterius of Amaseia, *Hom.* 11.1. GNys, *Contra Eunomium* 1.15, laughing, 3.10.50, 54, Eunomius as Demosthenes, with Chapter 1.

5. Archelaus as founder: see *Kingdom of Snow*, Chapter 1. GNaz, *Orat.* 43.25, second founder, 42, guardian, 63, "new city," with *Families and Friends*, Chapter 4, and *Kingdom of Snow*, Chapter 2, on the Basilias. For other examples of local notables being hailed as founders, see Strubbe (1984–1986) 289–301.

6. For Basil's failure to mention this Helladius, see *Kingdom of Snow*, Chapter 3.

7. Firmus of Caesarea, *Ep.* 43, Basilias; *Ep.* 17, second founder, addressed to Soterichus. *PLRE* 2:1022–23, suggests that Soterichus had influence at the court at Constantinople but was not necessarily holding an office; Calvet-Sebasti and Gatier (1989) 59, suggests that he may have been a vicar.

8. Later evaluations: Photius, *Bibliotheca* 40, with Chapter 8.

Preachers and Audiences Introduction

1. Drought: see *Kingdom of Snow*, Chapter 2. B, *Hom.* 14.4, drinking, with Lallemand (2001), for Basil's ideas about drunkenness; *Hom.* 21.9, fire.

2. Quotation about technical terms from Browning (1983) 50, in a fine discussion of diglossy, with Chapter 5, on the revival of classical Greek. Bishop Triphyllius in Cyprus: Sozomen, *HE* 1.11, referring to Mark 2:9. B, *De spiritu sancto* 7.16, language of countryfolk, with Courtonne (1934) 177–240, on Basil's use of rhetorical techniques in the *Hom. in Hexaemeron*.

3. Local dialects: *De viris illustribus urbis Romae* 76.1, with *Kingdom of Snow*, Chapter 1, on king Mithridates Eupator of Pontus. Regional language: B, *De spiritu sancto* 29.74. Heaven: GNys, *Contra Eunomium* 2.406. GNaz, *Orat.* 21.22, Tower of Babel; *Orat.* 23.12, fisherman, not Aristotle. For the survival of Cappadocian and other local languages in central Asia Minor, see Neumann (1980), and Mitchell (1993) 1:172–75.

4. Quotation about little town from Weber (1976) 235; note van der Meer (1961) 431: "The sermon was not only a form of popular education but also of popular entertainment." Midnight and noon: B, *Hom. in psalmos* 114.1, *PG* 29.484A. Holy Spirit: GNaz, *Ep.* 58.6–8, with *Families and Friends,* Chapter 10. Gallay (1943) 117n.4, dates GNaz, *Ep.* 58, to shortly after Gregory's assumption of his service at Nazianzus in 372, Gallay (1969) xx, to the end of 372, and Gallay (1964–1967) 1:73n.1, to 372 or 373. Hauschild (1990) 207, dates B, *Ep.* 71, apparently a reply to GNaz, *Ep.* 58, to 374.

5. Treatise and confession: GNys, *Ep.* 5.1–3. Actor: Libanius, *Ep.* 127.5. On sermons as dialogues, see Allen (1998) 252: "a two-way relationship in which the audience had a voice."

6. Bernardi (1968), provides a solid foundation for subsequent study of the sermons of the Cappadocian Fathers.

Chapter 6. The Six Days of Creation

1. Teacher: GNys, *Apologia in Hexaemeron, PG* 44.124A; note that only the title identified Peter as the recipient of this treatise, although Gregory mentioned another "book that we sent to your perfection," which was apparently *De opificio hominis,* also addressed to Peter. Commentary: Giet (1950) 7, "La plan suivi par Basile est avant tout exégétique"; for the longer tradition of commentaries on Genesis 1, see Robbins (1912), and van Winden (1988). Popularization: Amand de Mendieta (1978) 347, "un essai suggestif de vulgarisation scientifique au service de la foi chrétienne." Quotations from Rousseau (1994) 319, 320, 346, in a synthetic summation conflated from the nine sermons on the Hexaemeron, the two sermons on the creation of man sometimes attributed to Basil's authorship, and others of Basil's sermons.

2. GNaz, *Carm.* II.1.16.11–20, audience, 23–28, preferences, shouting.

3. GNaz, *Carm.* II.1.16.13, bees, 37, eloquence. Applauding me: Jerome, *Ep.* 52.8, with *Kingdom of Snow,* Chapter 8. For another discussion of Gregory's preaching techniques at Constantinople, see GNaz, *Carm.* II.1.11.1188–1259, with Beck (1977), and Spira (1985), on locating his sermons in the rhetorical tradition.

4. Byzantine commentators: Wyss (1983) 799–800, and Norris (1991) 29–30. Michael Psellus, *Caracteres Gregorii Theologi, Basilii Magni, Ioannis Chrysostomi et Gregorii Nysseni* 2, *PG* 122.901C: "What Demosthenes represents for the other community, that is, for the community of Hellenes [pagans], Gregory the Theologian represents for ours"; with the commentary in Mayer (1911). For the sophistication of audiences at different cities, see Demoen (1996) 134, in a comparison of Gregory's sermons at Nazianzus and Constantinople: "Gregory was much more sparing with pagan elements for his modest audience at home than for the inhabitants of the capital." Demophilus: *Suda* Δ.470. Slogans: GNys, *De deitate filii et spiritus sancti, PG* 46.557B, a sermon delivered at Constantinople in 383, with Bernardi (1968) 327–30.

5. Libanius at Constantinople: Libanius, *Orat.* 1.76. Listener: GNaz, *Orat.* 8.1.

6. Basil's oratory: GNaz, *Orat.* 43.77. Basil's audience: GNys, *Apologia in Hexaemeron, PG* 44.65A–B, with Bernardi (1968) 48–54, and Amand de Mendieta (1978) 351–57. Bernardi (1968) 388, praises Basil for "son souci de rester attentif aux

réactions de ceux qui l'écoutent"; MacMullen (1989), highlights but also overemphasizes the preacher's "distinctly upper-class audience" (p. 510); for introductions to the issues involving preachers and their audiences, see Allen (1997) 3–8, Cunningham and Allen (1998), and Mayer (1998). The best discussion of a preacher in action is van der Meer (1961) 412–32, on Augustine at Hippo.

7. Fasting: B, *Hom. in Hexaemeron* 8.8. Delivery during episcopacy: Giet (1950) 7. Bernardi (1968) 43–47, dates the sermons precisely to Monday through Friday, March 12–16, 378; Maraval (1988) 35–37, after redating Basil's death to 377, suggests March 374, before Basil became more concerned with the theology of the Holy Spirit. Rousseau (1994) 363, is content to date the sermons to Basil's final year, Amand de Mendieta and Rudberg (1997) XVII, to 378; Pouchet (1992b) 28–30, again supports March 378. Another possibility for the time of the year is late spring, since in a discussion of the seasons Basil noted that "now the sun is advancing toward the summer solstice": B, *Hom. in Hexaemeron* 6.8. For the custom of nonstop preaching during Lent, note B, *Hom.* 14.1: "I have continued preaching to you without interruption, night and day, during these seven weeks of fasting."

8. On conflation, see Rousseau (1994) 338: "The modern reader . . . is . . . obliged to grasp the work as a whole"—precisely what Basil's original listeners could not do, even at the end of the entire series of sermons. For a demonstration of the dangers of such synthetic readings, see Behr (1999).

9. Sources: even though B, *Hom. in Hexaemeron* 3.8, noted that "their own books" were contradictory, he mentioned no specific philosophical treatises. Giet (1950) 64–69, discusses the availability of texts and concludes, more out of hopefulness than on the basis of any evidence, that Basil was certainly never "l'homme d'un manuel"; Amand de Mendieta (1978) 357–65, surveys Basil's sources.

10. Moses: B, *Hom. in Hexaemeron* 1.1, including the puns on ἀρχή.

11. B, *Hom. in Hexaemeron* 1.2.

12. B, *Hom. in Hexaemeron* 1.5, discussion of ἀρχή, with Giet (1950) 110n.1; see Courtonne (1934) 16–54, on the sources for this first sermon, and Callahan (1958), on Basil's interaction with Greek philosophy.

13. B, *Hom. in Hexaemeron* 1.4, guffaw, 8, digression, 9, limits, 10, faith, 11, frivolity.

14. B, *Hom. in Hexaemeron* 1.11, bantering; 2.1, despair.

15. B, *Hom. in Hexaemeron* 2.1, purpose, 2, falsifiers (with Giet [1950] 143n.3), 4, Marcionites, Valentinians, Manichees, 6, Syrian, with Giet (1950) 54, 169n.3, who identifies this commentator as Theophilus of Antioch, Pouchet (1986) 259–68, (1992a) 358, as Diodorus of Tarsus, and Van Rompay (1992), as Eusebius of Emesa. Later traditions implausibly identified this Syrian exegete as the illustrious Ephraem of Edessa: see Rousseau (1957–1958) 279, 282–84. For Basil's connections with Syriac-speaking Christians, see Taylor (1997).

16. B, *Hom. in Hexaemeron* 2.5, tent. For the shift from philosophy to everyday examples, note Weber (1976) 76, on local dialects in France: "That was the nature of rural speech, poor in abstract terms, rich in concrete ones."

17. B, *Hom. in Hexaemeron* 2.4–5, evilness.

18. B, *Hom. in Hexaemeron* 2.8, day and night.

19. B, *Hom. in Hexaemeron* 3.1. Bernardi (1968) 42, suggests that each sermon required about fifty minutes for delivery.

20. B, *Hom. in Hexaemeron* 3.3, forges, wise men, 5, occupations, 8, philosophers. In *Ep.* 266.1 Basil compared himself and his indifference about false accusations to "workers in forges who are used to the din because their ears have been pummeled with noise."

21. B, *Hom. in Hexaemeron* 3.4, buildings and rocks. For rock-cut churches and monasteries, see Rodley (1985), Kostof (1989), and Chapter 9; for mining in Cappadocia, *Kingdom of Snow*, Chapter 1.

22. B, *Hom. in Hexaemeron* 3.2, 4, Person and Only-Begotten, 9, disagreement, with Giet (1950) 234n.3, who identifies these opponents as Origen and his followers.

23. B, *Hom. in Hexaemeron* 3.10, craftsman; 4.1, factory.

24. B, *Hom. in Hexaemeron* 4.1. These grumblings might imply that Basil's sermons were part of a municipal festival that included other entertainments, or that they were a substitute for such a municipal festival.

25. B, *Hom. in Hexaemeron* 4.5, Greek translation.

26. B, *Hom. in Hexaemeron* 4.2, demand (referring to *Hom. in Hexaemeron* 2.1), 3, rhetorical question, 4, contrary to experience.

27. B, *Hom. in Hexaemeron* 4.7, congregation.

28. B, *Hom. in Hexaemeron* 5.5, image of a sea. Since this was Basil's only sermon on this day, most commentators have assumed that he delivered it in the morning, and have then tried to explain the absence of a sermon in the evening: see Giet (1950) 318n.2. Although at the end of the sermon Basil decided that he had to stop because "the day will fail me" (*Hom. in Hexaemeron* 5.9), he made no explicit reference to morning or evening. So it is just as possible that Basil skipped the morning sermon and delivered this one in the evening. In fact, if it is correct that Basil initially intended to include the material in this sermon in his previous sermon, then presumably his original plan had been to deliver eight sermons in pairs on four days. In that case perhaps he inserted this single make-up sermon so that he could continue on the next day with his original sequence of paired sermons.

29. B, *Hom. in Hexaemeron* 5.5, black wheat, 7, almonds, with Broughton (1938) 611–12, on nuts in Asia Minor, and Sallares (1991) 479, on the identification of this wheat. Giet (1950) 290n.3, suggests that Basil derived his information from a manual or a florilegium.

30. B, *Hom. in Hexaemeron* 5.1, sun, 2, transience, 7, figs.

31. B, *Hom. in Hexaemeron* 5.2, marvel, 9, love; with Clark (1996) 325, on Christian exegesis: "The natural world is appropriated for human edification." For Archelaus' treatise, see *Kingdom of Snow*, Chapter 1.

32. B, *Hom. in Hexaemeron* 6.2–3, philology, 5–7, astrology. For the usage of φαῦσις, "illumination," see Giet (1950) 333n.4. On the challenge of astrology to Christian notions of free will, see Courtonne (1934) 99–110, and Moreschini and Sykes (1997) 174–94.

33. B, *Hom. in Hexaemeron* 6.1.

34. B, *Hom. in Hexaemeron* 6.1, flowers, 2, Persons.

35. B, *Hom. in Hexaemeron* 6.4, predicting weather, 8, seasons, 9, sun.

36. B, *Hom. in Hexaemeron* 6.10, moon, 11, tales.

37. B, *Hom. in Hexaemeron* 6.11, bread; 7.1, slime. In the ancient world people

preferred to eat wheat and often reserved barley for feeding livestock: see Brothwell (1988), and Sallares (1991) 285–86, 321, 367–68.

38. B, *Hom. in Hexaemeron* 7.2, 5, people on coast. For Basil's use of an epitome of Aristotle's zoology for *Hom. in Hexaemeron* 7–8, see Levie (1920). For ice fishing on a frozen river, see B, *Ep.* 329.

39. B, *Hom. in Hexaemeron* 7.1, souls, 3–4, examples.

40. B, *Hom. in Hexaemeron* 7.5–6, marriages. Recommendations: B, *Ep.* 188, Can. 9, *Ep.* 199, Can. 21, logic, with Chapter 2, on these canons. Note the wry assessment of Clark (1996) 321, on Basil's comments about wives and abusive husbands: "no doubt it woke up the congregation."

41. B, *Hom. in Hexaemeron* 7.6.

42. B, *Hom. in Hexaemeron* 8.1–2.

43. B, *Hom. in Hexaemeron* 8.2, explanation of silence. Giet (1950) 438n.1, argues that this reference to a distraction in the audience was a rhetorical device and that Basil could not have spoken at such length about birds simply as an extemporaneous digression. In fact, Basil was prepared to talk about birds, since he was now only delivering the comments he would have used the night before if he had not been overcome by poor health.

44. B, *Hom. in Hexaemeron* 8.2–3, learned observations, 4–6, examples; with Chapter 3, on the practical implications of these examples. The altruistic conduct of storks was so impressive that, according to Basil, "some call the repayment of benefactions ἀντιπελάργωσις, 'stork in return'" (*Hom. in Hexaemeron* 8.5). For this rare noun, see *Suda* A.2707.

45. B, *Hom. in Hexaemeron* 8.6, virgin birth, 8, transformation.

46. B, *Hom. in Hexaemeron* 8.7–8.

47. B, *Hom. in Hexaemeron* 9.1, with Lim (1990), for the connection between Basil's estimation of his audience and his opinions about allegorical interpretations.

48. B, *Hom. in Hexaemeron* 9.2–3, souls and rationality, 4, parents and children, "recent misfortune."

49. B, *Hom. in Hexaemeron* 9.6.

50. Basil had already used the argument that God's spoken commands implied the presence of another Person in the Trinity: see *Hom. in Hexaemeron* 3.2, 6.2.

51. On the disputed authorship of *Homiliae in hexaemeron* 10–11 = *Homiliae de creatione hominis* 1–2 (*CPG* 2:227–28, nos. 3215–16), see Smets and van Esbroeck (1970) 13–26, 116–26.

52. Ten thousand mouths: Theophilus of Antioch, *Ad Autolycum* 2.12.

53. Understanding: GNaz, *Orat.* 43.67. GNys, *Apologia in Hexaemeron*, *PG* 44.64C, complaint about the inadequacy of Basil's discussion of the sun, 65B, success, 68B–C, no contradiction, 124A, reference to "that earlier book" about the creation of man, with May (1972) 512–15, and Risch (1999) 1–11, on the differences between Basil's and Gregory's doctrines. Daniélou (1966) 162–63, and May (1971) 57, date the composition of Gregory of Nyssa's *De opificio hominis* to early 379, and of his *Apologia in Hexaemeron* to summer 379.

54. Basil's voice: GNaz, *Orat.* 43.65. Earthquake: GNys, *Dialogus de anima et resurrectione*, *PG* 46.97B.

55. Mold character: Isidore of Pelusium, *Ep.* 1.61, *PG* 78.224A. Clarity and

persuasiveness: Photius, *Bibliotheca* 141. Strabo, *Geographia* 12.2.7, summit of Mount Argaeus, with Beck (1977) 31–32, on the transitory nature of sermons. For the influence of Basil's *Hexaemeron*, see van Winden (1988) 1260, "das einflußreichste der nicht allegorisch deutenden."

56. Strabo, *Geographia* 11.5.6, snowshoeing and sledding in Armenia.

Chapter 7. The Cult of the Forty Martyrs

1. B, *Hom.* 19.6, one night, 8, mother and son. GNys, *Encomium in XL martyres* 1B, *PG* 46.768D, three nights, 769A–C, mother and son. Karlin-Hayter (1991), provides a helpful critical analysis primarily of the *Passio*, although her goal of finding "a brief and austere, but, above all, homogeneous, account, which . . . is entirely convincing" (p. 249) and "a fair approximation to the original" (p. 291), is doomed from the beginning. For the Greek hagiographical traditions about the Forty Martyrs, see Halkin (1957) 2:97–99, nos. 1201–8, (1969) 128–29.

2. Quotation about social discourse from Brakke (1995) 202, in a fine discussion of Athanasius' *Vita Antonii*.

3. Quotation about meaning from Fentress and Wickham (1992) 71.

4. See Karlin-Hayter (1991) 263, 291, for the *Passio* as an early version, 272, 275–87, for the names. Asia Minor was included in Licinius' territories from 313 to 324: see Barnes (1982) 81–82.

5. Licinius' orders to sacrifice: Eusebius, *HE* 10.8.10, *Vita Constantini* 1.54, with Barnes (1981) 70–72. Amaseia and Pontus: Eusebius, *HE* 10.8.15–18, *Vita Constantini* 2.1–2. Karlin-Hayter (1991) 271, 273–74, dates the martyrdom to the later third century.

6. *Passio XL martyrum* 4, recitation.

7. *Passio XL martyrum* 7, voice.

8. *Passio XL martyrum* 7, lake. *Testamentum XL martyrum* 1, ὑπὸ τὴν πόλιν Ζήλων ἐν τῷ χωρίῳ Σαρείν. In his critical apparatus von Gebhardt (1902) 166, suggested that πόλιν Ζήλων, "city of Zela," should perhaps be read as πολύζηλον (sc. ἐκκλησίαν), "much-admired (church)." For suggestions about the identification of Zela and the village of Sarim, see *Studia Pontica* 3.1: 235, 243, and Maraval (1985) 378n.1, "Sarim-les-Zéla est à chercher près de Zéla."

9. *Passio XL martyrum* 13, discovery.

10. B, *Hom.* 19.5, winter, 6, "fasting of forty days," with Bernardi (1968) 83–84, dating the oration to Basil's episcopacy, and below, for the date of the festival. Shrine at Caesarea: Gaudentius of Brescia, *Tractatus* 17.15, "insigne martyrium."

11. Shrine of St. Theodorus: GNys, *De Theodoro, PG* 46.737D. Bernardi (1968) 303, dates this sermon to February 381, Zuckerman (1991) 479–84, to February 380, and Esper (1984) 146–47, to before 376; Leemans (2001b), is an excellent attempt to imagine the audience of this sermon. For the cult of St. Theodorus, see Delehaye (1909) 11–43, and Halkin (1957) 2:281–86, nos. 1760–73, (1969) 181–82.

12. B, *Hom.* 19.2, oration and painting. For the use of gestures, see Aldrete (1999) 39, "a Roman orator would have been constantly in motion."

13. B, *Hom.* 19.1, praise, 3, edict, 6, clothing, 8, imitation. On Basil and the era of martyrs, see *Families and Friends*, Chapter 1.

14. B, *Hom.* 19.2, city, father, 5, lake, 8, towers.

15. B, *Hom.* 19.7, phalanx, 8, dancing.

16. For Basil and Eustathius, see *Families and Friends*, Chapters 1, 10; Basil and Neocaesarea, *Families and Friends*, Chapter 1. Note that when Gaudentius of Brescia received relics of the Forty Martyrs at Caesarea, he also learned their history, which was essentially a version of Basil's account: see Gaudentius of Brescia, *Tractatus* 17.17–33.

17. The common titles of Gregory's orations about the Forty Martyrs, as listed in *CPG* and elsewhere, readily cause confusion. The *Encomium in XL martyres* (= *CPG* 2:223, no. 3188) in fact consists of two separate orations, hereafter called *Encomium* 1A and *Encomium* 1B, that were delivered most likely in 383 on March 9 (the martyrs' festival) and March 10 respectively; for the dates, see Daniélou (1955) 362–63, and Bernardi (1968) 303. More tenuous is the suggestion of Leemans (2001a), who dates these orations during the mid-370s as a prelude to GNys, *In inscriptiones psalmorum*; in fact, the date of composition of this treatise is itself quite uncertain: see Heine (1995) 8–11. The *Encomium in XL martyres* 2 (= *CPG* 2:223, no. 3189) was, despite its numbering, delivered earlier. Daniélou (1955) 346–48, and Bernardi (1968) 303, date this earlier oration about the Forty Martyrs to March 9, 379, soon after Basil's death. The year of Basil's death is now debatable: see *Families and Friends*, Chapter 4. In addition, since Gregory seems to have delivered his orations on the Forty Martyrs in pairs on successive days, since he would certainly have delivered one on the martyrs' festival day, and since on this occasion he clearly distinguished between an oration "yesterday" and this oration "today" (*Encomium* 2, PG 46.773A), this *Encomium* 2 should be dated to March 10.

18. GNys, *Encomium in XL martyres* 2, PG 46.773A, goals, 788A–B, exhortations.

19. GNys, *Encomium in XL martyres* 2, PG 46.776A–B, Basil.

20. GNys, *Encomium in XL martyres* 2, PG 46.784B–785B, stories, 785B, laments.

21. GNys, *Encomium in XL martyres* 2, PG 46.784B, village. For families and cults in late Roman Gaul, see Van Dam (1985a) 207–17, (1993) 50–81.

22. GNys, *Encomium in XL martyres* 2, PG 46.776A, paradigm. For Gregory's dispute with Helladius, see Chapter 2.

23. GNys, *Encomium in XL martyres* 2, PG 46.785B, church.

24. GNys, *Ep.* 5.1, theology; *Ep.* 18.9, mockery; *Ep.* 19.15, election, 16, governor; *Ep.* 22.1, Jonah, with Maraval (1990a) 274n.1, for the suggestion that Gregory was here referring to his tenure at Sebasteia. Gregory's episcopacy at Sebasteia was probably in 379, and may have lasted several months: see Maraval (1990a) 29–31.

25. Peter at Constantinople: Theodoret, *HE* 5.8.4. Edict: *CTh* 16.1.3, with Maraval (1990a) 31, for the suggestion that Peter replaced a heterodox predecessor. Martyrium at Nyssa: GNys, *Ep.* 25, dated to after 381 by Maraval (1990a) 288n.1. Since the peristyle included "no fewer than forty columns" (GNys, *Ep.* 25.14), Klock (1984) 161, and Maraval (1990a) 298n.2, suggest that the shrine may have been dedicated to the Forty Martyrs. Cult of Peter: GNys, *Ep.* 1.5, "I had celebrated the festival of the most blessed Peter that had been held for the first time at Sebasteia. I was also commemorating with them the festivals for the holy martyrs that they customarily celebrate at the same time." For the identification of this St. Peter as the earlier bishop Peter, see Devos (1961b), Maraval and Hanriot (1984) 68, and Maraval

(1990a) 86–87. Peter's body had apparently been buried at another village, before now being moved back to Sebasteia: see *Passio Athenogenis* 37, with the discussion in Maraval (1990b) 14, 18.

26. Crowd: GNys, *Encomium in XL martyres* 1A, PG 46.749A, citing Luke 8:45.

27. GNys, *Encomium in XL martyres* 1A, PG 46.749B–C, readings. For citations from Psalms in the *Passio*, see the apparatus in von Gebhardt (1902) 172–80. For the use of Ephesians, note that the description of the martyrs in the *Testamentum* as "prisoners of Christ" was presumably modeled on Paul's description of himself in Ephesians 3:1, and that in the next day's sermon Gregory refered to Ephesians 6:11–17 in a discussion of the "armor of God": see GNys, *Encomium in XL martyres* 1B, PG 46.761C–D.

28. GNys, *Encomium in XL martyres* 1A, PG 46.752A–C, parents, 752D–753B, landmarks, 753D, martyrs.

29. GNys, *Encomium in XL martyres* 1A, PG 46.756A, holy field, 756B, narratives and weak voice, 756C–D, 757A–B, shouts.

30. GNys, *Encomium in XL martyres* 1B, PG 46.757A, hosts and guests, 757C, recitation.

31. GNys, *Encomium in XL martyres* 1B, PG 46.757C–D, garrison, 757D–760D, new story, 761B, lingering.

32. GNys, *Encomium in XL martyres* 1B, PG 46.765C, your miracles.

33. GNys, *Encomium in XL martyres* 1B, PG 46.760B, 768c, Job.

34. GNys, *Encomium in XL martyres* 1B, PG 46.765C, Lent, 765D, running with saints, 769D–772A, my oration, 772A–C, fiery sword. Bernardi (1968) 306n.18bis, argues that Gregory's reference to an earlier discussion implies that he had been in Sebasteia for some time.

35. Epitaph: *Studia Pontica* 3.1:159, no. 145a = Merkelbach and Stauber (2001) 382, no. 11/08/05. GNys, *Encomium in XL martyres* 2, PG 46.773B, διὰ τῆς μνήμης.

36. Gaudentius of Brescia, *Tractatus* 17.14–16, relics, 37, Assembly of Saints. Pulcheria: Sozomen, *HE* 9.2, with Holum (1982) 137. Group cults: Halkin (1957) 1:248, nos. 749–50, on Hieron and his thirty-two companions, 101, no. 1216, on the Forty-Five Martyrs, and Maraval (1985) 375.

37. Talk to each other: B, *Ep*. 9.3.

38. Ears and hands: Philostorgius, *HE* 8.3, mentioning Theodosius, bishop probably of Philadelphia in Lydia: see Socrates, *HE* 2.40.

39. Pitch of voice: Libanius, *Ep*. 481.4. For the importance of interpreting ancient orations as performances, see Gotoff (1993), on Cicero's speeches: "oratory invites comparison with theater" (p. 289).

The Life to Come Introduction

1. Descriptions from a text entitled "On physical characteristics, from the antiquarian discussions of ecclesiastical history by Elpius [or Ulpius] the Roman," preserved in a twelfth-century manuscript at Paris but composed apparently between the mid-ninth and the mid-tenth century: for the text and general discussions, see Chatzidakes (1938) 412–13, and Winkelmann (1990) 122–23, with Fitzgerald (1981),

for the iconography of Basil, and Tutorov (2000), for the iconography of Gregory of Nazianzus.

2. For Gregory of Nyssa's accounts of his brother and sister, see *Families and Friends*, Chapters 3, 6.

3. White spots: Philostorgius, *HE* 10.6. For ridicule of Eunomius' appearance, see Rufinus, *HE* 10.26: "the man was a leper in body and soul, and both inside and out he was afflicted with jaundice."

4. Nature: GNaz, *Carm.* II.1.41.55–56.

Chapter 8. Philostorgius at Constantinople

1. Philostorgius, *HE* 8.10, doctor Philostorgius, whose son, also a doctor, the historian Philostorgius had met, 9.9, hometown, family, with the correction of Eulampion's name in the critical apparatus of Bidez' edition. Borissus, "a village in the region of [the province of] Cappadocia Secunda," was about four miles southeast of Nazianzus: see Hild and Restle (1981) 159.

2. On Philostorgius' name, note that Φιλόστοργος, "affectionate," had once been a title used by the wives of Cappadocian kings: see Sullivan (1980) 1137–38; for its use in dedications among family members, see Veligianni (2001) 64. For Eunomius and Philostorgius, see Chapter 1.

3. Philostorgius' education: Bidez (1913) CIX–CXIII. For Gregory of Nazianzus and Julian, see *Kingdom of Snow*, Chapter 11. Philippus' (now lost) rebuttal: Socrates, *HE* 7.27, Photius, *Bibliotheca* 35. On Cyril's *Contra Iulianum*, see Wilken (1999).

4. Philostorgius, *HE* 8.14, writings against Porphyry by Methodius of Olympus, Eusebius of Caesarea, and Apollinarius of Laodicea, 10.10, his own refutation. Claim that Julian was "wiser than the old man from Tyre": Libanius, *Orat.* 18.178. For Porphyry and his Christian critics, see Wilken (1984) 126–63, and Digeser (1998), (2000) 91–114, 161–63.

5. Palladius, *Historia Lausiaca* 35.5, with Malingrey and Leclercq (1988) 1:10–18, Palladius' life, 39, familiarity with rhetorical techniques. Hypatius: Callinicus, *Vita Hypatii* 1.1–4, with Bartelink (1971) 17, for the chronology. Philostorgius, *HE* 2.5, Ulfilas' ancestors, from Sadagolthina, with Hild and Restle (1981) 268; 4.4, Eudoxius, from Arabissus in Armenia Secunda, with Hild and Restle (1981) 144–45; 5.5, Meletius, from Melitene in Armenia Secunda. For Eunomius, see Chapter 1; for Philostorgius' interest in churchmen as personalities and not just theologians, see Rusch (1974) 172.

6. Radiance: Callinicus, *Vita Hypatii* 1.6. Eunomians at Constantinople: Philostorgius, *HE* 12.11.

7. Philostorgius, *HE* 2.17, Constantine's statue, 3.2, Church of Apostles, 3.11, exotic animals, 11.3, Rufinus and Arcadius, 11.8, Gainas' head. For Theodosius' building projects, see *Kingdom of Snow*, Chapter 8. The relics of St. Timothy were brought to Constantinople in 356, those of St. Luke and St. Andrew in 357: see Jerome, *Chron.* s.a. 356, 357; *Consularia Constantinopolitana* s.a. 356, 357; *Chronicon Paschale* s.a. 356, 357; with Mango (1990).

8. Philostorgius, *HE* 2.9, traditions, 3.7–9, rivers, 10, Paradise; with Leppin (2001), on Philostorgius' loyalty to the Roman empire.

9. Signature: *Anthologia Graeca* 9.194; noted also by Photius, *Bibliotheca* 40.

Chapter 9. The Apocryphal Basil

1. Study at Constantinople: GNaz, *Orat.* 43.14, with *Families and Friends*, Chapter 1. For the construction at Constantinople under Constantine and Constantius, see Mango (1985) 23–42. Dedication of Church of Holy Wisdom on February 15, 360: Socrates, *HE* 2.43, Sozomen, *HE* 4.26.

2. Not visiting: B, *Ep.* 1, "the city on the Hellespont." This letter was written in autumn 357: see Hauschild (1990) 161n.1; for the identification of the city, see *Kingdom of Snow*, Chapter 3. Council at Constantinople in 360: B, *Adversus Eunomium* 1.2, with Chapter 1. Fish: B, *Hom. in Hexaemeron* 7.4–5, with Dagron (1995) 57, who notes that this migration into the Black Sea occurs in mid-spring.

3. For the diffusion of Gregory's panegyric, see Severus of Antioch, *Ep.* 8.1, tr. Brooks (1903–1904) 2:393, from the early sixth century: "The laudatory discourse also that was delivered upon Gregory the Wonder-worker we ourselves have known to be read in many churches, and in the royal city itself: similarly also that upon the great Basil"; also *Ep.* 1.1, 2, tr. 9–10, 13, for references to GNaz, *Orat.* 43, on the opposition to Basil's consecration as bishop of Caesarea. For the Greek hagiographical tradition about Basil, see Halkin (1957) 1:86–93, nos. 244–62, (1969) 40–43. Gregory's oration also became the source for an iconographical cycle of images of Basil's life: see Brubaker (1999) 137–41, commenting on an illustration in a manuscript of Gregory's orations and "its close adherence to Gregory's account of the saint's life" (p. 141).

4. *Buzandaran Patmut'iwnk'* 4.4, Nerses' consecration, 5, prayers, 6, exile, 7–8, Basil and Eusebius, 9, Basil's consecration, 10, Valens' death, tr. Garsoïan (1989) 111–32. Garsoïan's commentary is fundamental; see also Garsoïan (1989) 11, date of composition, 28–29, contamination by material about Basil, 40, anachronistic intrusion of Valens.

5. For Gregory the Illuminator, see *Kingdom of Snow*, Chapter 6. For the different versions of the death of Valens' son, see Socrates, *HE* 4.26 (death at Antioch), Sozomen, *HE* 6.16 (death apparently at Caesarea), and Theodoret, *HE* 4.19 (death at Caesarea), with *PLRE* 1:381, "Valentinianus Galates."

6. The account here relies on the German translation of this homily in von Zetterstéen (1934). This homily has sometimes been attributed, wrongly, to Amphilochius of Iconium: see *CPG* 2:241, no. 3252.

7. See Vööbus (1960), who argues that this homily borrowed episodes and characterizations from a Syriac biography of Rabbula, bishop of Edessa in the early fifth century.

8. This *Vita et miracula Basilii Magni* has also sometimes been attributed, wrongly, to Amphilochius of Iconium: see *CPG* 2:241, no. 3253; de Jerphanion (1938) 158, suggests that the author was a monk in Cappadocia or Lycaonia. The date of composition of this *Life* is uncertain. In the first half of the eighth century John of Damascus noted that Basil had once petitioned St. Mercurius for assistance in removing the emperor Julian. As the source for this story John mentioned "the *Life* of the blessed Basil [composed] by Helladius, his disciple and his successor in his episcopacy": see John of Damascus, *Orationes de imaginibus* 1, Testimonia, *PG* 94.1277B, with *Kingdom of Snow*, Chapter 10, for St. Mercurius. The *Life* mentioned a similar

story, and it claimed Helladius as the source for other stories. So perhaps John was referring to this *Life* as his source. Muraviev (2001), discusses the development of some of the legends in the *Life*; a Latin translation was available at Rome in the mid-ninth century: see de Jerphanion (1925–1936) 1:358n.3.

9. On Basil and Ephraem, see Rousseau (1957–1958) 90, "une histoire nostalgique."

10. Description of New Church and frescoes: de Jerphanion (1925–1936) 1:297–376, Rodley (1985) 213–22, and Kostof (1989) 95–105, 164–67. For the dating of the New Church to the mid-tenth century, see Epstein (1986) 29, and Jolivet-Lévy (1991) 108; for the imperial magistrates and local landowners who patronized the construction of these churches, Teteriatnikov (1996) 197–210. Inscriptions: Rott (1908) 228–29, and de Jerphanion (1925–1936) 1:358–65, (1938) 155–58. For other decorative scenes taken from the *Life*, see de Jerphanion (1925–1936) 2:52–53. Brubaker (1992), and Carr (1992), discuss a biographical icon of Basil that illustrated episodes in the *Life*.

11. Funeral riot: GNaz, *Orat.* 43.80.

12. Abyss: GNaz, *Carm.* II.1.10.25.

Chapter 10. The Autobiographies of Gregory of Nazianzus

1. GNaz, *Carm.* II.1.1.13, rescue, 255, passions. For the circumstances of Caesarius' death and the date of this poem, see *Families and Friends*, Chapters 2–3.

2. GNaz, *Carm.* II.1.1.139, doing good, 261–68, flight and weight.

3. GNaz, *Carm.* II.1.1.307–31, earlier misfortunes, 351, tremble, 367–92, parable, 424–66, Nonna's devotion, 556, winds, with *Families and Friends*, Chapter 5, on Gregory and his mother.

4. GNaz, *Carm.* II.1.1.108, "I am the only child left," 184, "no relatives helped me," 606–19, feuding among monks. For Basil's assistance, see Van Dam (1995) 125.

5. Quotation about narrative from Gusdorf (1980) 41.

6. Note Sykes (1985) 433, on Gregory's poems: "correctness of style provided an admirable protection of personality."

7. For Apollinarius' rewriting of the Bible, see *Kingdom of Snow*, Chapter 11. "New Psalms": GNaz, *Ep.* 101.73. Pagans, young people: GNaz, *Carm.* II.1.39.37–53, with Wyss (1949), a fine appreciation of Gregory as a poet, and Milovanovic-Barham (1997). For Gregory's theological poems, sometimes known as the *Arcana*, the "ineffable poems," see *Carm.* I.1.1–5, 7–9, with Moreschini and Sykes (1997) 66–67, dating these poems to 381 or early 382, and Van Dam (1998).

8. GNaz, *Carm.* II.1.39.24, toils, 37, laboring. On nonce words, note Moreschini and Sykes (1997) 60, "They are quite a marked feature of the poems."

9. For the notion of stuttering when writing autobiography, see Renza (1980) 279.

10. GNaz, *Carm.* II.1.12.14–15, assassins, 45, pain, 307–8, philosophy, 701–6, cat. McGuckin (2001), identifies Nectarius, Gregory's successor at Constantinople, as the primary object of his resentment.

11. GNaz, *Carm.* II.1.12.805, mother's vow, 818, another Gregory. Since Gregory implied that another bishop had not yet been selected, he presumably composed

this poem immediately after his departure from Constantinople: see Meier (1989) 17–18, on the date of composition.

12. GNaz, *Carm.* II.1.10.19, warrior; *Carm.* II.1.13.26, remedy; *Carm.* II.1.14.37, guardian; *Carm.* II.1.15.32, shifting powers; *Carm.* II.1.17.102, quiet life. The editors of *PG* 37 date all five poems to 381; Gallay (1943) 217, 253, dates *Carm.* II.1.10 to summer 381, and the other poems to 382.

13. GNaz, *Carm.* II.1.16.6, hand, 47–51, roosters, 76, fruit, with *Kingdom of Snow*, Chapter 8, on Gregory's tenure at Constantinople.

14. GNaz, *Carm.* II.1.16.103–4, groaning.

15. GNaz, *Carm.* II.1.5.8, my throne; *Carm.* II.1.16.76, this church. According to Socrates, *HE* 5.7, "emperors" later added a "huge church" to the original house-church. By the mid-fifth century this new Anastasia was conspicuous for its beauty and size: see Sozomen, *HE* 7.5. In an excellent survey of the later modifications, Snee (1998) 161 suggests that the emperor Theodosius was responsible for the construction of this new church. Nectarius, Gregory's successor as bishop of Constantinople, contributed marble panels to the new church: see Photius, *Bibliotheca* 59, for the accusation that John Chrysostom tried to sell these panels.

16. GNaz, *Carm.* II.1.11.1–2, trail, 9, once mine. Gallay (1943) 253, dates *Carm.* II.1.11 to early 382. Since in this poem Gregory stated that another bishop had already taken over his congregation, he apparently wrote it after *Carm.* II.1.12, not before, as claimed by Gallay (1943) 217, 253.

17. GNaz, *Carm.* II.1.11.57–92, mother, 112–13, passion, 330–32, sanctuary.

18. GNaz, *Carm.* II.1.11.345, 392, tyranny, 424, force, 607–8, arrival, 1048–49, 1057, watch and possibility of departure, 1111–12, thinking, 1370–91, shouting and demurral, 1525–38, consecration, 1747–48, departure, 1849–50, leave.

19. GNaz, *Carm.* II.1.11.1671–72, a life, 1810, canons, 1936, shroud, with Misch (1950) 2:616, on the conclusion to this poem: "the hero emerging from apparent defeat."

20. Bernardi (1995) 236–37, argues that Gregory revised *Carm.* II.1.11–12 in 389, shortly before his death. His arguments are suspect because they assume that Gregory was familiar with events in Italy. In *Carm.* II.1.11.1131–32 Gregory doubted whether there were any people "so far from the power that is now ruling Italy" who did not know about his troubles at Constantinople. Although Bernardi suggests that Gregory was here referring to the emperor Theodosius during his residence in Italy from 388 to 391, Jungck (1974) 197, argues, more plausibly, that Gregory was simply worried about his general reputation in the empire. In *Carm* II.1.12.125–27 Gregory mentioned that "the city of blessed Rome knew about this [success], in particular, I note, its foremost family, who happened to honor me with some esteem." Although Bernardi suggests that Gregory was referring to Theodosius and his family when they resided in Rome during summer 389, in fact, he seems to have been referring to his esteem while he was himself "present" (*Carm.* II.1.12.131) at "(New) Rome," that is, Constantinople. To one correspondent Gregory once conceded that he knew nothing about Italy: "I am ignorant about affairs in Italy" (*Ep.* 173.1). It is therefore unlikely that he would have included allusions to the imperial court's visit to Rome in his autobiographical poems. Gregory hence completed these two poems before serving again as bishop at Nazianzus, rather than revising them afterwards.

21. For the role of Gregory's will in helping him make the transition from

Constantinople back to Nazianzus, see Van Dam (1995). Beaucamp (1998), provides a new edition of the will and a full discussion of the legal aspects.

22. GNaz, *Carm.* II.1.19.51–53, father's throne, 72–74, grumbling; *Carm.* II.1.30. 67–86, critics. Gallay (1943) 220, suggests that Gregory composed *Carm.* II.1.19 in late 382, soon after assuming episcopal leadership at Nazianzus.

23. GNaz, *Carm.* II.1.19.29, reputation, 31, Job.

24. GNaz, *Carm.* II.1.68.39–41, great throne.

25. See *Families and Friends*, Chapter 3, on Caesarius, Chapter 4, on Gregory's anticipation about his burial with his father.

26. For the translation of Gregory's body, see *Synaxarium ecclesiae Constantinopolitanae*, ed. Delehaye (1902) xii–xiii, 422, and Clémencet (1885) 238. Constantine VII Porphyrogenitus, *Oratio de translatione Gregorii Theologi* 18, body, 19, study, foreigner, flock, 22, uncertainty about tomb, fragrance, 23, angels, 45, milk. For the attribution of this panegyric to Constantine, see Flusin (1998); Flusin (1999) 10–12, dates the arrival of Gregory's remains and the delivery of this panegyric to January 19, 946. In the mid-tenth century the bishop of Caesarea, Basil Minimus (Basil "the Least," so-called to distinguish himself from his homonymous predecessor, the original Basil the Great), composed a series of commentaries on various orations by Gregory of Nazianzus. He dedicated one of these commentaries to the emperor Constantine, perhaps to mark the translation of Gregory's remains: for the occasion, see Schmidt (2001) xii–xv, 3n.2. In the letter of dedication Basil praised the pleasure of Gregory's company to Constantine: see Basil Minimus, *Epistula nuncupatoria*, ed. Schmidt (2001) 4, "Is there anything more beloved for you or more precious than to see an image of Gregory and to publicize his works?"

27. Constantine VII Porphyrogenitus, *Oratio de translatione Gregorii Theologi* 25–26, suburbs, 45, protector, with Flusin (1999) 20, on the symmetry between Gregory's oration of departure (GNaz, *Orat.* 42) and Constantine's oration of welcome. Sarcophagus, spiritual beauty: Nicholas Mesarites, *Ecphrasis* 38.4, adapting the description of the "ruddy" David in 1 Samuel 16:12. Rituals: Constantine VII Porphyrogenitus, *De ceremoniis* 1.10, ed. Reiske, pp. 76–77, with Flusin (1998) 150–53, for the significance of these rituals for the relationship between emperors and patriarchs.

28. Constantine VII Porphyrogenitus, *Oratio de translatione Gregorii Theologi* 9, separation and return, 33, church.

29. Constantine VII Porphyrogenitus, *Oratio de translatione Gregorii Theologi* 13, home and father, 30, snow. Relics in the Anastasia: Symeon Magister, *Chronographia*, ed. Bekker (1838) 2:755, and *PG* 109.817B, with *Kingdom of Snow*, Chapter 8, for Gregory's service at Constantinople, and *Families and Friends*, Chapters 2, 5, for Gregory and his parents.

30. Narrator: GNaz, *Carm.* II.1.19.24–25. Gregory the Priest, *Vita Gregorii Theologi* 1, mason, 5, Gregory's baptism, 14, baptism of Maximus, 17, orations about Theodosius, 22, twelve years, poems as sources, 23, remember your Gregory. For the priority of this *Vita*, note that Gregory the Priest explicitly mentioned that he had used only Gregory's own writings: "no one has left us anything about him in writing" (*Vita* 1). Gallay (1943) xii–xiii, dates the *Vita* to the early seventh century, Lequeux (2001) 14–16, to the later sixth or early seventh century. For the sources,

including a discussion of additions and deviations, see Lequeux (2001) 21–28, and his excellent commentary. Note that when Gregory the Priest "quoted" from Gregory's orations, he was in fact inventing the quotations based on episodes from Gregory's poems: see *Vita* 15, with GNaz, *Carm.* II.1.11.956–98, and *Vita* 21, with GNaz, *Carm.* II.1.11.1828–55, 1881–1901. For the complaint by Sophronius, bishop of Jerusalem until 638, see Lequeux (2001) 15.

31. Theology itself: Nicetas the Paphlagonian, *Laudatio Gregorii* 1, with Rizzo (1976) 11–15, on Nicetas' sources. For the Greek hagiographical tradition about Gregory, see Halkin (1957) 1:235–37, nos. 723–29, (1969) 80; for the Latin tradition, Dolbeau (1989).

32. For the later use of GNaz, *Orat.* 43, *Carm.* II.1.11, and Gregory the Priest, *Vita Gregorii Theologi*, see Sevcenko (1996); for Gregory's autobiographical intrusions in his oration about Basil, see *Families and Friends*, Chapter 10. Even the extensive miniatures of Gregory's life that illustrated a deluxe ninth-century edition of his orations were remarkably faithful to his own accounts: see Brubaker (1999) 119–37. Quotation from Spacks (1976) 311.

Epilogue

1. Lupercus: *Suda* Λ.691, with *PLRE* 1:519, "Lupercus 1"; Kaster (1988) 305, suggests that the volume about καρίς ("shrimp") may in fact have discussed the quantity of the iota.

2. For the so-called "Cappadocian will" of Alexander, see Trumpf (1959) 256; for Digenes Akrites, *Kingdom of Snow*, Chapter 4. Texts about St. Georgius (George) are edited in Aufhauser (1911), who also, pp. 2n.2, 73–75, discusses the discrepancies over his homeland and the site of the conflict. Caesarea of Armenia: Burton (1934) 1:524, in the saga of Omar bin al-Nu'uman. Quotations about Cappadocia from the marvellous evocation of Fermor (1999) 79, 80, 87.

3. Ruins: Nicephorus Bryennius, *Hist.* 2.3.

Editions and Translations

In this book all translations from Greek and Latin texts are by the author. In this list of editions and translations full references for books and articles already cited in the notes are in the Bibliography.

The Cappadocian Fathers

Basil of Caesarea

Adversus Eunomium: ed. and tr. [French] Sesboüé, de Durand, and Doutreleau (1982–1983).

De spiritu sancto: ed. and tr. [French] B. Pruche, *Basile de Césarée, Traité du Saint-Esprit*. SChr. 17 (1947; 2nd ed., 1968)—tr. B. Jackson, in *St. Basil: Letters and Select Works*. NPNF, 2nd series, 8 (1895; reprint, 1978), pp. 2–50.

Epistulae: ed. and tr. R. J. Deferrari, *Saint Basil, The Letters*, 4 vols. LCL (1926–1934)—ed. and tr. [French] Y. Courtonne, *Saint Basile, Lettres*, 3 vols. Budé (1957–1966)—tr. [German] Hauschild (1973), (1990), (1993)—*Ep.* 1–46, ed. and tr. [Italian] M. Forlin Patrucco, *Basilio di Cesarea, Le lettere*, vol. 1 (Turin, 1983).

Homilia 7: ed. *PG* 31.277–304—ed. and tr. [French] Y. Courtonne, *Saint Basile: Homélies sur la richesse. Edition critique et exégétique* (Paris, 1935), pp. 38–71.

Homilia 14: ed. *PG* 31.444–64.

Homilia 18: ed. *PG* 31.489–508.

Homilia 19: ed. *PG* 31.508–25.

Homilia 23: ed. *PG* 31.589–600.

Homiliae in Hexaemeron: ed. Amand de Mendieta and Rudberg (1997)—ed. and tr. [French] Giet (1950)—tr. B. Jackson, in *St. Basil: Letters and Select Works*. NPNF, 2nd series, 8 (1895; reprint, 1978), pp. 52–107—tr. A. C. Way, *Saint Basil: Exegetic Homilies*. FC 46 (1963), pp. 3–150.

Homiliae in psalmos: ed. *PG* 29.209–494—tr. A. C. Way, *Saint Basil: Exegetic Homilies*. FC 46 (1963), pp. 151–359.

Gregory of Nazianzus

Carmina:

I.1.1–38 = *Carmina dogmatica*: ed. *PG* 37.397–522—*Carm.* I.1.1–5, 7–9: ed. and tr. Moreschini and Sykes (1997)—*Carm.* I.1.2, 11, 29–33, 35: tr. J. McGuckin, *Saint Gregory Nazianzen: Selected Poems* (Oxford, 1986), pp. 1–13.

II.1.1–99 = *Carmina de se ipso*: ed. *PG* 37.969–1452—*Carm*. II.1.1, 11, 12: tr. D. M. Meehan, *Saint Gregory of Nazianzus: Three Poems. Concerning His Own Affairs, Concerning Himself and the Bishops, Concerning His Own Life*. FC 75 (1987)—*Carm*. II.1.11: ed. and tr. [German] Jungck (1974)—*Carm*. II.1.11, 19, 34, 39, 92: tr. C. White, *Gregory of Nazianzus: Autobiographical Poems*. Cambridge Medieval Classics 6 (Cambridge, 1996)—*Carm*. II.1.12: ed. and tr. [German] Meier (1989)—*Carm*. II.1.24–25, 69–70, 76–77: tr. J. McGuckin, *Saint Gregory Nazianzen: Selected Poems* (Oxford, 1986), pp. 14–17.

Epigrammata: ed. *PG* 38.81–130—*Epigram*. 26–29, 47–94 are included in *Anthologia Graeca* 8: ed. and tr. W. R. Paton, *The Greek Anthology*, vol. 2. LCL (1917), pp. 472–505 (see *CPG* 2:192, for a concordance).

Epistulae: ed. Gallay (1969)—*Ep*. 1–100, 103–201, 203–42, 244–49: ed. and tr. [French] Gallay (1964–1967)—*Ep*. 101–2, 202: ed. and tr. [French] Gallay and Jourjon (1974)—tr. [German] M. Wittig, *Gregor von Nazianz: Briefe*. Bibliothek der griechischen Literatur, Abteilung Patristik, Bd. 13 (Stuttgart, 1981)—selections tr. C. G. Browne and J. E. Swallow, in *S. Cyril of Jerusalem. S. Gregory Nazianzen*. NPNF, 2nd series, 7 (1894; reprint, 1978), pp. 437–82.

Orationes: *Orat*. 4–5: ed. and tr. [French] J. Bernardi, *Grégoire de Nazianze: Discours 4–5, Contre Julien*. SChr. 309 (1983)—*Orat*. 6–12: ed. and tr. [French] M.-A. Calvet-Sebasti, *Grégoire de Nazianze: Discours 6–12*. SChr. 405 (1995)—*Orat*. 20–23: ed. and tr. [French] J. Mossay and G. Lafontaine, *Grégoire de Nazianze: Discours 20–23*. SChr. 270 (1980)—*Orat*. 32–37: ed. and tr. [French] C. Moreschini and P. Gallay, *Grégoire de Nazianze: Discours 32–37*. SChr. 318 (1985)—*Orat*. 42–43: ed. and tr. [French] J. Bernardi, *Grégoire de Nazianze: Discours 42–43*. SChr. 384 (1992)—*Orat*. 43: ed. and tr. [French] F. Boulenger, *Grégoire de Nazianze: Discours funèbres en l'honneur de son frère Césaire et de Basile de Césarée* (Paris, 1908), pp. 58–231—*Orat*. 1–3, 7–8, 12, 16, 18, 21, 27–31, 33–34, 37–43, 45: tr. C. G. Browne and J. E. Swallow, in *S. Cyril of Jerusalem. S. Gregory Nazianzen*. NPNF, 2nd series, 7 (1894; reprint, 1978), pp. 203–434.

Gregory of Nyssa

Apologia in Hexaemeron: ed. *PG* 46.61–124—tr. [German] Risch (1999), pp. 58–102.

Contra Eunomium: ed. W. Jaeger, *Gregorii Nysseni Contra Eunomium libri, Pars prior: Liber I et II (vulgo I et XIIв)*, and *Gregorii Nysseni Contra Eunomium libri, Pars altera: Liber III (vulgo III–XII). Refutatio confessionis Eunomii (vulgo Lib. II)*. GNO 1–2 (2nd ed., 1960)—tr. W. Moore, H. A. Wilson, H. C. Ogle, and M. Day, in *Select Writings and Letters of Gregory, Bishop of Nyssa*. NPNF, 2nd series, 5 (1893; reprint, 1976), pp. 35–100, 250–314, 135–248 [in that order]—*Contra Eunomium* 1: tr. S. G. Hall, in Mateo-Seco and Bastero (1988), pp. 35–135.

De deitate filii et spiritus sancti: ed. *PG* 46.553–76.

De opificio hominis: ed. *PG* 44.125–256—tr. H. A. Wilson, in *Select Writings and Letters of Gregory, Bishop of Nyssa*. NPNF, 2nd series, 5 (1893; reprint, 1976), pp. 387–427.

De Theodoro: ed. J. P. Cavarnos, in *Gregorii Nysseni Sermones, pars II*. GNO 10.1 (1990), pp. 59–71; reference numbers from *PG* 46.736–48.

Dialogus de anima et resurrectione: ed. *PG* 46.12–160—tr. W. Moore, in *Select Writings and Letters of Gregory, Bishop of Nyssa.* NPNF, 2nd series, 5 (1893; reprint, 1976), pp. 430–68—tr. V. W. Callahan, *Saint Gregory of Nyssa: Ascetical Works.* FC 58 (1967), pp. 198–272.

Encomia in XL martyres 1A, 1B, 2: ed. O. Lendle, in *Gregorii Nysseni Sermones, pars II.* GNO 10.1 (1990), pp. 135–69; reference numbers from *PG* 46.749–88.

Epistulae: ed. G. Pasquali, *Gregorii Nysseni Epistulae.* GNO 8.2 (2nd ed., 1959)—ed. and tr. [French] Maraval (1990a)—*Ep.* 29–30, 2, 4–18, 20, 25, 3, 1 [in that order]: tr. W. Moore, H. C. Ogle, and H. A. Wilson, in *Select Writings and Letters of Gregory, Bishop of Nyssa.* NPNF, 2nd series, 5 (1893; reprint, 1976), pp. 33–34, 382–83, 527–48.

In Basilium fratrem: ed. and tr. J. A. Stein, *Encomium of Saint Gregory Bishop of Nyssa on His Brother Saint Basil Archbishop of Cappadocian Caesarea.* Catholic University of America Patristic Studies 17 (Washington, D. C., 1928)—ed. O. Lendle, in *Gregorii Nysseni Sermones, pars II.* GNO 10.1 (1990), pp. 107–34.

In inscriptiones psalmorum: ed. J. McDonough, in *Gregorii Nysseni In inscriptiones Psalmorum, In sextum Psalmum, In Ecclesiasten homiliae.* GNO 5 (1962), pp. 24–175—tr. Heine (1995), pp. 83–213.

Refutatio confessionis Eunomii: ed. W. Jaeger, *Gregorii Nysseni Contra Eunomium libri, Pars altera: Liber III (vulgo III–XII). Refutatio confessionis Eunomii (vulgo Lib. II).* GNO 2 (1960), pp. 312–410—tr. H. C. Ogle and H. A. Wilson, in *Select Writings and Letters of Gregory, Bishop of Nyssa.* NPNF, 2nd series, 5 (1893; reprint, 1976), pp. 101–34.

Vita Gregorii Thaumaturgi: ed. G. Heil, in *Gregorii Nysseni Sermones, pars II.* GNO 10.1 (1990), pp. 1–57; reference numbers from *PG* 46.893–957—tr. Slusser (1998), pp. 41–87.

Vita Macrinae: ed. V. W. Callahan, in *Gregorii Nysseni opera ascetica.* GNO 8.1 (1952), pp. 370–414—tr. V. W. Callahan, *Saint Gregory of Nyssa: Ascetical Works.* FC 58 (1967), pp. 163–91—ed. and tr. [French] P. Maraval, *Grégoire de Nysse: Vie de sainte Macrine.* SChr. 178 (1971).

Ancient Authors and Texts

Ammianus Marcellinus, *Res gestae:* ed. and tr. J. C. Rolfe, *Ammianus Marcellinus,* 3 vols. LCL (1935–1940).

Anonymus Valesianus, Pars posterior: ed. and tr. J. C. Rolfe, *Ammianus Marcellinus,* vol. 3. LCL (1939), pp. 530–69.

Anthologia Graeca: ed. and tr. W. R. Paton, *The Greek Anthology,* 5 vols. LCL (1916–1918).

Anthologia Latina: ed. D. R. Shackleton Bailey, *Anthologia Latina, I: Carmina in codicibus scripta.* Fasc. 1: *Libri Salmasiani aliorumque carmina.* Teubner (1982).

Asterius of Amaseia, *Homiliae* 1–14: ed. C. Datema, *Asterius of Amasea: Homilies I–XIV. Text, Introduction and Notes* (Leiden, 1970).

Athanasius, *De synodis Arimini in Italia et Seleuciae in Isauria:* ed. Opitz (1935–1941), pp. 231–78—tr. A. Robertson, *Select Writings and Letters of Athanasius, Bishop of Alexandria.* NPNF, 2nd series, 4 (1892; reprint, 1991), pp. 451–80.

Basil of Ancyra, *De virginitate*: ed. *PG* 30.669–809.

Buzandaran Patmut'iwnk': tr. Garsoïan (1989).

Callinicus, *Vita Hypatii*: ed. and tr. [French] G. J. M. Bartelink, *Callinicos: Vie d'Hypatios*. SChr. 177 (1971).

Chronicon Paschale: ed. L. Dindorf, *Chronicon Paschale ad exemplar Vaticanum*, vol. 1. Corpus Scriptorum Historiae Byzantinae (Bonn, 1832)—tr. M. Whitby and M. Whitby, *Chronicon Paschale 284–628 AD*. TTH 7 (1989).

CJ = *Codex Justinianus*: ed. P.Krueger, *Codex Iustinianus*. Corpus Iuris Civilis 2 (11th ed., 1954; reprint, Hildesheim, 1989).

Constantine VII Porphyrogenitus, *De ceremoniis*: ed. J. J. Reiske, *Constantini Porphyrogeniti imperatoris de ceremoniis aulae byzantinae libri duo*, vol. 1. Corpus Scriptorum Historiae Byzantinae (Bonn, 1829).

———, *De thematibus*: ed. Pertusi (1952).

———, *Oratio de translatione Gregorii Theologi*: ed. and tr. [French] Flusin (1999), pp. 40–81.

Consularia Constantinopolitana: ed. R. W. Burgess, *The* Chronicle *of Hydatius and the* Consularia Constantinopolitana: *Two Contemporary Accounts of the Final Years of the Roman Empire* (Oxford, 1993), pp. 215–45.

Council of Constantinople, *Canones*: ed. J. B. Pitra, *Iuris ecclesiastici graecorum historia et monumenta iussu Pii IX. pont. max.*, vol. 1 (Rome, 1864), pp. 507–9.

CTh = *Codex Theodosianus*: ed. Th. Mommsen, *Codex Theodosianus 1.2: Theodosiani libri XVI cum Constitutionibus Sirmondi[a]nis* (Berlin, 1905)—tr. C.Pharr et al., *The Theodosian Code and Novels and the Sirmondian Constitutions* (1952; reprint, Westport, Conn., 1969), pp. 3–486.

Cyril of Scythopolis, *Vita Theodosii*: ed. E. Schwartz, *Kyrillos von Skythopolis*. Texte und Untersuchungen 49.2 (Leipzig, 1939), pp. 235–41—tr. R. M. Price, *Cyril of Scythopolis: The Lives of the Monks of Palestine*. Cistercian Studies Series 114 (Kalamazoo, Mich., 1991), pp. 262–67.

De viris illustribus urbis Romae: ed. F. Pichlmayr and R. Gruendel, *Sexti Aurelii Victoris Liber de Caesaribus*. Teubner (1970), pp. 25–74.

Epiphanius, *Ancoratus*: ed. K. Holl, *Epiphanius (Ancoratus und Panarion), 1: Ancoratus und Panarion Haer. 1–33*. GCS 25 (1915), pp. 1–149.

———, *Panarion* (+ *Rescriptum ad Acacium et Paulum* and *Recapitulatio brevis*): ed. K. Holl, *Epiphanius (Ancoratus und Panarion)*, 3 vols. GCS 25, 31, 37 (1915–1933)—tr. F. Williams, *The Panarion of Epiphanius of Salamis*, 2 vols. Nag Hammadi and Manichaean Studies 35–36 (Leiden, 1987–1994)—selections tr. P. R. Amidon, *The* Panarion *of St. Epiphanius, Bishop of Salamis: Selected Passages* (New York and Oxford, 1990).

Eunomius, *Apologia*: ed. and tr. [French] Sesboüé, de Durand and Doutreleau (1982–1983), vol. 2, pp. 234–99—ed. and tr. Vaggione (1987), pp. 34–75.

———, *Expositio fidei*: ed. and tr. Vaggione (1987), pp. 150–59.

Eusebius of Caesarea, *De martyribus Palaestinae*, recensio brevior: ed. E. Schwartz, *Eusebius Werke 2: Die Kirchengeschichte. Die lateinische Übersetzung des Rufinus*, 3 vols. GCS 9.1–3 (1903–1909), vol. 2, pp. 907–50—"Recensio prolixior" and "Recensio brevior": tr. H. J. Lawlor and J. E. L. Oulton, *Eusebius, Bishop of*

Caesarea: The Ecclesiastical History and The Martyrs of Palestine, vol. 1 (1927; reprint, London, 1954), pp. 327–400.

——, *HE = Historia ecclesiastica*: ed. E. Schwartz, *Eusebius Werke 2: Die Kirchengeschichte. Die lateinische Übersetzung des Rufinus*, 3 vols. GCS 9.1–3 (1903–1909)—tr. K. Lake, J. E. L. Oulton, and H. J. Lawlor, *Eusebius: The Ecclesiastical History*, 2 vols. LCL (1926–1932).

——, *Vita Constantini*: ed. F. Winkelmann, *Eusebius Werke 1.1: Über das Leben des Kaisers Konstantin*. GCS (2nd ed., 1991)—tr. A. Cameron and S. G. Hall, *Eusebius: Life of Constantine. Introduction, Translation, and Commentary* (Oxford, 1999).

Firmus of Caesarea, *Epistulae*: ed. and tr. [French] Calvet-Sebasti and Gatier (1989).

Gaudentius of Brescia, *Tractatus*: ed. A. Glueck, *S. Gaudentii episcopi Brixiensis Tractatus*. CSEL 68 (1936).

Gregory Thaumaturgus, *Oratio panegyrica in Origenem*: ed. and tr. [French] H. Crouzel, *Grégoire le Thaumaturge: Remerciement à Origène, suivi de la lettre d'Origène à Grégoire*. SChr. 148 (1969), pp. 94–183—tr. Slusser (1998), pp. 91–126.

Gregory the Priest, *Vita Gregorii Theologi*: ed. and tr. [French] Lequeux (2001), pp. 120–201.

[Hesychius of Jerusalem,] *Martyrium Longini* and *Passio et capitis inventio Longini*: ed. and tr. [French] Aubineau (1978–1980), vol. 2, pp. 817–44, 872–901.

Isidore of Seville, *Etymologiae*: ed. W. M. Lindsay, *Isidori Hispalensis episcopi Etymologiarum sive Originum libri XX*, 2 vols. Oxford Classical Texts (Oxford, 1911).

Jerome, *Chronicon*: ed. R. Helm, *Eusebius Werke 7: Die Chronik des Hieronymus. Hieronymi Chronicon*. GCS 47 (2nd ed., 1956)—*Chron.* s. a. 327 to end: tr. M. D. Donalson, *A Translation of Jerome's* Chronicon *with Historical Commentary* (Lewiston, Pa., 1996), pp. 39–57.

——, *De viris illustribus*: ed. E. C. Richardson, *Hieronymus: Liber de viris inlustribus. Gennadius: Liber de viris inlustribus*. Texte und Untersuchungen 14.1 (Leipzig, 1896), pp. 1–56—tr. T. P. Halton, *Saint Jerome: On Illustrious Men*. FC 100 (1999).

——, *Epistulae*: ed. I. Hilberg, *Sancti Eusebii Hieronymi Epistulae*, 3 vols. CSEL 54–56 (1910–1918)—ed. and tr. [French] J. Labourt, *Jérôme: Correspondance*, 8 vols. Budé (1949–1963)—selections tr. W. H. Fremantle, *St. Jerome: Letters and Select Works*. NPNF, 2nd series, 6 (1892; reprint, 1954), pp. 1–295.

John Diacrinomenus, *HE = Historia ecclesiastica*, fragmenta 1–2 (= *Epitome* 525–561): ed. G. C. Hansen, *Theodoros Anagnostes: Kirchengeschichte*. GCS (1971), pp. 152–57.

John of Antioch, *Fragmenta*: ed. C. Müller, *Fragmenta Historicorum Graecorum*, vol. 4 (Paris, 1851), pp. 538–622; vol. 5.1 (Paris, 1870), pp. 27–38.

John of Damascus, *Orationes de imaginibus*: ed. *PG* 94.1232–1420—tr. D. Anderson, *St. John of Damascus: On the Divine Images. Three Apologies Against Those Who Attack the Divine Images* (Crestwood, N.Y., 1980).

Josephus, *Antiquitates Iudaicae*: ed. and tr. H. St. J. Thackeray, R. Marcus, A. Wikgren, and L. H. Feldman, *Josephus*, vols. 4–10. LCL (1930–1965).

Julian, *Epistulae*: ed. and tr. W. C. Wright, *The Works of the Emperor Julian*, vol. 3. LCL (1923), pp. 2–303.

Lactantius, *De mortibus persecutorum*: ed. and tr. J. L. Creed, *Lactantius: De Mortibus Persecutorum*. Oxford Early Christian Texts (Oxford, 1984).

Libanius, *Epistulae* and *Epistularum commercium*: ed. R. Foerster, *Libanii opera*, vols. 10–11. Teubner (1921–1922)—selections ed. and tr. A. F. Norman, *Libanius: Autobiography and Selected Letters*, 2 vols. LCL (1992).

———, *Orationes*: ed. R. Foerster, *Libanii opera*, vols. 1–4. Teubner (1903–1908)— *Orat.* 1: ed. and tr. A. F. Norman, *Libanius: Autobiography and Selected Letters*, vol. 1. LCL (1992), pp. 52–337—*Orat.* 2, 12–24, 30, 33, 45, 47–50: ed. and tr. A. F. Norman, *Libanius: Selected Works*, 2 vols. LCL (1969–1977)—*Orat.* 3, 11, 31, 34, 36, 42–43, 58, 62: tr. A. F. Norman, *Antioch as a Centre of Hellenic Culture as Observed by Libanius*. TTH 34 (2000).

Mark the Deacon, *Vita Porphyrii*: ed. and tr. [French] Grégoire and Kugener (1930).

Menander Rhetor, *Treatises* I–II: ed. and tr. Russell and Wilson (1981), pp. 2–225.

Mosaicarum et Romanarum legum collatio: ed. J. Baviera, *Fontes iuris romani ante-justiniani, Pars altera: Auctores* (Florence, 1968), pp. 544–89.

Nemesius of Emesa, *De natura hominis*: ed. M. Morani, *Nemesii Emeseni De natura hominis*. Teubner (1987).

Nicephorus Bryennius, *Historia*: ed. and tr. [French] P. Gautier, *Nicéphore Bryennios: Histoire. Introduction, texte, traduction et notes*. Corpus Fontium Historiae Byzantinae 9 (Brussels, 1975).

Nicetas the Paphlagonian, *Laudatio Gregorii*: ed. and trans. Rizzo (1976).

Nicholas Mesarites, *Ecphrasis*: ed. and tr. G. Downey, "Nikolaos Mesarites: Description of the Church of the Holy Apostles at Constantinople. Greek Text Edited with Translation, Commentary and Introduction," *Transactions of the American Philosophical Society* n.s. 47.6 (1957) 861–918.

Palladius, *Historia Lausiaca*: ed. C. Butler, *The Lausiac History of Palladius, II: The Greek Text Edited with Introduction and Notes*. Texts and Studies 6.2 (Cambridge, 1904)—tr. R. T. Meyer, *Palladius: The Lausiac History*. ACW 34 (1964).

Parastaseis syntomoi chronikai: ed. T. Preger, *Scriptores originum Constantinopolitanarum*, vol. 1. Teubner (1901), pp. 19–73—tr. A. Cameron and J. Herrin, *Constantinople in the Early Eighth Century: The* Parastaseis Syntomoi Chronikai (Leiden, 1984), pp. 56–165.

Passio Athenogenis: ed. and tr. [French] Maraval (1990b), pp. 30–85.

Passio XL martyrum: ed. von Gebhardt (1902), pp. 171–81.

Periplus Ponti Euxini: ed. C. Müller, *Fragmenta historicorum graecorum*, vol. 5.1 (Paris, 1870), pp. 174–84.

Philostorgius, *HE = Historia ecclesiastica*: ed. J. Bidez, *Philostorgius Kirchengeschichte. Mit dem Leben des Lucian von Antiochien und den Fragmenten eines arianischen Historiographen*. GCS 21 (1913); rev. F. Winkelmann, 2nd ed. (1972), 3rd ed. (1981)—tr. E. Walford, *The Ecclesiastical History of Sozomen, Comprising a History of the Church, from A.D. 324 to A.D. 440. Translated from the Greek: with a Memoir of the Author. Also the Ecclesiastical History of Philostorgius, as Epitomised by Photius, Patriarch of Constantinople*. Bohn's Ecclesiastical Library (London, 1855), pp. 429–521.

Philostratus, *Vitae sophistarum*: ed. and tr. W. C. Wright, *Philostratus and Eunapius: The Lives of the Sophists*. LCL (1921), pp. 2–315.

Photius, *Bibliotheca*: ed. and tr. [French] R. Henry, *Photius: Bibliothèque*, 8 vols., and Index, ed. J. Schamp. Budé (1959–1991).

Plutarch, *Lucullus*: ed. and tr. B. Perrin, *Plutarch's Lives*, vol. 2. LCL (1914), pp. 470–611.

Procopius, *Anecdota* and *Bellum Persicum*: ed. and tr. H. B. Dewing, *Procopius*, vols. 1–6. LCL (1914–1935).

Rufinus, *HE* = *Historia ecclesiastica*: ed. T. Mommsen, in *Eusebius Werke 2: Die Kirchengeschichte. Die lateinische Übersetzung des Rufinus*, ed. E. Schwartz, vols. 1–2. GCS 9.1–2 (1903–1908)—*HE* 10–11: tr. P. R. Amidon, *The Church History of Rufinus of Aquileia. Books 10 and 11* (New York, 1997).

Severus of Antioch, *Epistulae*: tr. Brooks (1903–1904).

Socrates, *HE* = *Historia ecclesiastica*: ed. G. C. Hansen, with M. Sirinian, *Sokrates: Kirchengeschichte*. GCS, Neue Folge 1 (1995)—tr. A. C. Zenos, in *Socrates, Sozomenus: Church Histories*. NPNF, 2nd series, 2 (1890; reprint, 1973), pp. 1–178.

Sozomen, *HE* = *Historia ecclesiastica*: ed. J. Bidez, *Sozomenus: Kirchengeschichte*. GCS 50 (1960); rev. G. C. Hansen. GCS, Neue Folge 4 (2nd ed., 1995)—tr. C. D. Hartranft, in *Socrates, Sozomenus: Church Histories*. NPNF, 2nd series, 2 (1890; reprint, 1973), pp. 236–427.

Strabo, *Geographia*: ed. and tr. H. L. Jones, *The Geography of Strabo*, 8 vols. LCL (1917–1932).

Suda: ed. A. Adler, *Suidae Lexicon*, 5 vols. (1928–1938; reprint, Stuttgart, 1967–1971).

Synodicon vetus: ed. and tr. J. Duffy and J. Parker, *The* Synodicon Vetus: *Text, Translation, and Notes*. Corpus Fontium Historiae Byzantinae 15 (Washington, D.C., 1979), pp. 2–143.

Testamentum XL martyrum: ed. von Gebhardt (1902), pp. 166–70—ed. and tr. H. Musurillo, *The Acts of the Christian Martyrs: Introduction, Texts and Translations*. Oxford Early Christian Texts (Oxford, 1972), pp. 354–61.

Theodore of Mopsuestia, *Contra Eunomium*: tr. Vaggione (1980).

Theodoret, *HE* = *Historia ecclesiastica*: ed. L. Parmentier, *Theodoret: Kirchengeschichte*. GCS 19 (1911); 2nd ed. rev. F. Scheidweiler. GCS 44 (1954); 3rd ed. rev. G. C. Hansen. GCS, Neue Folge 5 (1998)—tr. B. Jackson, in *Theodoret, Jerome, Gennadius, Rufinus: Historical Writings, Etc*. NPNF, 2nd series, 3 (1892; reprint, 1989), pp. 33–159.

Theophilus of Antioch, *Ad Autolycum*: ed. and tr. R. M. Grant, *Theophilus of Antioch: Ad Autolycum*. Oxford Early Christian Texts (Oxford, 1970).

Vita et miracula Basilii Magni: ed. and tr. [Latin] F. Combefis, *SS. Patrum Amphilochii Iconiensis, Methodii Patarensis, et Andreae Cretensis opera omnia, quae reperiri potuerunt. Nunc primum, magnam partem tenebris eruta, latina reddita, ac recognita, notisque illustrata* (Paris, 1644), pp. 155–225; Latin translation reprinted in *PG* 29, pp. ccxciv–cccxvi.

Bibliography

Abramowski, L. (1976). "Das Bekenntnis des Gregor Thaumaturgus bei Gregor von Nyssa und das Problem seiner Echtheit." *Zeitschrift für Kirchengeschichte* 87: 145–66.

Aldrete, G. S. (1999). *Gestures and Acclamations in Ancient Rome*. Baltimore and London.

Allen, P. (1997). "John Chrysostom's Homilies on I and II Thessalonians: The Preacher and His Audience." In *Studia Patristica, Vol. XXXI, Papers Presented at the Twelfth International Conference on Patristic Studies Held in Oxford 1995. Preaching, Second Century, Tertullian to Arnobius, Egypt Before Nicaea*, ed. E. A. Livingstone, pp. 3–21. Leuven.

———. (1998). "The Identity of Sixth-Century Preachers and Audiences in Byzantium." In *Identities in the Eastern Mediterranean in Antiquity*, ed. G. Clarke. = *Mediterranean Archaeology* 11:245–53.

Amand de Mendieta, E. (1978). "Les neuf homélies de Basile de Césarée sur l'Hexaéméron." *Byzantion* 48:337–68.

Amand de Mendieta, E., and S. Y. Rudberg, ed. (1997). *Basilius von Caesarea: Homilien zum Hexaemeron*. GCS, Neue Folge, Band 2. Berlin.

Anastos, M. V. (1981). "Basil's Κατὰ Εὐνομίου: A Critical Analysis." In *Basil of Caesarea: Christian, Humanist, Ascetic: A Sixteen-Hundredth Anniversary Symposium*, ed. P. J. Fedwick, 1:67–136. Toronto.

Anderson, J. G. C. (1903). *A Journey of Exploration in Pontus*. = *Studia Pontica* 1. Brussels.

Arjava, A. (1996). *Women and Law in Late Antiquity*. Oxford.

Aubineau, M., ed. and tr. (1978–1980). *Les homélies festales d'Hésychius de Jérusalem*, 2 vols. Subsidia Hagiographica 59. Brussels.

Aufhauser, J. B. (1911). *Das Drachenwunder des heiligen Georg in der griechischen und lateinischen Überlieferung*. Byzantinisches Archiv 5. Leipzig.

Azéma, Y., ed. and tr. (1964). *Théodoret de Cyr: Correspondance II (Epist. Sirm. 1–95)*. SChr. 98. Paris.

Bagnall, R. S. (1993). *Egypt in Late Antiquity*. Princeton, N.J.

Bannon, C. J. (1997). *The Brothers of Romulus: Fraternal Pietas in Roman Law, Literature, and Society*. Princeton, N.J.

Barnes, M. R. (1993). "The Background and Use of Eunomius' Causal Language." In *Arianism After Arius: Essays on the Development of the Fourth Century Trinitarian Conflicts*, ed. M. R. Barnes and D. H. Williams, pp. 217–36. Edinburgh.

Barnes, T. D. (1981). *Constantine and Eusebius*. Cambridge, Mass.

———. (1982). *The New Empire of Diocletian and Constantine*. Cambridge, Mass.

————. (1993). *Athanasius and Constantius: Theology and Politics in the Constantinian Empire*. Cambridge, Mass.

Bartelink, G. J. M., ed. and tr. (1971). *Callinicos: Vie d'Hypatios*. SChr. 177. Paris.

Beaucamp, J. (1998). "Le testament de Grégoire de Nazianze." In *Fontes Minores X*, ed. L. Burgmann, pp. 1–100. Forschungen zur Byzantinischen Rechtsgeschichte 22. Frankfurt.

Beck, H.-G. (1977). "Rede als Kunstwerk und Bekenntnis: Gregor von Nazianz." *Akademie der Wissenschaften, philosophisch-historische Klasse, Sitzungsberichte, Jahrgang 1977, Heft 4*. Munich.

Behr, J. (1999). "The Rational Animal: A Rereading of Gregory of Nyssa's *De hominis opificio*." *Journal of Early Christian Studies* 7:219–47.

Bekker, I., ed. (1838). *Theophanes Continuatus, Ioannes Cameniata, Symeon Magister, Georgius Monachus*, 2 vols. Corpus Scriptorum Historiae Byzantinae 33. Bonn.

Berges, D., and J. Nollé (2000). *Tyana: Archäologisch-historische Untersuchungen zum südwestlichen Kappadokien*, 2 vols. Inschriften griechischer Städte aus Kleinasien 55.1–2. Bonn.

Bernardi, J. (1968). *La prédication des Pères Cappadociens: La prédicateur et son auditoire*. Paris.

————. (1995). *Saint Grégoire de Nazianze: Le théologien et son temps (330–390)*. Paris.

Bidez, J. (1913). "Einleitung." In J. Bidez, ed., *Philostorgius Kirchengeschichte: Mit dem Leben des Lucian von Antiochien und den Fragmenten eines arianischen Historiographen*, pp. IX–CLXVII. GCS 21. Leipzig [same pagination in 3rd ed., 1981].

Bland, R. (1991). "The Last Coinage of Caesarea in Cappadocia." In *Ermanno A. Arslan Studia Dicata, Parte I, Monetazione greca e greco-imperiale*, ed. R. Martini and N. Vismara, pp. 213–58. Glaux 7. Milan.

Blok, A. (1974). *The Mafia of a Sicilian Village, 1860–1960: A Study of Violent Peasant Entrepreneurs*. New York.

Böhm, T. (2001). "Basil of Caesarea, *Adversus Eunomium* I–III and Ps. Basil, *Adversus Eunomium* IV–V." In *Studia Patristica, Vol. XXXVII, Papers Presented at the Thirteenth International Conference on Patristic Studies Held in Oxford 1999. Cappadocian Writers, Other Greek Writers*, ed. M. F. Wiles and E. J. Yarnold, with P. M. Parvis, pp. 20–26. Leuven.

Bourdieu, P. (1976). "Marriage Strategies as Strategies of Social Reproduction." In *Family and Society: Selections from the Annales, économies, sociétés, civilisations*, ed. R. Forster and O. Ranum, tr. E. Forster and P. M. Ranum, pp. 117–44. Baltimore.

Bradley, K. R. (1991). *Discovering the Roman Family: Studies in Roman Social History*. New York.

Brakke, D. (1995). *Athanasius and the Politics of Asceticism*. Oxford.

Braund, D. (1986). "The Caucasian Frontier: Myth, Exploration and the Dynamics of Imperialism." In *The Defence of the Roman and Byzantine East: Proceedings of a Colloquium Held at the University of Sheffield in April 1986*, ed. P. Freeman and D. Kennedy, pp. 31–49. British Archaeological Reports, International Series 297. Oxford.

van Bremen, R. (1996). *The Limits of Participation: Women and Civic Life in the Greek East in the Hellenistic and Roman Periods*. Amsterdam.

Brennecke, H. C. (1988). *Studien zur Geschichte der Homöer: Der Osten bis zum Ende der homöischen Reichskirche.* Beiträge zur Historischen Theologie 73. Tubingen.

Brooks, E. W., tr. (1903–1904). *The Sixth Book of the Select Letters of Severus Patriarch of Antioch in the Syriac Version of Athanasius of Nisibis, Vol. II (Translation),* 2 vols. London and Oxford.

Brothwell, D. R. (1988). "Foodstuffs, Cooking, and Drugs." In *Civilization of the Ancient Mediterranean: Greece and Rome,* ed. M. Grant and R. Kitzinger, 1:247–61. New York.

Broughton, T. R. S. (1938). "Roman Asia Minor." In *An Economic Survey of Ancient Rome,* ed. T. Frank, 4:499–918. Baltimore.

Browning, R. (1983). *Medieval and Modern Greek.* 2nd ed. Cambridge.

Brubaker, L. (1992). "The Vita Icon of Saint Basil: Iconography." In *Four Icons in the Menil Collection,* ed. B. Davezac, pp. 70–93. Houston.

———. (1999). *Vision and Meaning in Ninth-Century Byzantium: Image as Exegesis in the Homilies of Gregory of Nazianzus.* Cambridge.

Burrus, V. (1995). *The Making of a Heretic: Gender, Authority, and the Priscillianist Controversy.* Berkeley, Calif.

———. (2000). *"Begotten, Not Made": Conceiving Manhood in Late Antiquity.* Stanford, Calif.

Burton, R. F. (1934). *The Book of the Thousand Nights and a Night: A Plain and Literal Translation of the Arabian Nights Entertainments,* 2 vols. New York.

Callahan, J. F. (1958). "Greek Philosophy and the Cappadocian Cosmology." *Dumbarton Oaks Papers* 12:29–57.

Calvet-Sebasti, M.-A., and P.-L. Gatier, ed. and tr. (1989). *Firmus de Césarée: Lettres.* SChr. 350. Paris.

Cameron, A. (1985). "Polyonomy in the Late Roman Aristocracy: The Case of Petronius Probus." *Journal of Roman Studies* 75:164–82.

Carr, A. W. (1992). "The Vita Icon of Saint Basil: Notes on a Byzantine Object." In *Four Icons in the Menil Collection,* ed. B. Davezac, pp. 94–105. Houston.

Cavalcanti, E. (1976). *Studi Eunomiani.* Orientalia Christiana Analecta 202. Rome.

Cavallin, A. (1944). *Studien zu den Briefen des hl. Basilius.* Lund.

Chatzidakes, M. (1938). "Ἐκ τῶν Ἐλπίου τοῦ Ῥωμαίου." *Epeteris Hetaireias Byzantinon Spoudon* 14:393–414.

Clark, E. A. (1992). *The Origenist Controversy: The Cultural Construction of an Early Christian Debate.* Princeton, N.J.

———. (1999). *Reading Renunciation: Asceticism and Scripture in Early Christianity.* Princeton, N.J.

Clark, G. (1996). "Cosmic Sympathies: Nature as the Expression of Divine Purpose." In *Human Landscapes in Classical Antiquity: Environment and Culture,* ed. G. Shipley and J. Salmon, pp. 310–29. London and New York.

Clarke, K. (1999). *Between Geography and History: Hellenistic Constructions of the Roman World.* Oxford.

Clémencet, C. (1885). "Vita sancti Gregorii Theologi episcopi Constantinopolitani ex ipsius potissimum scriptis adornata." In *PG* 35, col. 147–242. Paris.

Courtonne, Y. (1934). *Saint Basile et l'hellénisme: Etude sur la rencontre de la pensée chrétienne avec la sagesse antique dans l'Hexaéméron de Basile le Grand.* Paris.

Crouzel, H. (1970). "L'école d'Origène à Césarée: Postscriptum à une édition de Grégoire le Thaumaturge." *Bulletin de littérature ecclésiastique* 71:15–27.

Cumont, F., and E. Cumont (1906). *Voyage d'exploration archéologique dans le Pont et la Petite Arménie.* = *Studia Pontica* 2. Brussels.

Cunningham, M. B., and P. Allen (1998). "Introduction." In *Preacher and Audience: Studies in Early Christian and Byzantine Homiletics,* ed. M. B. Cunningham and P. Allen, pp. 1–20. A New History of the Sermon 1. Leiden.

Dagron, G. (1969). "Aux origines de la civilisation byzantine: Langue du culture et langue d'état." *Revue historique* 241:23–56.

———. (1984). *Constantinople imaginaire: Etudes sur le recueil des* Patria. Bibliothèque byzantine, Etudes 8. Paris.

———. (1995). "Poissons, pêcheurs et poissonniers de Constantinople." In *Constantinople and Its Hinterland: Papers from the Twenty-Seventh Spring Symposium of Byzantine Studies, Oxford, April 1993,* ed. C. Mango, G. Dagron, and G. Greatrex, pp. 57–73. Society for the Promotion of Byzantine Studies, Publications 3. Aldershot.

Daniélou, J. (1955). "La chronologie des sermons de Grégoire de Nysse." *Revue des sciences religieuses* 29:346–72.

———. (1956). "Eunome l'Arien et l'exégèse néo-platonicienne du Cratyle." *Revue des études grecques* 69:412–32.

———. (1966). "La chronologie des oeuvres de Grégoire de Nysse." *Studia Patristica* 7 = *Texte und Untersuchungen* 92:159–69.

Delehaye, H., ed. (1902). *Synaxarium ecclesiae Constantinopolitanae e codice Sirmondiano nunc Berolinensi adiectis synaxariis selectis.* = Propylaeum ad Acta Sanctorum Novembris. Brussels.

———. (1909). *Les légendes grecques des saints militaires.* Paris.

Demoen, K. (1996). *Pagan and Biblical Exempla in Gregory Nazianzen: A Study in Rhetoric and Hermeneutics.* CChr., Lingua Patrum 2. Turnhout.

Devos, P. (1961a). "S. Grégoire de Nazianze et Hellade de Césarée en Cappadoce." *Analecta Bollandiana* 79:91–101.

———. (1961b). "S. Pierre Ier, évêque de Sébastée, dans une lettre de s. Grégoire de Nazianze." *Analecta Bollandiana* 79:346–60.

Digeser, E. D. (1998). "Lactantius, Porphyry, and the Debate over Religious Toleration." *Journal of Roman Studies* 88:129–46.

———. (2000). *The Making of a Christian Empire: Lactantius and Rome.* Ithaca, N.Y.

Di Maio, M. (1978). "The Transfer of the Remains of the Emperor Julian from Tarsus to Constantinople." *Byzantion* 48:43–50.

Dixon, S. (1992). *The Roman Family.* Baltimore and London.

Dolbeau, F. (1989). "Recherches sur les oeuvres littéraires du pape Gélase II. A.—Une vie inédite de Grégoire de Nazianze (*BHL* 3668d), attribuable à Jean de Gaète." *Analecta Bollandiana* 107:65–127.

Downey, G. (1961). *A History of Antioch in Syria from Seleucus to the Arab Conquest.* Princeton, N.J.

Drecoll, V. H. (1996). *Die Entwicklung der Trinitätslehre des Basilius von Cäsarea: Sein Weg vom Homöusianer zum Neonizäner.* Forschungen zur Kirchen- und Dogmengeschichte 66. Göttingen.

Dueck, D. (2000). *Strabo of Amasia: A Greek Man of Letters in Augustan Rome.* London and New York.

Easterling, P., and R. Miles (1999). "Dramatic Identities: Tragedy in Late Antiquity." In *Constructing Identities in Late Antiquity,* ed. R. Miles, pp. 95–111. London and New York.

Eck, W. (1978). "Der Einfluß der konstantinischen Wende auf die Auswahl der Bischöfe im 4. u. 5. Jahrhundert." *Chiron* 8:561–85.

Emmett Nobbs, A. (1990). "Philostorgius' View of the Past." In *Reading the Past in Late Antiquity,* ed. G. Clarke, B. Croke, A. Emmett Nobbs, and R. Mortley, pp. 251–64. Rushcutters Bay.

Epstein, A. W. (1986). *Tokalı Kilise: Tenth-Century Metropolitan Art in Byzantine Cappadocia.* Dumbarton Oaks Studies 22. Washington, D.C.

van Esbroeck, M. (1988). "L'aspect cosmologique de la philosophie d'Eunome pour la réprise de l'Hexaémeron basilien par Grégoire de Nysse." In *El "Contra Eunomium I" in la producción literaria de Gregorio de Nisa: VI Coloquio Internacional sobre Gregorio de Nisa,* ed. L. F. Mateo-Seco and J. L. Bastero, pp. 203–16. Pamplona.

Esper, M. (1984). "Enkomiastik und Christianismos in Gregors epideiktischer Rede auf den Heiligen Theodor." In *The Biographical Works of Gregory of Nyssa: Proceedings of the Fifth International Colloquium on Gregory of Nyssa (Mainz, 6–10 September 1982),* ed. A. Spira, pp. 145–59. Patristic Monograph Series 12. Cambridge, Mass.

Evans Grubbs, J. (1989). "Abduction Marriage in Antiquity: A Law of Constantine (*CTh* IX.24.1) and Its Social Context." *Journal of Roman Studies* 79:59–83.

———. (1995). *Law and Family in Late Antiquity: The Emperor Constantine's Marriage Legislation.* Oxford.

Fentress, J., and C. Wickham (1992). *Social Memory.* Oxford.

Fermor, P. L. (1999). "The Rock Monasteries of Cappadocia." In P. L. Fermor, *A Time to Keep Silence,* pp. 79–87. Reprint, Pleasantville, N.Y.

Fitzgerald, W. (1981). "Notes on the Iconography of Saint Basil the Great." In *Basil of Caesarea: Christian, Humanist, Ascetic: A Sixteen-Hundredth Anniversary Symposium,* ed. P. J. Fedwick, 2:533–63. Toronto.

Flusin, B. (1998). "L'empereur et le théologien: A propos du retour des reliques de Grégoire de Nazianze (*BHG* 728)." In *AETOΣ : Studies in Honour of Cyril Mango Presented to Him on April 14, 1998,* ed. I. Ševčenko and I. Hutter, pp. 137–53. Stuttgart and Leipzig.

———. (1999). "Le panégyrique de Constantin VII Porphyrogénète pour la translation des reliques de Grégoire le Théologien (*BHG* 728)." *Revue des études byzantines* 57:5–97.

Foss, C. (1987). "St. Autonomus and His Church in Bithynia." *Dumbarton Oaks Papers* 41:187–98. Reprinted in C. Foss, *History and Archaeology of Byzantine Asia Minor,* Chapter 5. Aldershot, 1990.

———. (1995). "Nicomedia and Constantinople." In *Constantinople and Its Hinterland. Papers from the Twenty-Seventh Spring Symposium of Byzantine Studies, Oxford, April 1993,* ed. C. Mango, G. Dagron, and G. Greatrex, pp. 181–90. Society for the Promotion of Byzantine Studies, Publications 3. Aldershot.

Fowden, G. (1978). "Bishops and Temples in the Eastern Roman Empire A.D. 320–435." *Journal of Theological Studies* n.s. 29:53–78.

Froidevaux, L. (1929). "Le symbole de saint Grégoire le Thaumaturge." *Recherches de science religieuse* 19:193–247.

Gain, B. (1985). *L'église de Cappadoce au IVᵉ siècle d'après la correspondance de Basile de Césarée (330–379)*. Orientalia Christiana Analecta 225. Rome.

Gallay, P. (1943). *La vie de saint Grégoire de Nazianze*. Lyon and Paris.

———, ed. and tr. (1964–1967). *Saint Grégoire de Nazianze: Lettres*, 2 vols. Budé. Paris.

———, ed. (1969). *Gregor von Nazianz: Briefe*. GCS 53. Berlin.

Gallay, P., and M. Jourjon, ed. and tr. (1974). *Grégoire de Nazianze: Lettres théologiques*. SChr. 208. Paris.

———, ed. and tr. (1978). *Grégoire de Nazianze: Discours 27–31 (Discours théologiques)*. SChr. 250. Paris.

Gardner, J. F. (1993). *Being a Roman Citizen*. London and New York.

Garsoïan, N. G. (1989). *The Epic Histories Attributed to Pʿawstos Buzand (Buzandaran Patmutʿiwnkʿ)*. Cambridge, Mass.

von Gebhardt, O., ed. (1902). *Acta martyrum selecta: Ausgewählte Märtyreracten und andere Urkunden aus der Verfolgungszeit der christlichen Kirche*. Berlin.

Giet, S. (1941). *Les idées et l'action sociales de saint Basile*. Paris.

———, ed. and tr. (1950). *Basile de Césarée: Homélies sur l'Hexaéméron*. SChr. 26. Paris.

———. (1955). "Saint Basile et le concile de Constantinople de 360." *Journal of Theological Studies* n.s. 6:94–99.

Gleason, M. W. (1995). *Making Men: Sophists and Self-Presentation in Ancient Rome*. Princeton, N.J.

Gotoff, H. (1993). "Oratory: The Art of Illusion." *Harvard Studies in Classical Philology* 95:289–313.

Gould, G. E. (1989). "Basil of Caesarea and Gregory of Nyssa on the Beatitudes." In *Studia Patristica, Vol. XXII, Papers Presented to the Tenth International Conference on Patristic Studies Held in Oxford 1987. Cappadocian Fathers, Chrysostom and his Greek Contemporaries, Augustine, Donatism and Pelagianism*, ed. E. A. Livingstone, pp. 14–22. Leuven.

Gowers, E. (1993). *The Loaded Table: Representations of Food in Roman Literature*. Oxford.

Gregg, R. C., and D. E. Groh (1981). *Early Arianism—A View of Salvation*. Philadelphia.

Grégoire, H., and M.-A. Kugener, ed. and tr. (1930). *Marc le Diacre: Vie de Porphyre évêque de Gaza*. Collection Byzantine publiée sous le patronage de l'Association Guillaume Budé. Paris.

Gribomont, J. (1981). "Notes biographiques sur s. Basile le Grand." In *Basil of Caesarea: Christian, Humanist, Ascetic: A Sixteen-Hundredth Anniversary Symposium*, ed. P. J. Fedwick, 1:21–48. Toronto.

Grierson, P. (1962). "The Tombs and Obits of the Byzantine Emperors (337–1042)." *Dumbarton Oaks Papers* 16:1–60.

Grillmeier, A. (1975). *Christ in Christian Tradition, Vol. 1, From the Apostolic Age to Chalcedon (451)*, tr. J. Bowden. 2nd ed. London and Oxford.

Gusdorf, G. (1980). "Conditions and Limits of Autobiography." In *Autobiography: Essays Theoretical and Critical*, ed. J. Olney, pp. 28–48. Princeton, N.J.

Haas, C. (1997). *Alexandria in Late Antiquity: Topography and Social Conflict.* Baltimore.

Halkin, F. (1957). *Bibliotheca hagiographica graecae.* Subsidia Hagiographica 8a. 3rd ed. Brussels.

———. (1969). *Auctarium bibliothecae hagiographicae graecae.* Subsidia Hagiographica 47. Brussels.

Hanson, R. P. C. (1988). *The Search for the Christian Doctrine of God: The Arian Controversy 318–381.* Edinburgh.

Harper, R. P. (1968). "Tituli Comanorum Cappadociae." *Anatolian Studies* 18:93–147.

Hauschild, W.-D., tr. (1973). *Basilius von Caesarea: Briefe, Zweiter Teil.* Bibliothek der griechischen Literatur, Abteilung Patristik, Bd. 3. Stuttgart.

———, tr. (1990). *Basilius von Caesarea: Briefe, Erster Teil.* Bibliothek der griechischen Literatur, Abteilung Patristik, Bd. 32. Stuttgart.

———, tr. (1993). *Basilius von Caesarea: Briefe, Dritter Teil.* Bibliothek der griechischen Literatur, Abteilung Patristik, Bd. 37. Stuttgart.

Heather, P. (1998). "Senators and Senates." In *The Cambridge Ancient History, Vol. XIII, The Late Empire, A.D. 337–425,* ed. A. Cameron and P. Garnsey, pp. 184–210. Cambridge.

Heather, P., and J. Matthews (1991). *The Goths in the Fourth Century.* TTH 11. Liverpool.

Heine, R. E. (1995). *Gregory of Nyssa's Treatise on the Inscriptions of the Psalms: Introduction, Translation, and Notes.* Oxford.

Hild, F., and M. Restle (1981). *Kappadokien (Kappadokia, Charsianon, Sebasteia und Lykandos). = Tabula Imperii Byzantini,* ed. H. Hunger, Bd. 2. Österreichische Akademie der Wissenschaften, philosophisch-historische Klasse, Denkschriften, Bd. 149. Vienna.

Holum, K. G. (1982). *Theodosian Empresses: Women and Imperial Dominion in Late Antiquity.* Berkeley, Calif.

Honigmann, E. (1961). *Trois mémoires posthumes d'histoire et de géographie de l'Orient chrétien,* ed. P. Devos. Subsidia Hagiographica 35. Brussels.

Honoré, T. (1978). *Tribonian.* Ithaca, N.Y.

Hopwood, K. (1989). "Consent and Control: How the Peace Was Kept in Rough Cilicia." In *The Eastern Frontier of the Roman Empire: Proceedings of a Colloquium Held at Ankara in September 1988,* ed. D. H. French and C. S. Lightfoot, pp. 191–201. British Institute of Archaeology at Ankara, Monograph 11 = British Archaeological Reports, International Series 553.1. Oxford.

Horden, P., and N. Purcell (2000). *The Corrupting Sea: A Study of Mediterranean History.* Oxford.

Jaeger, W. (1960). "Prolegomena." In *Gregorii Nysseni Contra Eunomium libri, Pars altera: Liber III (vulgo III–XII). Refutatio confessionis Eunomii (vulgo Lib. II),* ed. W. Jaeger, pp. v–lxxi. GNO 2. Leiden.

de Jerphanion, G. (1925–1936). *Une nouvelle province de l'art byzantin: Les églises rupestres de Cappadoce, Texte,* 2 vols. Bibliothèque archéologique et historique 5–6. Paris.

———. (1938). "Histoires de saint Basile dans les peintures cappadociennes et dans les peintures romaines du Moyen Age." In G. de Jerphanion, *La voix des monuments: Etudes d'archéologie, nouvelle série,* pp. 153–73. Rome and Paris. Reprinted from *Byzantion* 6 (1931): 535–58.

Johnson, M. J. (1991). "On the Burial Places of the Valentinian Dynasty." *Historia* 40:501–6.

Jolivet-Lévy, C. (1991). *Les églises byzantines de Cappadoce: Le programme iconographique de l'abside et de ses abords.* Paris.

Jones, A. H. M. (1940). *The Greek City from Alexander to Justinian.* Oxford.

———. (1964). *The Later Roman Empire 284–602: A Social, Economic, and Administrative Survey,* 2 or 3 vols. (continuous pagination). Oxford and Norman, Okla.

———. (1971). *The Cities of the Eastern Roman Provinces.* 2nd ed. Oxford.

Jones, C. P. (1978). *The Roman World of Dio Chrysostom.* Cambridge, Mass.

Jungck, C., ed. and tr. (1974). *Gregor von Nazianz: De vita sua.* Heidelberg.

Karlin-Hayter, P. (1991). "Passio of the XL Martyrs of Sebasteia. The Greek Tradition: The Earliest Account (*BHG* 1201)." *Analecta Bollandiana* 109:249–304.

Kaster, R. A. (1988). *Guardians of Language: The Grammarian and Society in Late Antiquity.* Berkeley, Calif.

Klock, C. (1984). "Architektur im Dienste der Heiligenverehrung: Gregory von Nyssa als Kirchenbauer (Ep. 25)." In *The Biographical Works of Gregory of Nyssa: Proceedings of the Fifth International Colloquium on Gregory of Nyssa (Mainz, 6–10 September 1982),* ed. A. Spira, pp. 161–80. Patristic Monograph Series 12. Cambridge, Mass.

Knauber, A. (1968). "Das Anliegen der Schule des Origenes zu Cäsarea." *Münchener Theologische Zeitschrift* 19:182–203.

Köttig, B. (1962). "Gregor von Nyssa's Wallfahrtskritik." In *Studia Patristica* 5, ed. F. L. Cross. = *Texte und Untersuchungen* 80:360–67. Berlin.

Kopecek, T. A. (1973). "The Social Class of the Cappadocian Fathers." *Church History* 42:453–66.

———. (1979). *A History of Neo-Arianism,* 2 vols. Patristic Monograph Series 8. Cambridge, Mass.

Kostof, S. (1989). *Caves of God: Cappadocia and Its Churches.* Revised ed. Oxford.

Kurmann, A. (1988). *Gregor von Nazianz: Oratio 4, Gegen Julian. Ein Kommentar.* Schweizerische Beiträge zur Altertumswissenschaft 19. Basel.

Laiou, A. E. (1993). "Sex, Consent, and Coercion in Byzantium." In *Consent and Coercion to Sex and Marriage in Ancient and Medieval Societies,* ed. A. E. Laiou, pp. 109–221. Washington, D.C.

Lallemand, A. (2001). "L'ivresse chez Basile et Grégoire de Nysse." In *Studia Patristica, Vol. XXXVII, Papers Presented at the Thirteenth International Conference on Patristic Studies Held in Oxford 1999. Cappadocian Writers, Other Greek Writers,* ed. M. F. Wiles and E. J. Yarnold, with P. M. Parvis, pp. 133–39. Leuven.

Lampe, G. W. H. (1961). *A Patristic Greek Lexicon.* Oxford.

Lane Fox, R. (1987). *Pagans and Christians.* New York.

Le Boulluec, A. (2000). "Orthodoxie et hérésie aux premiers siècles dans l'historiographie récente." In *Orthodoxie, christianisme, histoire: Orthodoxy, Christianity, History,* ed. S. Elm, E. Rebillard, and A. Romano, pp. 303–19. Collection de l'Ecole française de Rome 270. Rome.

Lee, A. D. (1988). "Close-Kin Marriage in Late Antique Mesopotamia." *Greek, Roman and Byzantine Studies* 29:403–13.

Leemans, J. (2001a). "On the Date of Gregory of Nyssa's First Homilies on the Forty Martyrs of Sebaste (1A and 1B)." *Journal of Theological Studies* n.s. 52:93–97.

———. (2001b). "A Preacher-Audience Oriented Analysis of Gregory of Nyssa's Homily on Theodore the Recruit." In *Studia Patristica, Vol. XXXVII, Papers Presented at the Thirteenth International Conference on Patristic Studies Held in Oxford 1999. Cappadocian Writers, Other Greek Writers*, ed. M. F. Wiles and E. J. Yarnold, with P. M. Parvis, pp. 140–46. Leuven.

Lenski, N. (1999). "Basil and the Isaurian Uprising of A.D. 375." *Phoenix* 53:308–29.

Leppin, H. (2001). "Heretical Historiography: Philostorgius." In *Studia Patristica, Vol. XXXIV, Papers Presented at the Thirteenth International Conference on Patristic Studies Held in Oxford 1999. Historica, Biblica, Theologica et Philosophica*, ed. M. F. Wiles and E. J. Yarnold, with P. M. Parvis, pp. 111–24. Leuven.

Lequeux, X., ed. and tr. (2001). *Gregorii Presbyteri Vita sancti Gregorii Theologi.* CChr., Series graeca 44 = Corpus Nazianzenum 11. Turnhout and Leuven.

Levie, J. (1920). "Les sources de la septième et de la huitième homélie de saint Basile sur l'Hexaéméron." *Musée belge* 19–24:113–49.

Lim, R. (1990). "The Politics of Interpretation in Basil of Caesarea's *Hexaemeron.*" *Vigiliae Christianae* 44:351–70.

———. (1995). *Public Disputation, Power, and Social Order in Late Antiquity.* Berkeley, Calif.

Lipatov, N. A. (2001). "*The Statement of Faith* Attributed to St. Basil the Great." In *Studia Patristica, Vol. XXXVII, Papers Presented at the Thirteenth International Conference on Patristic Studies Held in Oxford 1999. Cappadocian Writers, Other Greek Writers*, ed. M. F. Wiles and E. J. Yarnold, with P. M. Parvis, pp. 147–59. Leuven.

MacMullen, R. (1989). "The Preacher's Audience (AD 350–400)." *Journal of Theological Studies* n.s. 40:503–11.

———. (1990). *Changes in the Roman Empire: Essays in the Ordinary.* Princeton, N.J.

Magie, D. (1950). *Roman Rule in Asia Minor to the End of the Third Century After Christ*, 2 vols. Princeton, N.J.

Malingrey, A.-M. and P. Leclercq, ed. and tr. (1988). *Palladios: Dialogue sur la vie de Jean Chrysostome*, 2 vols. SChr. 341–42. Paris.

Mango, C. (1985). *Le développement urbain de Constantinople (IVᵉ–VIIᵉ siècles).* Travaux et Mémoires du Centre de recherche d'histoire et civilisation de Byzance. Collège de France, Monographies 2. Paris.

———. (1990). "Constantine's Mausoleum and the Translation of Relics." *Byzantinische Zeitschrift* 83:51–62. Reprinted in C. Mango, *Studies on Constantinople*, Chapter 5. Aldershot, 1993.

Maraval, P. (1985). *Lieux saints et pèlerinages d'Orient: Histoire et géographie des origines à la conquête arabe.* Paris.

———. (1986). "Un lecteur ancien de la 'Vie de Macrine' de Grégoire de Nysse." *Analecta Bollandiana* 104:187–90.

———. (1988). "La date de la mort de Basile de Césarée." *Revue des études augustiniennes* 34:25–38.

————, ed. and tr. (1990a). *Grégoire de Nysse: Lettres*. SChr. 363. Paris.

————, ed. and tr. (1990b). *La passion inédite de S. Athénogène de Pédachthoé en Cappadoce (BHG 197b)*. Subsidia Hagiographica 75. Brussels.

Maraval, P., and A. Hanriot (1984). "L'authenticité de la Lettre 1 de Grégoire de Nysse." *Analecta Bollandiana* 102:61–70.

Mateo-Seco, L. F., and J. L. Bastero, ed. (1988). *El "Contra Eunomium I" in la producción literaria de Gregorio de Nisa: VI Coloquio internacional sobre Gregorio de Nisa*. Pamplona.

Mathews, T. F. (1993). *The Clash of Gods: A Reinterpretation of Early Christian Art*. Princeton, N.J.

Matthews, J. (1975). *Western Aristocracies and Imperial Court, A.D. 364–425*. Oxford.

May, G. (1966). "Gregor von Nyssa in der Kirchenpolitik seiner Zeit." *Jahrbuch der österreichischen byzantinischen Gesellschaft* 15:105–32.

————. (1971). "Die Chronologie des Lebens und der Werke des Gregor von Nyssa." In *Ecriture et culture philosophique dans la pensée de Grégoire de Nysse*, ed. M. Harl, pp. 51–66. Leiden.

————. (1972). "Einige Bemerkungen über das Verhältnis Gregors von Nyssa zu Basilios dem Grossen." In *Epektasis: Mélanges patristiques offerts au Cardinal Jean Daniélou*, ed. J. Fontaine and C. Kannengiesser, pp. 509–15. Paris.

Mayer, A. (1911). "Psellos' Rede über den rhetorischen Charakter des Gregorios von Nazianz." *Byzantinische Zeitschrift* 20:27–100.

Mayer, W. (1998). "John Chrysostom: Extraordinary Preacher, Ordinary Audience." In *Preacher and Audience: Studies in Early Christian and Byzantine Homiletics*, ed. M. B. Cunningham and P. Allen, pp. 105–37. A New History of the Sermon 1. Leiden.

McGuckin, J. A. (2001). "Autobiography as Apologia in St. Gregory of Nazianzus." In *Studia Patristica, Vol. XXXVII, Papers Presented at the Thirteenth International Conference on Patristic Studies Held in Oxford 1999. Cappadocian Writers, Other Greek Writers*, ed. M. F. Wiles and E. J. Yarnold, with P. M. Parvis, pp. 160–77. Leuven.

McLynn, N. (1994). *Ambrose of Milan: Church and Court in a Christian Capital*. Berkeley, Calif.

————. (1997). "The Voice of Conscience: Gregory Nazianzen in Retirement." In *Vescovi e pastori in epoca teodosiana: In occasione del XVI centenario della consacrazione episcopale di S. Agostino, 396–1996. XXV Incontro di studiosi dell'antichità cristiana, Roma, 8–11 maggio 1996*, 2:299–308. Studia Ephemeridis "Augustinianum" 58. Rome.

van der Meer, F. (1961). *Augustine the Bishop: The Life and Work of a Father of the Church*, tr. B. Battershaw and G. R. Lamb. London and New York.

Meier, B., ed. and tr. (1989). *Gregor von Nazianz: Über die Bischöfe (Carmen 2,1,12). Einleitung, Text, Übersetzung, Kommentar*. Studien zur Geschichte und Kultur des Altertums, Neue Folge, 2. Reihe: Forschungen zu Gregor von Nazianz 7. Paderborn.

Meredith, A. (1976). "Traditional Apologetic in the *Contra Eunomium* of Gregory of Nyssa." In *Studia Patristica, Vol. XIV, Papers Presented to the Sixth International Conference on Patristic Studies Held in Oxford 1971. Part III:Tertullian,*

Origenism, Gnostica, Cappadocian Fathers, Augustiniana, ed. E. A. Livingstone, pp. 315–19. Texte und Untersuchungen 117. Berlin.

Merkelbach, R. and J. Stauber (2001). *Steinepigramme aus dem griechischen Osten 2: Die Nordküste Kleinasiens (Marmarameer und Pontos)*. Munich and Leipzig.

Millar, F. (1999). "The Greek East and Roman Law: The Dossier of M. Cn. Licinius Rufinus." *Journal of Roman Studies* 89:90–108.

Milovanovic-Barham, C. (1997). "Gregory of Nazianzus: Ars Poetica (In suos versus: Carmen 2.1.39)." *Journal of Early Christian Studies* 5:497–510.

Misch, G. (1950). *A History of Autobiography in Antiquity*, tr. E. W. Dickes, 2 vols. London.

Mitchell, S. (1977). "R. E. C. A. M. Notes and Studies No. 1: Inscriptions of Ancyra." *Anatolian Studies* 27:63–103.

———. (1982). "The Life of Saint Theodotus of Ancyra." *Anatolian Studies* 32:93–113.

———. (1993). *Anatolia: Land, Men, and Gods in Asia Minor*, 2 vols. Oxford.

———. (1999). "The Life and *Lives* of Gregory Thaumaturgus." In *Portraits of Spiritual Authority: Religious Power in Early Christianity, Byzantium and the Christian Orient*, ed. J. W. Drijvers and J. W. Watt, pp. 99–138. Religions in the Graeco-Roman World 137. Leiden.

Morani, M., ed. (1987). *Nemesii Emeseni De natura hominis*. Teubner. Leipzig.

Moraux, P. (1959). *Une imprécation funéraire à Néocésarée*. Bibliothèque archéologique et historique de l'Institut français d'archéologie d'Istanbul 4. Paris.

Moreschini, C., and D. A. Sykes, ed. and tr. (1997). *St Gregory of Nazianzus: Poemata Arcana*. Oxford.

Mosshammer, A. A. (1990). "Disclosing But Not Disclosed: Gregory of Nyssa as Deconstructionist." In *Studien zu Gregor von Nyssa und der christlichen Spätantike*, ed. H. R. Drobner and C. Klock, pp. 99–122. Supplements to Vigiliae Christianae 12. Leiden.

Mudd, M. M. (1989). *Studies in the Reign of Constantius II*. New York.

Muraviev, A. (2001). "The Syriac Julian Romance as a Source of the Life of St. Basil the Great." In *Studia Patristica, Vol. XXXVII, Papers Presented at the Thirteenth International Conference on Patristic Studies Held in Oxford 1999. Cappadocian Writers, Other Greek Writers*, ed. M. F. Wiles and E. J. Yarnold, with P. M. Parvis, pp. 240–49. Leuven.

Neumann, G. (1980). "Kleinasien." In *Die Sprachen im römischen Reich der Kaiserzeit*, ed. G. Neumann and J. Untermann, pp. 167–85. Bonner Jahrbücher, Beiheft 40. Cologne.

Norris, F. W. (1985). "The Authenticity of Gregory Nazianzen's Five Theological Orations." *Vigiliae Christianae* 39:331–39.

———. (1991). *Faith Gives Fullness to Reasoning: The Five Theological Orations of Gregory Nazianzen. Introduction and Commentary*. Supplements to Vigiliae Christianae 13. Leiden.

Opitz, H.-G., ed. (1935–1941). *Athanasius Werke, Zweiter Band, Erster Teil: Die Apologien*. Berlin and Leipzig.

O'Roark, D. (1996). "Close-Kin Marriage in Late Antiquity: The Evidence of Chrysostom." *Greek, Roman, and Byzantine Studies* 37:399–411.

Otis, B. (1958). "Cappadocian Thought as a Coherent System." *Dumbarton Oaks Papers* 12:95–124.

Pagels, E. (1979). *The Gnostic Gospels.* New York.

Panichi, S. (2000). "La Cappadocia." In *Strabone e l'Asia Minore,* ed. A. M. Biraschi and G. Salmeri, pp. 509–41. Incontri Perugini de storia della storiografia antica e sul mundo antico 10. Naples.

Parmentier, L. (1909). "Eunomios tachygraphe." *Revue de philologie* 33:238–45.

Pasquali, G. (1923). "Le lettere di Gregorio di Nissa." *Studi italiani di filologia classica* n.s. 3:75–136.

Patlagean, E. (1977). *Pauvreté économique et pauvreté sociale à Byzance, 4ᵉ–7ᵉ siècles.* Paris.

Peachin, M. (2001). "Friendship and Abuse at the Dinner Table." In *Aspects of Friendship in the Graeco-Roman World: Proceedings of a Conference Held at the Seminar für Alte Geschichte, Heidelberg, on 10–11 June, 2000,* ed. M. Peachin, pp. 135–44. Journal of Roman Archaeology, Supplementary Series 43. Portsmouth, R.I.

Pelikan, J. (1993). *Christianity and Classical Culture: The Metamorphosis of Natural Theology in the Christian Encounter with Hellenism.* New Haven, Conn.

Pertusi, A., ed. (1952). *Constantino Porfirogenito: De thematibus. Introduzione—Testo critico—Commento.* Studi et Testi 160. Vatican City.

Petit, P. (1955). *Libanius et la vie municipale à Antioche au IVᵉ siècle après J.-C.* Institut français d'archéologie de Beyrouth, Bibliothèque archéologique et historique 62. Paris.

Pouchet, R. (1986). "Les rapports de Basile de Césarée avec Diodore de Tarse." *Bulletin de littérature ecclésiastique* 87:243–72.

———. (1992a). *Basile le Grand et son univers d'amis d'après sa correspondance: Une stratégie de communion.* Studia Ephemeridis "Augustinianum" 36. Rome.

———. (1992b). "La date de l'élection épiscopale de saint Basile et celle de sa mort." *Revue d'histoire ecclésiastique* 87:5–33.

Pourkier, A. (1992). *L'hérésiologie chez Epiphane de Salamine.* Christianisme antique 4. Paris.

Price, M. J., and B. L. Trell (1977). *Coins and Their Cities: Architecture on the Ancient Coins of Greece, Rome, and Palestine.* London and Detroit.

Price, S. R. F. (1984). *Rituals and Power: The Roman Imperial Cult in Asia Minor.* Cambridge.

Ramsay, W. M. (1890). *The Historical Geography of Asia Minor.* London.

Renza, L. A. (1980). "The Veto of the Imagination: A Theory of Autobiography." In *Autobiography: Essays Theoretical and Critical,* ed. J. Olney, pp. 268–95. Princeton, N.J.

Riedinger, R. (1981). "Das Bekenntnis des Gregor Thaumaturgus bei Sophronius von Jerusalem und Macarius von Antiocheia." *Zeitschrift für Kirchengeschichte* 92:311–14.

Risch, F. X., tr. (1992). *Pseudo-Basilius: Adversus Eunomium IV–V. Einleitung, Übersetzung und Kommentar.* Supplements to Vigiliae Christianae 16. Leiden.

———, tr. (1999). *Gregor von Nyssa: Über das Sechstagewerk. Verteidigungsschrift an seinen Bruder Petrus.* Bibliothek der griechischen Literatur, Abteilung Patristik, Bd. 49. Stuttgart.

Rist, J. M. (1981). "Basil's 'Neoplatonism': Its Background and Nature." In *Basil of Caesarea: Christian, Humanist, Ascetic: A Sixteen-Hundredth Anniversary Symposium,* ed. P. J. Fedwick, 1:137–220. Toronto.

Rizzo, J. J., ed. and tr. (1976). *The Encomium of Gregory Nazianzen by Nicetas the Paphlagonian.* Subsidia Hagiographica 58. Brussels.

Robbins, F. E. (1912). *The Hexaemeral Literature: A Study of the Greek and Latin Commentaries on Genesis.* Chicago.

Robert, L. (1963). *Noms indigènes dans l'Asie-Mineure gréco-romaine: Première partie.* Bibliothèque archéologique et historique de l'Institut français d'archéologie d'Istanbul. Paris.

Rochette, B. (1997). *Le latin dans le monde grec: Recherches sur la diffusion de la langue et des lettres latines dans les provinces hellénophones de l'Empire romain.* Collection Latomus 233. Brussels.

Rodley, L. (1985). *Cave Monasteries of Byzantine Cappadocia.* Cambridge.

Rott, H. (1908). *Kleinasiatische Denkmäler aus Pisidien, Pamphylien, Kappadokien und Lydien.* Studien über christliche Denkmäler, Neue Folge 5–6. Leipzig.

Rousseau, O. (1957–1958). "La recontre de saint Ephrem et de saint Basile." *Orient syrien* 2:261–84, and 3:73–90.

Rousseau, P. (1994). *Basil of Caesarea.* Berkeley, Calif.

Rusch, W. G. (1974). "A la recherche de l'Athanase historique." In *Politique et théologie chez Athanase d'Alexandrie: Actes du Colloque de Chantilly, 23–25 septembre 1973*, ed. C. Kannengiesser, pp. 161–77. Théologie historique 27. Paris.

Russell, D. A., and N. G. Wilson, eds. and tr. (1981). *Menander Rhetor.* Oxford.

Sallares, R. (1991). *The Ecology of the Ancient Greek World.* London.

Salway, B. (1994). "What's in a Name? A Survey of Roman Onomastic Practice from c. 700 B.C. to A.D. 700." *Journal of Roman Studies* 84:124–45.

Schmidt, T. S., ed. and tr. (2001). *Basilii Minimi in Gregorii Nazianzeni orationem XXXVIII Commentarii.* CChr., Series graeca 46 = Corpus Nazianzenum 13. Turnhout and Leuven.

Scholten, C. (1992). "Die Chorbischof bei Basilius." *Zeitschrift für Kirchengeschichte* 103:149–73.

Seeck, O. (1919). *Regesten der Kaiser und Päpste für die Jahre 311 bis 476 n. Chr. Vorarbeit zu einer Prosopographie der christlichen Kaiserzeit.* Stuttgart.

Sesboüé, B., G.-M. de Durand, and L. Doutreleau, ed. and tr. (1982–1983). *Basile de Césarée: Contre Eunome suivi de Eunome: Apologie*, 2 vols. SChr. 299, 305. Paris.

Ševčenko, I. (1996). "The Logos on Gregory of Nazianzus by Theodore Metochites." In *Geschichte und Kultur der Palaiologenzeit: Referate des Internationalen Symposions zu Ehren von Herbert Hunger (Wien, 30. November bis 3. Dezember 1994)*, ed. W. Seibt, pp. 221–33. Österreichische Akademie der Wissenschaften, philosophisch-historische Klasse, Denkschriften, Bd. 241. Veroffentlichungen der Kommission für Byzantinistik, Bd. 8. Vienna.

Shaw, B. D. (1993). "The Bandit." In *The Romans*, ed. A. Giardina, pp. 300–341. Chicago.

Shaw, B. D., and R. P. Saller (1984). "Close-Kin Marriage in Roman Society?" *Man* n.s. 19:432–44.

Slusser, M., tr. (1998). *St. Gregory Thaumaturgus: Life and Works.* FC 98. Washington, D.C.

Smets, A., and M. van Esbroeck, ed. and tr. (1970). *Basile de Césarée: Sur l'origine de l'homme (Hom. X et XI de l'Hexaéméron).* SChr. 160. Paris.

Snee, R. (1998). "Gregory Nazianzen's Anastasia Church: Arianism, the Goths, and Hagiography." *Dumbarton Oaks Papers* 52:157–86.

Spacks, P. M. (1976). *Imagining a Self: Autobiography and Novel in Eighteenth-Century England.* Cambridge, Mass.

Spira, A. (1985). "Volkstümlichkeit und Kunst in der griechischen Väterpredigt des 4. Jahrhunderts." *Jahrbuch der österreichischen Byzantinistik* 35:55–73.

Spoerl, K. M. (1993). "The Schism at Antioch Since Cavallera." In *Arianism After Arius: Essays on the Development of the Fourth Century Trinitarian Conflicts,* ed. M. R. Barnes and D. H. Williams, pp. 101–26. Edinburgh.

Stead, C. (1994). *Philosophy in Christian Antiquity.* Cambridge.

Strubbe, J. H. M. (1984–1986). "Gründer kleinasiatischer Städte: Fiktion und Realität." *Ancient Society* 15–17:253–304.

Sullivan, R. D. (1980). "The Dynasty of Cappadocia." In *Aufstieg und Niedergang der römischen Welt,* vol. 2.7.2, ed. H. Temporini, pp. 1125–68. Berlin and New York.

Swain, S. (1996). *Hellenism and Empire: Language, Classicism, and Power in the Greek World AD 50–250.* Oxford.

Sykes, D. A. (1985). "Gregory Nazianzen as Didactic Poet." In *Studia Patristica* 16.2, ed. E. A. Livingstone. = *Texte und Untersuchungen* 129:433–37. Berlin.

Taylor, D. G. K. (1997). "Basil of Caesarea's Contacts with Syriac-Speaking Christians." In *Studia Patristica, Vol. XXXII, Papers Presented at the Twelfth International Conference on Patristic Studies Held in Oxford 1995. Athanasius and His Opponents, Cappadocian Fathers, Other Greek Writers After Nicaea,* ed. E. A. Livingstone, pp. 213–19. Leuven.

Teteriatnikov, N. B. (1996). *The Liturgical Planning of Byzantine Churches in Cappadocia.* Orientalia Christiana Analecta 252. Rome.

Treggiari, S. (1991). *Roman Marriage: Iusti coniuges from the Time of Cicero to the Time of Ulpian.* Oxford.

Trombley, F. R. (1993). *Hellenic Religion and Christianization c. 370–529,* 2 vols. Religions in the Graeco-Roman World 115.1–2. Leiden.

Trumpf, J. (1959). "Alexanders kappadokisches Testament." *Byzantinische Zeitschrift* 52:253–56.

Tsananas, G. (1980). "Humor bei Basilius dem Grossen." In *Philoxenia: Prof. Dr. Bernhard Kötting gewidmet von seinen griechischen Schülern,* ed. A. Kallis, pp. 259–79. Munster.

Tutorov, B. (2000). "Grégoire de Nazianze dans le décor monumental." In *Studia Nazianzenica I,* ed. B. Coulie, pp. 273–82. CChr., Series graeca 41 = Corpus Nazianzenum 8. Turnhout.

Uthemann, K.-H. (1993). "Die Sprache der Theologie nach Eunomius von Cyzicus." *Zeitschrift für Kirchengeschichte* 104:143–75.

Vaggione, R. P. (1980). "Some Neglected Fragments of Theodore of Mopsuestia's Contra Eunomium." *Journal of Theological Studies* n.s. 31:403–70.

———, ed. and tr. (1987). *Eunomius: The Extant Works.* Oxford.

———. (1993). "Of Monks and Lounge Lizards: 'Arians,' Polemics and Asceticism in the Roman East." In *Arianism After Arius: Essays on the Development of the Fourth Century Trinitarian Conflicts,* ed. M. R. Barnes and D. H. Williams, pp. 181–214. Edinburgh.

———. (2000). *Eunomius of Cyzicus and the Nicene Revolution.* Oxford.

Van Dam, R. (1982). "Hagiography and History: The Life of Gregory Thaumaturgus." *Classical Antiquity* 1:272–308.

———. (1985a). *Leadership and Community in Late Antique Gaul.* Berkeley, Calif.

———. (1985b). "From Paganism to Christianity at Late Antique Gaza." *Viator* 16:1–20.

———. (1986). "Emperor, Bishops, and Friends in Late Antique Cappadocia." *Journal of Theological Studies* n.s. 37:53–76.

———. (1993). *Saints and Their Miracles in Late Antique Gaul.* Princeton, N.J.

———. (1995). "Self-Representation in the Will of Gregory of Nazianzus." *Journal of Theological Studies* n.s. 46:118–48.

———. (1996). "Governors of Cappadocia During the Fourth Century." In *Late Antiquity and Byzantium*, ed. R. W. Mathisen. = *Medieval Prosopography* 17:7–93.

———. (1998). Review of Moreschini and Sykes (1997). *Journal of Theological Studies* n.s. 49:386–88.

Van Nijf, O. (1999). "Athletics, Festivals and Greek Identity in the Roman East." *Proceedings of the Cambridge Philological Society* 45:176–200.

———. (2001). "Local Heroes: Athletics, Festivals and Elite Self-Fashioning in the Roman East." In *Being Greek Under Rome: Cultural Identity, the Second Sophistic and the Development of Empire*, ed. S. Goldhill, pp. 306–34. Cambridge.

Van Rompay, L. (1992). "L'informateur syrien de Basile de Césarée: A propos de Genèse 1,2." *Orientalia Christiana Periodica* 58:245–51.

Vandenbussche, E. (1944–1945). "La part de la dialectique dans la théologie d'Eunomius 'le technologue'." *Revue d'histoire ecclésiastique* 40:47–72.

Veligianni, C. (2001). "*Philos* und *Philos*-Komposita in den griechischen Inschriften der Kaiserzeit." In *Aspects of Friendship in the Graeco-Roman World: Proceedings of a Conference Held at the Seminar für Alte Geschichte, Heidelberg, on 10–11 June, 2000*, ed. M. Peachin, pp. 63–80. Journal of Roman Archaeology, Supplementary Series 43. Portsmouth, R.I.

Vööbus, A. (1960). "Das literarische Verhältnis zwischen der Biographie des Rabbūlā und dem Pseudo-Amphilochianischen Panegyrikus über Basilius." *Oriens Christianus* 44:40–45.

Walker, P. W. L. (1990). *Holy City, Holy Places? Christian Attitudes to Jerusalem and the Holy Land in the Fourth Century.* Oxford.

Wallraff, M. (1997). "Il «Sinodo di tutte le eresie» a Costantinopoli (383)." In *Vescovi e pastori in epoca teodosiana: In occasione del XVI centenario della consacrazione episcopale di S. Agostino, 396–1996. XXV Incontro di studiosi dell'antichità cristiana, Roma, 8–11 maggio 1996*, 2:271–79. Studia Ephemeridis "Augustinianum" 58. Rome.

Weber, E. (1976). *Peasants into Frenchmen: The Modernization of Rural France, 1870–1914.* Stanford, Calif.

Wickham, L. R. (1968). "The *Syntagmation* of Aetius the Anomean." *Journal of Theological Studies* n.s. 19:532–69.

———. (1969). "The Date of Eunomius' *Apology*: A Reconsideration." *Journal of Theological Studies* n.s. 20:231–40.

Wiles, M. (1989). "Eunomius: Hair-Splitting Dialectician or Defender of the Accessibility of Salvation." In *The Making of Orthodoxy: Essays in Honour of Henry Chadwick*, ed. R. Williams, pp. 157–72. Cambridge.

———. (1996). *Archetypal Heresy: Arianism through the Centuries*. Oxford.

Wiles, M., and R. C. Gregg (1985). "Asterius: A New Chapter in the History of Arianism." In *Arianism: Historical and Theological Reassessments. Papers from the Ninth International Conference on Patristic Studies, September 5–10, 1983, Oxford, England*, ed. R. C. Gregg, pp. 111–51. Patristic Monograph Series 11. Cambridge, Mass.

Wilken, R. L. (1984). *The Christians As the Romans Saw Them*. New Haven, Conn.

———. (1999). "Cyril of Alexandria's *Contra Iulianum*." In *The Limits of Ancient Christianity: Essays on Late Antique Thought and Culture in Honor of R. A. Markus*, ed. W. E. Klingshirn and M. Vessey, pp. 42–55. Ann Arbor, Mich.

Williams, R. (1987). *Arius: Heresy and Tradition*. London.

van Winden, J. C. M. (1988). "Hexaemeron." In *Reallexikon für Antike und Christentum: Sachwörterbuch zur Auseinandersetzung des Christentums mit der antiken Welt*, ed. E. Dassmann et al., vol. 14, col. 1250–69. Stuttgart.

Winkelmann, F. (1990). "'Über die körperlichen Merkmale der gottbeseelten Väter': Zu einem Malerbuch aus der Zeit zwischen 836 und 913." In *Fest und Alltag in Byzanz*, ed. G. Prinzing and D. Simon, pp. 107–27. Munich.

Wolfram, H. (1988). *History of the Goths*, tr. T. J. Dunlap. Berkeley, Calif.

Woodhead, A. G., ed. (1962). *Supplementum epigraphicum graecum*, vol. 18. Leiden.

Wyss, B. (1949). "Gregor von Nazianz: Ein griechisch-christlicher Dichter des 4. Jahrhunderts." *Museum Helveticum* 6:177–210.

———. (1983). "Gregor II (Gregor von Nazianz)." In *Reallexikon für Antike und Christentum: Sachwörterbuch zur Auseinandersetzung des Christentums mit der antiken Welt*, ed. E. Dassmann et al., vol. 12, col. 793–863. Stuttgart.

———. (1984). "Gregor von Nazianz oder Gregory von Nyssa? (Greg. Naz. epist. 249 Gallay / Greg. Nyss. epist. 1 Pasquali)." In *Mémorial André-Jean Festugière: Antiquité païenne et chrétienne*, ed. E. Lucchesi and H. D. Saffrey, pp. 153–62. Cahiers d'orientalisme 10. Geneva.

von Zetterstéen, K. (1934). "Eine Homilie des Amphilochius von Iconium über Basilius von Caesarea." *Oriens Christianus* 31:67–98.

Zgusta, L. (1964). *Kleinasiatische Personennamen*. Prague.

Zuckerman, C. (1991). "Cappadocian Fathers and the Goths." *Travaux et Mémoires* 11:473–86.

Index